TRUE CONFESSIONS

FRANCIS X. MAIER

TRUE CONFESSIONS

Voices of Faith from a Life in the Church

With an introduction by
Archbishop Emeritus Charles J. Chaput, O.F.M. Cap.

IGNATIUS PRESS   SAN FRANCISCO

Cover design by Enrique Aguilar

© 2024 by Ignatius Press, San Francisco
All rights reserved
ISBN 978-1-62164-624-2 (PB)
ISBN 978-1-64229-270-1 (eBook)
Library of Congress Control Number 2023945900
Printed in the United States of America ∞

For SMM. She lived it.

After this, many of his disciples drew back and no longer walked with him. Jesus said to the Twelve, "Will you also go away?" Simon Peter answered him, "Lord, to whom shall we go? You have the words of eternal life."

—*John 6:66–68*

CONTENTS

INTRODUCTION

Mater et Magistra

The book in your hands began, in late 2020, with the Scripture verses on the epigraph page. They anchor not merely this text, but the entire Christian life. I'll return to those verses, to the nature of this book, and to its author in a moment. But I'll do it in a roundabout way. So I hope you'll bear with me.

Two saints have shaped the course of my life. The first is Francis of Assisi. The second is Augustine of Hippo. As a boy and young man I was educated by Capuchin Franciscans. Through them, I encountered Francis. The sheer radicalism he brought to pursuing God—his abandonment of the world and its vanities, from his family's wealth to his very self—lit a forest fire, all consuming, in my imagination. Later, as a priest and bishop, I was drawn to Augustine as the pastor I wanted myself to be: a man of strong mind, passion for the faith, love for his people, and courage in turbulent times not unlike our own. Nothing compares to his *Confessions*. It speaks to the restless heart in every generation.

What interests me here, though, is both men's lay roots. Franciscan life began as a lay vocation, not a clerical one. Francis never became a priest. Tradition holds that he once served as a deacon at a Christmas Mass, but the evidence is thin. I don't personally believe Francis was ever ordained. Few of his earliest brothers were clerics. As for Augustine, he was a prominent convert and brilliant lay scholar ... clearly too prominent and too brilliant, because the Christians of Hippo pressed him into becoming a priest and later their bishop. He did that priestly ministry for decades with astonishing piety and skill. But it was never the path he intended as a rising young master of rhetoric.

Baptism is the cornerstone of the Christian faith. No baptized layperson is "ordinary" or unimportant. It subtracts nothing from the

11

dignity of the priesthood to note that I've always found as much energy and faith in the laity as in the clergy; sometimes even more. In Scripture, most of Jesus' followers were everyday men and women. And I've always seen the Gospel message as applying equally to all of us who are baptized, and not in some special way to clergy or religious. As a young man, I wanted to be a Capuchin both earlier and more intensely than I wanted to be a priest. I saw the simplicity of Francis as the main vocation of my religious order, not the priesthood itself. Of course I'm profoundly happy to be a priest. Looking back, I'm sure God called me to that path. But I was very conscious that I was called *from the laity*, and that ordination doesn't make a man better than or different from the laity, other than the new responsibilities it gives him, including the duty to be an icon of Christ for others.

Working with talented laypeople as a priest and bishop gave me a deep admiration for their service. Collaborating with laypersons was both fruitful and often less complex than working with clergy. Laypeople tend to have a natural respect for their bishop. Clergy, especially diocesan clergy, have a closer but also more ambivalent relationship with their bishop. The reason is simple: He's a brother and a father, but also "the boss". Explaining and navigating that particular human terrain, though, would need a different introduction to a different book.

So, back to the task at hand: Why the book you're holding matters.

I was a teenager when Pope John XXIII issued his great encyclical *Mater et Magistra* (Mother and Teacher) in 1961. I was already in seminary with the Capuchins and eager to follow St. Francis. I wanted a demanding life, and the Capuchins, who began as a rigorous reform community within the larger Franciscan family, were the obvious path for me. With them, life made sense. I was on fire for the Gospel and the Church. I had an appetite for God and the energy of a very young heart. So I found the pope's words electrifying. His message was filled with confidence and joy:

> Mother and Teacher of all nations—such is the Catholic Church in the mind of her Founder, Jesus Christ; to hold the world in an embrace of love, that men, in every age, should find in her their own completeness in a higher order of living, and their ultimate salvation. She is "the pillar and ground of the truth." To her was entrusted

by her holy Founder the twofold task of giving life to her children and of teaching them and guiding them—both as individuals and as nations—with maternal care. Great is their dignity, a dignity which she has always guarded most zealously and held in the highest esteem.

Christianity is the meeting-point of earth and heaven. It lays claim to the whole man, body and soul, intellect and will, inducing him to raise his mind above the changing conditions of this earthly existence and reach upwards for the eternal life of heaven, where one day he will find his unfailing happiness and peace. (Nos. 1–2)

John XXIII was a saint. And as a leader, he did not disappoint. A year and a half later, in October 1962 and just two weeks after I turned 18, he convened the Second Vatican Council. As a global gathering of bishops, Vatican II had the task of bringing the Church into better engagement with the modern world without damaging the continuity and integrity of her teaching. In his remarks opening the Council, the pope stressed that

the very serious matters and questions which need to be solved by the human race have not changed after almost twenty centuries. For Christ Jesus still stands at the center of history and life: people either embrace him and his Church and so enjoy the benefits of light, goodness, order, and peace, or they live without him or act against him and deliberately remain outside the Church, so that confusion arises among them, their relationships are embittered, and the danger of bloody wars impends.

Despite such challenges, he added, "The Council which is now beginning rises in the Church like a day shining with the most splendid light. It is only the dawn, but already how delightfully are our hearts affected by the first rays of the rising sun! Everything here breathes holiness and stirs up joy. For we see the stars by their brilliance increasing the majesty of this temple."

Vatican documents, as vital as they are, can sometimes read like a cure for insomnia. Not so with the words and work of John XXIII, and I quote them here for a simple reason. They testify to the Catholic hopes of the early 1960s. European Christianity had a brief but vigorous resurgence in the 10 or 12 years following the end of World War II. An open, fruitful dialogue between the Church and the world seemed uniquely possible. The Council produced 16 documents alive with reform, renewal, energy, and zeal. It was an extraordinary time. It ignited the spirit of millions of Christians worldwide, including seminarians like my Capuchin brothers and me.

The Council closed in 1965. I was ordained a priest in 1970. I went on to teach in seminary, to parish work in Colorado, and later, to provincial Capuchin leadership. In the five short years between the Council's end and my ordination, the world changed fundamentally, and not in a kind way for the Church. By 1969–1970, a young theologian was noting that "the road to the moon is easier to find than the road to man himself." And: "Man is the hope of mankind, as he certainly is also the hell of mankind and a constant threat to mankind." And finally: "[T]he faith is being shaken to its foundation by the crisis of the present."

The young theologian's name was Joseph Ratzinger.

As I write these words in 2023, more than 60 years have passed since the beauty of John XXIII's opening Council words. The Church has lost ground in nearly every materially advanced nation. Internal disputes over the Council's meaning persist. In some ways, they've grown worse. Conflicts about the nature of Catholic teaching on sexuality and other key matters can be intense. It's easy to lose heart in the confusion of the times. But I'll offer a useful piece of advice: *Don't make that mistake.*

Francis and Augustine lived in equally difficult, and arguably worse, times. Yet Francis the saint had a passionate joy rooted in the Gospel. And he lived that joy so well because he let the Word of God possess and transform him. He got out of God's way by giving himself entirely to God. And when he did, God renewed the Church of his day through his service. Augustine the saint had a very different personality, but he lived that same joy. And, crucially, Augustine the bishop reminded his people, again and again, that complaining about the darkness of the times is useless. We *are* the times. We *make* the times. And it's up to us to make them better.

None of us is powerless. The power of the (seemingly) powerless resides in a person's refusal to live a lie; to live instead in the truth, whatever the cost. Each of our choices and actions matters. Each contributes, in a small but material way, to renewing or degrading the character of the times. As the *Letter to Diognetus* stressed in the second century A.D., "The Christian is to the world what the soul is to the body." And the power of Christian witness—your Christian witness and mine—is multiplied in the *ekklesia*, the "calling out" of individual believers into public assembly in the family of the Church. Simply put: There's strength in numbers, especially when Christians believe and work together.

John XXIII described the Church as *mater et magistra* for a reason. The Church is never merely an institution, never merely a creature of this world, and always far greater than the sins of her leaders and people. At heart, the Church is a "she", not an "it": the Bride of Jesus Christ; a mother of tenderness and the teacher of truth. And even in an age that derides her and dismisses the need for a God; even in an age when her weakness is often brutally obvious; the Church is younger, stronger, and more beautiful than her enemies have the capacity to understand or see. But the author of this book *does* see that beauty. And he records it, with affection and candor, through the lens of his own experience and the experience of many others ... all of them faithful; and all of them, like Simon Peter, unwilling to abandon "the words of eternal life" or the Lord who speaks them.

So, a few final words about the author.

I met Fran in Rapid City, in February 1997. He arrived a week or so before I was publicly announced as Denver's new archbishop. He'd been sent by Denver's diocesan leadership team with their report on the state of the archdiocese. And he no doubt had the task of bringing back some intel on the new boss. I'd heard of Fran from a bishop friend who told me I'd be lucky to work with him, and I knew his background in a vague way. I'd already had good working friendships with lay colleagues and staff in South Dakota. Kerry Kober, my personal secretary, gave invaluable support to my ministry in Rapid City and later in Denver and Philadelphia. I took Vatican II's words on the importance of the lay vocation seriously. So, Fran was the natural place to look for help in building the same kind of lay and clergy collaboration in Denver.

In Denver, I named Fran as my chancellor and senior aide very quickly. In Philadelphia he served as my senior adviser and special assistant: a different title, but the same tasks. His strengths were obvious. As a married man with children, including a son with Down syndrome, he understood the terrain of lay life in an intimate way. He had energy, maturity, and discretion. He listened carefully. He had strong communication skills. He knew theology and Church history. He knew public policy. And he wasn't scandalized by the uglier problems of Church life, which made his counsel in difficult matters that much more valuable.

In 26 years of working together, I've never had a moment when I questioned Fran's ability or character. Not once. He was a vital help at three different Roman synods. He was a key aide with multiple legal strategies, seminars, conferences, and workshops; books and lectures; a World Meeting of Families; and numerous sensitive affairs. His energy inspired other laypersons to have confidence in doing the same. My hopes for laypeople collaborating fruitfully with bishops were proven practical and true by our own work together. And I'm convinced that bishops who lack or avoid working with laity as closely as Fran and I worked together are hobbled in some crucial ways.

In Denver, in the early years of our collaboration, I sometimes stopped by Fran's office at the end of the day to think out loud or exchange ideas. I asked him once why he worked for the Church when he could do something else that paid more. He looked at me quizzically, and then said, "Because I love her."

That's the man who wrote this book. That's why you need to read it.

+ *Charles J. Chaput, O.F.M. Cap.*
Archbishop Emeritus of Philadelphia
June 22, 2023
Feast of Saints Thomas More and John Fisher

AUTHOR'S PREFACE

Writing about the Church toward the end of a career spent in and around her structures is a strange business: You know too much and too little at the same time. Too much, because decades of experience teach you what likely will and likely won't work in serving her mission. Too little, because times and circumstances change, and the same learned skills that once made you effective can also blind you to new ideas and solutions that might be fruitful.

That obviously hasn't stopped me. But the reader is duly warned.

This book is a snapshot of the Catholic Church in the United States in the third decade of the 21st century: Who she is; where she is culturally; how she got there; and her prospects for the future, with a special emphasis on the nature of the lay vocation. It's deliberately not a data dump or a work of sociology, but rather a collection of lived experiences and insights from a variety of real people. It doesn't claim to be comprehensive; given the size and diversity of the Church, how could it be? It *does* claim to be—and is—truthful and revealing about a large segment of American Catholic life at a specific point in time.

The author's perspective is based on three facts: 15 years as editor in chief of a national Catholic newsweekly; 27 years in senior diocesan service; and 103 personal, in-depth interviews conducted over a 17-month period, December 2020 through May 2022. Additional interviews have been added along the way in the course of writing.

The initial interviews included 30 bishops. Two of them had recently retired. The rest were active in their ministries at the time of their interviews. They included metropolitans and suffragans, as well as two auxiliaries, from 25 states and one foreign country. Another two bishops did not respond to interview requests. A third—Scotland's Archbishop Philip Tartaglia of Glasgow, a friend I assisted during the 2015 synod on the family in Rome—died two weeks before our interview could be conducted. I've reserved any comments from my former employer Archbishop Charles Chaput for inclusion among the long-form interviews in the afterword. All other bishop interviews were conducted anonymously, at my request, to ensure a candid exchange.

The text's remaining interviews included 16 extended conversations with priests, deacons, and consecrated/religious; and 57 with laypersons—men and women—from various personal backgrounds. Comments from the men and women in chapter 5 are also anonymous at the request of several, for reasons similar to my conversations with bishops.

Each of the interviews ranged from 7,000 to more than 10,000 words when transcribed. All of them, no surprise, needed significant editing and condensing. Every interviewee named in the text had the opportunity to review, correct, and approve the material quoted. As it turned out, the changes were very few. To the best of my ability, all anonymous interviews included herein accurately reflect what was actually said. No attempt was made to eliminate unwelcome or inconvenient views, or to force the content in directions unintended by the person speaking. I already know my own opinions. I often publish them. The point of *this* book was to hear the experiences, insights, and opinions of others ... and to share them without an interpretive filter.

With the exception of chapters 1 and 11, all chapters are a blend of brief commentary and direct interviews. Readers are welcome to browse specific chapters and interviews in whatever order they choose. But starting at the start and pursuing the text to its end may be the more fruitful route. Extremes on both ends of the ecclesial spectrum have been excluded. The focus of this text is people who love Jesus Christ and their Christian faith more than they love themselves, or at least sincerely try; persons who accept, believe, and are attempting faithfully to live the teachings of the Catholic Church ... often at personal cost.

As the reader will discover, this does not preclude ample criticism of her failures, her foibles, her structures, and her leaders.

CHAPTER ONE

Ordinary Time

Framing the Moment

I'm reminded of two good men. The first is John Tracy Ellis, who said that, in reality, there were never any "good old days" in the Church. We've always been a mix of success and disaster. The second is an African bishop who got up years ago at one of the synods and said, "Maybe you gentlemen from Europe and America didn't get the memo, but Constantine is dead. And so is his style of Church."

—From a bishop, urban diocese

U.S. Highway 6 crosses the Continental Divide through Loveland Pass, 60 miles west of Denver. The altitude is just shy of 12,000 feet. Before Interstate 70 tunneled through the mountains, U.S. 6 was a main route across the Rockies. It snakes upward to the crest along wooded slopes that drop sharply away. During the Colorado winters, snows are heavy. Plows struggle to keep the road open. But summers are another matter. Several times each summer, during the years we lived in Denver, my wife, Suann, and I would rise at 3 A.M., drive to the pass, and then hike a mile or so along the Divide. Even for people accustomed to Denver's "Mile High City" breathing, the air at 12,000 feet can be demanding. It's cold and thin in the lungs, but also clean and exhilarating. We'd scrabble along the rocks puffing in the dark to a favorite vantage point.

And then we would wait.

Some moments are sacramental. It's the only word to describe them. They point to something more; something behind and above the world. As we watched, the sunrise would spread its carpet of rays first across the forests below, then briefly turn the mountains a shade of rose, and then wash over us and the whole Divide like a wave of pure light ... all in silence.

I believe in God for many reasons, but first among them is beauty. Beauty is transfiguring. The beauty of the world, the beauty of my wife's face, the beauty of family and good friendships: All these things feed the soul, the interior essence that makes us human. They speak of a loving design that connects us to and beyond each other, transcends dead matter, and gives life its meaning. In other words, they speak of an Author, whom the modern spirit, bent and blinded by its own self-flattery, refuses to see. But as the great Jesuit theologian Henri de Lubac once said, choosing to shut our eyes does not destroy the sun, even if we're later "shocked at not seeing what we prevent ourselves from seeing".

The sin of the modern era is pride, and pride makes the proud stupid. To borrow a thought attributed to George Orwell—himself no friend of the Catholic Church, but an honest voice nonetheless—some ideas are so stupid that only an intellectual can believe them. The key word in that preceding sentence is "believe". There are no unbelievers. All humans believe in something, including self-described atheists. They then construct their approach to the world grounded on that belief. "There is no God" is merely a different and defective statement of creed, because if God is really God, he can never be scientifically measured and disproven. Thus, as Lubac noted, modern atheism is not a negative, but a perverse positive; not an absence of belief, but a conscious *antitheism* built upon a resentment toward God and a choice to struggle against Providence. In the process, antitheism results not in the death of God, but the death of those things that make humans uniquely human.

I believe in God because he loves us, and because the people I've loved and trusted, loved him first and long before I did. My mother was a keenly intelligent woman; a woman of character and ideas. But she never went beyond high school in her education because her family was poor, and she needed to help support her nine siblings. She was also a person of deep Irish faith, with a special devotion to Thérèse of Lisieux. She told me a curious story as a young boy. It happened before I was born. My father's job had moved my family from city to city four times in a dozen years. It was a heavy burden on their marriage, the source of both bitter conflict and fatigue. There finally came a morning in mid-winter one year when my father left home to prepare for another, fifth, mandatory job transfer. In my mother's words, it was the low point of their life together. It was also the same morning she finished a novena to Thérèse. Around noon that day, again in her words, with all the windows sealed against the cold, the home filled with an overpowering fragrance of roses, the flower of Thérèse. And then a few minutes later, my father walked in to say that his transfer had been canceled. They never moved again.

As a child, this made a huge impression on me. My mother had begged; Thérèse had listened. The miraculous was real. But as I grew older, finished university and graduate studies, married, had children, and buried myself in work, the story took on a purely nostalgic glow; the implausible product of a very good woman with an overzealous imagination. The memory faded. I'm not like my mother. My faith has always been, in large part, a left-brain affair.

But I'm not quite finished.

When Suann and I and our first child moved to Los Angeles in the early 1970s, we went through a decade of financial and material stress. But over time, things worked out. And I remember walking with our four-year-old daughter one day in the mid-1980s, telling her that God was good, that she was the proof of it, and that he had never left us, never let us down. She smiled. It made her happy.

Now, at the time we lived on a divided street: two lanes one way, two lanes the other, separated by a 30-yard-wide divider of grass, where we would sometimes play with the kids. The area was residential. The posted speed was slow. But traffic was always very heavy and the actual speeds high. After walking with my daughter that day, we crossed over to the median to toss a football around with my sons. And when I looked over to my daughter, she was stepping back into the street to cross back to our home. As a parent, there's a kind of paralysis that sets in when you see something very bad about to happen to your child, something you have no power to avert. But without looking, and purely by chance, she chose the exact moment when no traffic was passing. I ran into the street, grabbed her, and jumped to the other side. Precisely *then*, the traffic resumed. And here's the oddest thing, or rather the numinous thing: Unexpected, unexplained, and as clear and firm as a man standing at my shoulder, I heard a voice say, *I'm still here.*

Sound unlikely? Sure. Laugh at it, ignore it, dismiss it. But I don't. Nor will I ever.

ঌ ঌ ঌ

Loving God and loving the Church are two different, if related, things.

I love the Church because she is my home, my extended family, the mother who takes us back whatever our failures and mistakes. I love her for the grandeur of the art, music, law, architecture, and literature she has inspired. I love her for the brilliance of her intellectual legacy, which has no parallel in human experience. I love her for the good that remains in the civilization she shaped. I love her for her patience and mercy. I love her because she treasures and refuses to abandon the weak. I love her above all because what she teaches is salvific and true. There has never been a Christianity without the Church. She's essential to the Christian life. The Church preceded the Gospels, not the other way around. And the Christian faith has never been *merely* a personal relationship with God, as important as that is. It has always been, beginning in the Upper Room, an assembly of believing friends, an *ekklesia*—a Church.

I love the Church despite the sins of her leaders and her people. Including my own.

Human beings are imperfect creatures. They inhabit and shepherd the Church, and that has consequences. Not all of them welcome. Hierarchy and institutions are necessary to any long-term community. They help sustain and harmonize its life. They also too easily breed tumors, even in the life of faith. Thus, there's never really been a golden age in the life of the Church; it's always been a patchwork of light and dark, saint and sinner. That's the nature of ordinary time. The epistles of Paul, John, and Jude, written with the death and resurrection of Jesus still fresh in the memory, make that vividly clear. Ordinary Time in the liturgical calendar of the Church brackets the great feasts of Christmas, Easter, and Pentecost, and the seasons of Advent and Lent. It's where we live the ordinary joys and sorrows, passions and apathies, achievements and car wrecks that constitute everyday life. And as with individuals, so also with the Church.

I've worked in and around the Church for 45 years. And because of the access and the duties that the work involved, I've seen both the best and the worst of clergy life, including the life of bishops, in a way few laypeople ever do. Those memories shape this text. It's been a great life with too many blessings to count. I love the Church more today than when I started. I admire priests and the priesthood more today than when I began. And the bishops I've worked with and for have been uniformly honorable men trying to do their best for their people. I respect any man who takes on the office of pastor— whether priest in his parish or bishop in his diocese—with devotion and humility, because somebody in the Church needs to lead. Somebody needs to be the dad. And it can be thankless work.

Having said that though, I'll add this simple fact. I'm angry much of the time. Most of the people I know are angry about something most of the time. And if you multiply that by 50 or 90 or 200 million people, you get a sense of the real virus infecting so much of current American life. Anger is now the pervasive background radiation to our politics, our court battles, and our conflicts within the Church. And it won't be going away any time soon. The irony of course is that we live in the wealthiest, most successful democratic republic in history. Even many of our poor are rich by the standards of half the world's population. So how do we account for the anger? Bishops in the Church tend to get blamed for everything. And sometimes they earn it. But bishops didn't invent the birth control pill. They didn't create the sexual anarchy that flowed from it. Bishops didn't invent the transistor, or the microchip, or the cell phone, or video games, or gay dating apps, or the internet cocoon of pornography that's destroyed millions of families and vocations. And bishops don't have a magic wand to cancel out the massively negative influence of popular culture on their people.

We're living through a sea change in our politics, economy, culture, and self-understanding. And the Church has survived such changes before. But what's unique about our current moment is what the social researcher Hartmut Rosa calls "acceleration and alienation". Science and technology are changing not just the *way* we think and act. They're also speeding up the *rate* of change. This disrupts organizations and behaviors. It undermines traditional loyalties and social stability. And it renders individuals confused and frustrated. Which then leads to a sense of powerlessness. Which then triggers anger. Which eventually burns us out in exhaustion. Which then easily leads to cynicism, or acedia, or despair, or all three.

So what does that mean for the Church? Simply put: For the next 25 years or more, the time ahead will be "ordinary" only in light of Christian history and its challenges. The road will be rough in terms of Church resources, attendance, infrastructure, and social influence. And if current trends continue, the attitudes of our culture toward Catholic belief are unlikely to improve. We can mitigate the pain with good planning and new evangelical energy. But we can't quick-fix problems we behaved ourselves into. We're suffering from outside factors we couldn't predict and can't control. But we're also harvesting the effects of a century of Catholic assimilation and naïve optimism about the compatibility of Catholic teaching and American culture. I've always believed in our potential as Catholic Christians to be a leaven in American life. It just hasn't worked out that way. Of course, that can change. But it requires leaders, and their people, who think in terms of the long haul and commit to missionary witness as their first priority in thought and deed.

$\approx$ $\approx$ $\approx$

Descending from the crest of the Continental Divide to metropolitan Denver involves a 3 to 6 percent angle of decline. That sounds modest. But it's the opposite, especially at high speeds on a narrow, winding interstate blasted through rock and squeezed between mountains. There comes a moment, though, when the mountains part. Denver appears in the distance below. And beyond it, the Great Plains stretch out flat and away for another 800 miles.

As metaphors go, it's not a bad one for the Christian's pilgrimage in the world. The beauty of the peaks might be transfiguring. But we live out our duties, our loves, our burdens, and our witness on the plains. And it demands conversion, because we're each a mixture of clay and spirit, carbon and grace; a cocktail of skepticism and hope. *Skepticism*, because unless we're experts at lying to ourselves, we all do finally know our sins. We all have a secret laboratory tucked away in our hearts where we perfect the flavor of our resentments and refine the elegance of our alibis. But *hope* is also part of the cocktail, because despite our weaknesses, we're each capable of courage, charity, and mercy. And Scripture testifies, again and again, to the fact that God never abandons his people ... because he loves us.

This is why the great French Catholic writer Georges Bernanos described the virtue of hope as "despair, overcome". And it's why Augustine of Hippo should be the patron saint of our age. Augustine was never an optimist but always a man of hope. He lived at the end of a world; a Roman world unraveling into confusion, and not so different from our own. But in the face of all the fear and violence of his time, he wrote two books—his *Confessions* and *The City of God*—that still, after 1,600 years, rank among the greatest works of human genius. He could do that because he had hope. He had hope because he had faith. And he had faith because he pursued and encountered God as a vivid, personal presence in his life; the source of his joy and confidence. And he never let the distractions and anxieties of his times dim that experience.

We need to remember Augustine and his world. We also need to learn from them. Augustine lived in an apocalyptic time. Today, so do we. But the word "apocalypse", as Carl Trueman suggests later in these pages, is easily misunderstood. It comes from the Greek words *apokalypsis* and *apokalyptein*, which mean to uncover things concealed. An apocalypse may or may not involve suffering, but it always involves revealing certain truths about ourselves and our times.

Many of us—maybe most American Catholics—still believe that we live in a familiar country with a familiar history, familiar rules, a familiar division of power, and a familiar personal role in governance through the ballot box. That country is draining away. And retrieving the best of the America we once lived in won't be achieved with the standard civic pieties, ecclesial attitudes, and framework of thought that so many of us grew up with. Some of what's now advanced as "good for America" is bad for the Church and toxic for a life of faith.

America has deep Christian roots in the early Puritan experience. I was raised in a Catholic family with a strong love of Church and a strong love of country in equal measure. Our eldest son attended West Point. It was a source of huge pride for my wife and me. The question that my wife and I, and many others like us, now face is simply this: *What happened to the country we once knew*, a country where

civic duty and religious faith seemed to coexist naturally and rein-
force each other?

Some of the shrewdest thinking about the Catholic role in the
American experiment came from John Courtney Murray, the Jesuit
priest and scholar. Murray was a key player in the 20th-century
development of positive Catholic attitudes toward religious freedom
and American democracy. He saw clearly that the United States is a
product of Protestant and Enlightenment thought. But he believed
that Catholics could not only "fit into" American life, but also thrive
here by contributing their faith to the moral health of the country.
And that's been proven true ... at least in part. We Catholics have
done very well in America. Arguably too well for our own good.

Today Murray is probably best remembered for his work on Vatican II's Declaration on Religious Liberty and for his book *We Hold
These Truths*, a book quite favorable toward America and its possibilities. But there's another side to Murray that's a useful footnote
to his body of work. In 1940, he delivered a series of lectures that
became an essay entitled "The Construction of a Christian Culture".
And in it, he said the following about the country he loved:

> American culture, as it exists, is actually the quintessence of all that
> is decadent in the culture of the Western Christian world. It would
> seem to be erected on the triple denial that has corrupted Christian
> culture at its roots, the denial of metaphysical reality, of the primacy
> of the spiritual over the material, of the social over the individual....
> ... Its most striking characteristic is its profound materialism....
> It has given citizens everything to live for and nothing to die for.
> And its achievement may be summed up thus: It has gained a conti-
> nent and lost its own soul.

Elsewhere in the same text he said, "In view of the fact that American
culture is built on the negation of all that Christianity stands for, it
would seem that our first step toward the construction of a Christian
culture should be the destruction of the existing one. In the presence
of a Frankenstein, one does not reach for baptismal water, but for
a bludgeon."

Murray wrote those words more than 80 years ago. His sympathy
for the American experiment was very real. But it hinged on our

nation preserving its biblical leaven and Catholics staying faithful to their religious identity. Neither has happened. Just the opposite. The America of 2023 would be unrecognizable to the John Courtney Murray of 1940 or even 1960.

The Church is the soul of the world and the leaven of a just society. To live that mandate, she needs to recover her health and mission. But an illness can be addressed and healed only when it's named.

Which is the work of the voices that follow.

CHAPTER TWO

Life at the Top

Bishops Speak

As an auxiliary, you learn the ropes but can dodge some of the difficult issues. When you're the ordinary, the buck stops with you. And it's almost like you're no longer a real person; you're this entity. Your whole life really does change because you can no longer be who you are. You always have to be "the bishop".

—From a bishop, urban/rural diocese

Once upon a time, being a bishop came with privileged social standing and considerable public influence. Any man in the job today with similar appetites is in the wrong line of work. The ministry of bishop in the 21st-century United States has a rather different flavor.

Plenty of social data exists on the lives of American bishops. Readers might be interested to know that the average Latin rite ordinary—i.e., the bishop actually in charge of a diocese, as opposed to an auxiliary—sleeps 6.49 hours a night and prays 1.80 hours a day. He works 6.33 days and about 51 hours each week. Ordinaries rank the *National Catholic Reporter* lowest on a list of religious news publications they typically read. They rank the Fox network as their most frequently watched television news source. Some 72 percent of ordinaries (and 88 percent of auxiliaries; they're not the boss) feel accepted by most of their priests. Barely 3 percent rank criticism from priests as a serious problem. And 97 percent list administering the sacraments and celebrating the liturgy as their greatest joy.

These and other facts, many of them useful, can be found in the 2019 book *Catholic Bishops in the United States: Church Leadership in the Third Millennium* (Oxford). It's based on the findings of a 2016 survey by the Center for Applied Research in the Apostolate.

The purpose of this chapter is different.

Over the decades that I served in and around the Church, the bishops I met and worked with were consistently good men. There were exceptions. There always will be. But most bishops did, and do, their honest best for their people and priests. Their personalities, skill sets, and resources vary widely. It's an all-consuming job in a tough cultural environment. And the "collegiality" of bishops doesn't preclude antagonism and conflicts among them. Leaders with different views don't always get along, even when they sign their correspondence "fraternally yours". The point is this: Survey data on a computer screen or a printed page lack a human dimension, and bishops are very much human creatures. So here, in these pages, bishops speak for themselves.

Most, though not all, of the men interviewed for this chapter were appointed as bishops by John Paul II or Benedict XVI. Predictably, most have a special affection for those two popes. Their feelings toward Pope Francis, as seen in some of their comments, are more complex. Attitudes range from support to confusion to deep frustration, though always within a basic fidelity. Popes have a unique role in the Church as guarantors of her unity. They therefore figure inevitably into the ministry of every bishop. It's also worth noting that popes, like bishops, come and go; that the Church survives their passing; and that bishops appointed by John XXIII and Paul VI often had similar mixed feelings toward the popes who followed those men: John Paul II and Benedict XVI. Bishops named by Francis may one day deal with the same mixed feelings toward *his* successors. Such is the nature of things.

ॐ ॐ ॐ

I. From a bishop, urban/rural diocese

We're a poor, essentially rural diocese. Frankly I was surprised when I got here that people were as deeply spiritual as they are. There's a lot of devotion to the angels and saints, the traditional Latin Mass, a strong interest in vocations. These things have a rich environment here. The Catholic population is small. The people we interact with are pretty firm Evangelicals. But a number of the public officials are Catholic. Our relations with local and state leaders are generally good. So we have an outsized influence. What I do hear, is that people are losing what little respect they had for the federal government. There's a sense that it's not being honest with us and hurting people needlessly; but at the same time, it's ineffective on a whole range of issues.

On the matter of Pope Francis: The media shape most of our perceptions about him, and the media are largely corrupt. When Francis arrived on the scene he was lionized as a savior for being "open" and nice and accepting of all sorts of progressive ideas. But every time he shows himself to be genuinely Catholic—as he often does—suddenly he's the boogeyman again. Yes, he shoots from the hip. Yes, he's unreasonably negative toward capitalism. And I don't think his pontificate's focus on climate and the environment makes much sense, given all the other urgent issues we face. But most people still have a positive view of him, and so do I. On my *ad limina* visit, I was very impressed with his energy and personal warmth. Francis also seems to be looking for pastorally oriented men as bishops; guys who've been engaged in pastoral work. And that's an appropriate thing to do. If you get careerists and technicians as bishops, guys who've spent most of their time just doing chancery work, it can really influence their episcopal ministry, and not in a good way.

Finally, on the issue of priestly "loneliness": It's actually married people who imagine that celibacy is so hard; we celibates think marriage is hard. Remember that we hear a *lot* of confessions, and a lot of those confessions come from husbands and wives. The more dysfunctional a culture becomes around issues of sexuality, the more a celibate witness is valuable and needed. We can't allow numbers to dictate whether celibacy is good or not. It doesn't at all follow that we'll get more priests if we do away with celibacy. That's not how God works with almost anything. The loneliest persons in the world are the husband and wife sitting in a room and unable to talk to each other because of their bitterness and frustration. For me, that would be an unbearable feeling. So yes, priests do experience loneliness, but that's because they're human. Every living person will experience loneliness. And without God, I don't know how anyone could make sense of it.

2. From a bishop, urban/rural diocese

It's a strange time. This is a vibrant diocese in a fairly religious region. When I was made bishop here I didn't have to come too far from where I was already serving. In some ways it's like a dream, a good dream. Our senior political leaders are regular churchgoers. I have the governor's cell number. He has mine. We're not chums or anything, but we're comfortable reaching out to each other directly if a relevant issue comes up. We have generally good relations with local and state government, built up over many years. All of which is positive. But I've been startled by how politics now infects every aspect of life. Even within the Church, even here, the default position is always political. Whenever we're planning something, especially something new, immediately you get people lining up to oppose it, just to prevent somebody else from getting what he or she wants. It's hard to reflect prayerfully together and make plans within the diocese without first sanitizing everybody's feelings and disarming different camps.

I've been very edified by the imagination and creativity of our priests. They're really good men. I couldn't ask for better. But like the people they serve, their morale took a heavy hit from COVID and all the social and political bitterness of the last few years. We've had some mental health problems in the presbyterate and a lot of stress that parishioners often don't see. Catholic Leadership Institute helped us with listening sessions around the diocese, and then with our planning and visioning for the future. That's made a difference. In the United States, we've always been very well organized as a Church with parishes, schools, and other institutions. Those things served us well for a long time. But right now, some of those structures no longer serve us. On many days, they feel more like dead weight. We don't want to be foolish and just blow things up. But in looking to the future, other than the things given to us by the Lord himself, things in sacred tradition, I believe everything should be up for discussion about whether and how well it fits into our mission. Difficult times are difficult. That's their nature. But they also make us think more clearly about who we are, what we're doing, and why.

I actually have a lot of joy. And also a lot of hope. We're not going to recapture what we had in the past. But I don't think the Lord is calling us in that direction anyway. He's calling us, laypeople and priests alike, to be missionaries again. He's asking us to collaborate, to be patient with each other, to mentor each other, to share the leadership in our parishes, to be prayerful, and to have a little courage. It's his Church. That's how he'll create the future.

ɛʋ ɛʋ ɛʋ

3. From a bishop, urban diocese

One of the things that really refreshed my spirit a few years ago was traveling in Eastern Europe and meeting some of the underground bishops from the Soviet era. Back then they survived by being ambulance drivers or coal stokers or night watchmen. I visited their homes. They had very few material things, and they lived very simply. But there was a peace about them that moved me and made me compare their experiences with my own. My diocese is poor. It hasn't always been shepherded well. We have a lot of financial and morale problems. But we all still live pretty comfortably. In fact, there's a bourgeois quality to a lot of Church life in this country, and it cripples us with blind spots. It deadens our faith's eschatological dimension. We forget that our lives will culminate outside of this world and be judged by our connection to the needs and sufferings of others.

The Church is the Body of Christ, and we have his promise that she will not die. But we need to be better at remembering that the Christian life is a life of giving, a life lived for others, a life of gift. It's not a competition. It's not a race for comfort. We're all called to humble service. And unless we recover that awareness, a lot of things are going to break up and fall down, like a house of cards, or a house built on sand.

I've thought a lot about the "crises" in our culture and in our Church. A big one, probably the main one, is a crisis of fatherhood—fatherhood in our families, fatherhood among priests, and especially

fatherhood among bishops. I was on retreat a year or so ago, and
the retreat master pushed me very hard to examine the questions of
fatherhood, fidelity, and betrayal. We all have frictions and disap-
pointments with friends and family members. But some of the hardest
experiences in my life have been with clergy, and of those clergy,
most of them were bishops. Why is that? Maybe it's just my bad
luck. But I think it's a more widespread misuse of ecclesial authority
and power.

Right now I'm dealing with post-traumatic shock in many of my
priests who've been manhandled. Some of them might deserve to
be slapped on the side of the head, but no one in their past—least
of all the bishop—dealt with their spiritual weakness and disordered
behavior in a genuine, fatherly way. I have one young priest whose
dad totally rejected him and never speaks to him. Never. It's the
most deforming issue in his life, and it demands a huge emotional
effort to work through. So, I suppose the lesson is this: The men
whom the Church calls to be bishops—myself included—need to be
better fathers to their priests. We need to exercise our ministry with
real paternal care for the priests who serve our people, the priests on
whom our people depend.

ॐ ॐ ॐ

4. From a bishop, urban diocese

In our diocese most of the civil authorities are Catholic. Some are
better Catholics than others, but most of them are Catholic. Secularism is growing, especially among our Latino population. But the
Catholic culture is still there; not as strong as we want it to be, but
we're at least holding our own. We get a lot of newcomers moving
here from other states, and that's great for the Church in one sense,
but dangerous in another. It can make us complacent and mask the
number of people falling away. Our politics are fairly conservative
because we have a lot of people who fled here at some point from
places like Nicaragua, Honduras, Colombia, and Venezuela, because
of Marxist violence or persecution. For a lot of my people, communists are just Democrats in a hurry.

The biggest surprise for me in becoming a bishop was that I was too
young. At least I assumed so. I did come from a very strong Catholic

family. But I'd never studied in Rome, never been a seminary rector, hadn't worked in a chancery, and didn't have a canon law degree. My background was pastoral work, and I knew a couple of languages from working with immigrants. The hardest things for me now in my ministry are the personnel challenges, and I don't mean character issues, but the three-dimensional chess I have to play with pastors because some of our parishes celebrate Mass in multiple languages. It keeps me awake at night. But generally speaking, I'm very happy with the men coming out of our seminary. They're a lot more intentional than my own age cohort was. They understand what the stakes are. And they're "conservative" in the best sense of the word: orthodox and faithful in belief, but pastoral and human in their manner.

I do know that many of my priests have misgivings about Pope Francis. Especially the Latin American Jesuits working here. Francis didn't do well as a Jesuit provincial in Argentina, and Jesuits have long memories. One of them calls him "our Trump". But I tell people they're wrong. I think Francis may actually be a genius. We live in a moment when every major institution—government, academia, entertainment, the news media, religion—all seem to be discredited. So Francis becomes the head of the longest-lived institution in history, the papacy. And what does he do? He presents himself, from the very first day, as *anti-institutional*. Which immediately explains why the secular world is attracted to him, and so many otherwise alienated people seem to admire him. I was on a walking pilgrimage with a priest friend recently, and my friend complained to me that "Francis never says anything nice about priests." My answer was, "Oh really, you're worried about that? Have you ever heard him say anything nice about bishops?"

ᘓᕒ ᘓᕒ ᘓᕒ

5. From a bishop, urban diocese

Among my people, at least, there's the same divide you'll find in the public square. Some are perfectly happy to depend on the government. They believe it should be doing and providing more. They think the Church should actually be more like the government. And then a lot of others are suspicious now of any kind of government effort to impose even commonsense restrictions on anything. Meanwhile, the ability of the Church to affect the culture positively is diminishing. One reason for that is our congregations reflect the same intense antagonisms you'll find in our wider society. Another is the simple fact that we're losing strength. And political leaders know it. I can write pastoral letters, make statements, record videos, engage in focus groups and town halls, all those things. But the reality is that the Church is not on the upswing, but on the downswing. And our political leadership exploits that. So mainly I'm stuck playing defense.

We just don't have the conceptual tools as a society anymore to bring about a healthy and respectful dialogue, let alone find common ground. The tools are gone, and the main one missing is an acceptance, even unconsciously, of the natural moral law. The disappearance of natural law thinking has had a huge effect on the diminishment of religion, but also on people's ability to intuit that some things are always right, other things are always wrong, and how to properly apply prudential reasoning to things in the middle. We used to have a substratum of commonly held moral sanity that helped people on both sides of a dispute come together. Again, that's gone.

Social media have made our discourse much nastier, more brittle, and apocalyptic. Catholic media often ape and add to the confusion. And compounding the problem is our forgetfulness of history. As a nation, we've never been very good at history; now we barely know it at all. The reason for that is our educational system. We've created two generations of people who really don't know their heritage, and then we wonder why they're willing to part with it so easily. I believe that was done on purpose by people in authority. And I think it bodes ill for our democratic structures and representative form of government.

Sometimes I wish we'd never had a Catholic president. We'd be better off for it. We've celebrated our assimilation. Now we're paying the price for it. At some point, a wholehearted identification with the Catholic faith was surpassed by the desire to "fit in" and succeed in the broader culture. The rosary of a man like Joe Biden is a bit like a perfume bottle. It's empty, but you can still catch the scent of the perfume now and again.

॰ॐ ॰ॐ ॰ॐ

6. From a bishop, urban/rural diocese

I was a vicar general before becoming a bishop, so the content of the job wasn't a surprise. But it's easy when you're behind the throne whispering your advice into the ear of your boss. You can be wrong and not have to live with it. A bishop owns his decisions. That's why I value the bishops' conference. It's fraternal in the true sense of the word, where you can walk up and talk to anybody and get his advice as a brother. I did have a few surprises. I have a great diocese; it's not "radical" at all. Our people are faithful and pretty conservative. But I still get pushback from the fringes in the Church. Somebody is always unhappy. Somebody always thinks I'm doing the job wrong. So, I can't imagine what it's like to be in a place like Chicago or one of the dioceses where the bishops were off the wall for years. I was surprised too by my first visit to our Extraordinary Form parish. I was expecting a lot of old people, more or less trying to get back to the past through the old Latin Mass. It was the opposite: a lot of young singles and families who had no memory of the 1950s and therefore no nostalgia. They just wanted something grounded and beautiful.

The thing that really shook me, though, was a conversation I had with an exorcist, a very good man, and then reading some of his redacted reports. They were deeply sobering. I don't think people have any idea of how much genuine, satanic evil is out there, the demons that can be present in a person, and the way they can enter a human being through the senses, from the misuse of technology, from generational curses, or through the role of other sins, like free-masonry, in someone's history. I know that can sound implausible. Everything is psychology these days. Most people don't have a grasp of real evil. That's because we haven't preached it. And one of the devil's favorite tactics is to get us to believe that he doesn't exist. But he's very real and very active. People who doubt that are putting themselves in serious danger.

The key thing we need to keep in mind is that helping people means leading them to the truth. We can "accompany" people all day long, and that's good if it finally leads them to the right desti-nation. Otherwise it's just the blind leading the blind. I find that many people are hungry for the truth because they get so much equivocation and deceit. They deal with people every day who try to mold reality into some political framework. It deforms the soul, and people sooner or later can sense they're being lied to. And that's an opening for the Gospel.

🙋 🙋 🙋

7. From a bishop, urban diocese

We're living in unprecedented times, and I don't know what God is up to. I serve in a very secular environment, a kind of poster child for the political divides of the day. For the civil authorities here, the Church is irrelevant. A fly in the ointment.

Within the Church, there's a purification going on, a winnowing of the flock. A lot of our Catholic people think that being a good Christian boils down to loving everybody, embracing and not judging them, and being inclusive and welcoming. If we did that, we could just limp along, try to make everyone happy, and keep them in the fold at all costs. The trouble is, that's not Christianity. It's not the faith of the Catholic Church. It's not the truth Jesus taught. As a Church we need to get back to apostolic mission, to preaching and living the whole Word of God. I want everyone to have the necessities of a decent life. I want every person to have the basic things that support his or her God-given dignity, and part of the Church's mission is helping to provide that. But my job isn't ensuring people's material happiness. My job is leading people to a transformative encounter with Jesus Christ, for the sake of their salvation. My task is the salvation of a man's or a woman's soul. So I find it distressing, frankly, when some of our Church leaders seem to worry more about the climate of the planet than the climate of faith, the *crisis* of faith, in our own house.

Pope Francis has a great love for the poor. His heart is genuine. He's committed to the social mission of the Church. He deserves our gratitude for refocusing our attention on the reality of evil, and the importance of the corporal and spiritual works of mercy. But a pope should be the principle of unity in the Church, and instead Francis fosters ambiguity, which feeds division. His distaste for the United States and its bishops is obvious and unwarranted. His manner is authoritarian. And it's revealing that not a single seminarian inspired by Francis has come to this diocese during his tenure. A Church under pressure needs something better than this.

$\gg$ $\gg$ $\gg$

8. From a bishop, urban diocese

I know a lot of dioceses suffer from "empty building" syndrome. That's not our problem here. We don't have any empty buildings. We're constantly building new churches, schools, Newman Centers, that sort of thing. So we're very much in that mode. We've been one of the fastest-growing regions in the country for the past few years. We put a big emphasis on evangelizing through our Catholic schools. We're not in the business of getting kids into Ivy League universities. We make that very clear to parents. Our schools are academically strong, but that's secondary to developing mature young men and women in Christ. We hire teachers and staff accordingly. The key thing is leadership. I've made sure that every one of our schools is under a pastor who's committed to serving as its spiritual father. We want no separation between the interests of families in our schools and the families in our parishes.

For me, our culture has two big wounds. The first is our appetite for sterility. Contraception steals something from the soul. If you're a layperson, there's no way to make up for not having children; for not welcoming new life. And it has a ripple effect. It damages the whole of society, including the integrity of family structure and the consolations of old age. The other wound is our crisis in the identity and mission of men. We're made in God's image, male and female. Men and women both need to flourish in their particular ways. Our culture now aggressively undermines the identity of women, but men even more so. It strips away the reasons why men should be strong and unselfish and courageous. It's very much a work of the devil and a matter of spiritual warfare, because it attacks the nature of who and what human beings are, and why we're here. Our hearts were made for God. They're made for goodness, beauty, fruitfulness, and truth. We long for those things. We starve and become bitter without them.

I do worry about how I can keep our people's focus on the Lord. I worry about how I can help them better engage the culture. There are times when I tell God, "I don't have a clue what you want me to do in this situation." But for the most part I'm very peaceful. I don't have trouble sleeping. I'm the kind of person who's almost always hopeful, because I really do trust that Jesus makes all things new. I don't know why he chose me as a bishop, but I trust that he did. And I figure that if he can work through me, he can work through anybody.

❧ ❧ ❧

9. From a bishop, urban diocese

I have a good diocese in a friendly state. When I was appointed here, I got a personal, handwritten note from the governor welcoming me. I couldn't believe it, especially given the atmosphere of the state I was coming from. When protestors disrupted a pro-life Mass at our cathedral, shouting at children and screaming "This Church teaches hate!", a number of state legislators immediately reached out to us, wanting to find ways to prevent that in the future. And I honestly don't feel a lot of division in the U.S. hierarchy. Neither do my bishop friends. Maybe I'm being naïve. I know there are troublesome pockets, but I just stay away from them. I have my own diocese to run. I'm not worried about other dioceses. I need to stay focused on what's happening here.

In my experience, most bishops are like that. They're normal guys trying to do their best. You meet an occasional climber or stuffed shirt, but at the end of the day, they all want to do what's best for their people. They're loyal men of the Church. I don't know any one of them who's disloyal. It's a good brotherhood, and we need that because the office of bishop is a kind of giant problem-solving machine, and the problems never stop. I worry about my priests staying healthy. I worry about my people staying faithful to the Church. I worry about paying for schools that have great academics but don't really teach the faith. I worry about Pope Francis because he's a pastor, and pastors aren't always clear. They often speak in informal, pastoral ways that can easily be misunderstood or twisted out of context ... and some people are happy to do that. And I worry about persons I might hurt by the decisions I need to make. That's the stuff that keeps me awake at night, because the people I've pastored through-out my priesthood have been generous and grateful and good, and they deserve the best I've got.

What I don't worry about is the future. I have a lot of hope. We'll be a smaller Church but a stronger one. I believe that. A big, luke-warm Church attracts nobody; it converts no one. The good news is that I can see all the faith we'll need for the future in some of the young people I meet.

ЗО ЗО ЗО

10. From a bishop, urban/rural diocese

Over the last few years, it's struck me that we're very much in an Old Testament moment; a moment when many people in the Church today, like the people of Israel, have abandoned faith in God while still giving him lip service. In their heart of hearts, a lot of folks who claim to be Christian don't really believe in the authority of Jesus Christ. Even some of my brother bishops are actually more influ-enced by the culture than by the Gospel. I wonder if they've ever really encountered Jesus Christ. The same applies to many priests. The basic questions that every believer needs to answer and be able to articulate are very simple: How has Jesus Christ changed my life, and what's my relationship with him?

We need to take the words of Jesus seriously. We need to be *in* the world, but not *of* the world. And communicating that effectively at the local level depends on the pastor. The pastor is essential. His skill and his personality determine whether a parish will thrive, floun-der, or decline. Which means you need a man in that role who has truly encountered Jesus Christ. That's why I see a "spirituality year" before men enter the seminary as so important. Men thinking about the priesthood need a year of withdrawal from the noise of the world to focus on conversion of the heart and growing in intimacy with God. Without a deeply rooted relationship with Jesus, a man can't be faithful to his promises, especially today. The seminary formation I got in the 1970s didn't have that. I had to find it on my own. I read everything good I could get my hands on. Dietrich Bonhoeffer's book *The Cost of Discipleship* had a big influence on me.

I worry very much about our young people; their suicide rate, and how unhappy they often are. Today's sexual confusion has left so many young people deeply wounded, badly hurt, and really struggling. I hear it all the time in the confessional. They feel lied to. They were told that hooking up would make them happy, and instead they end up sleeping with people whose names they don't even know. As a country, we've created a lot of human wreckage. So I've stopped putting my hope in programs and leaders. The only person who gives me hope is Jesus Christ. He doesn't disappoint.

ॐ ॐ ॐ

11. From a bishop, urban/rural diocese

I was blessed to serve as an auxiliary bishop before I took over a diocese. A lot of priests go straight from being a pastor to being an ordinary. That can be tough. As an auxiliary, you learn the ropes but can dodge some of the difficult issues. When you're the ordinary, the buck stops with you. And it's almost like, you're no longer a real person; you're this entity. Your whole life really does change because you can no longer be who you are. You always have to be "the bishop". The hardest thing for me has been dealing with the scandals in the Church, at both the universal and local levels, especially when you're dealing with your own priests who've done stupid or evil things and you need to make hard decisions. It breaks my heart, but it's necessary for the sake of the faithful.

On the matter of selecting new bishops: For me, the main issues with any candidate for the episcopacy are simple. How many vocations has this priest helped cultivate? If he's a pastor, is he living his priesthood as a true shepherd of souls? Is his parish dynamic? How well does he work with laypeople? If a guy lacks an advanced degree, but he's getting vocations, and his parish is hitting on all eight cylinders with lots of good things happening—I'd take somebody like that as bishop material any day over a talented, brilliant intellectual. I do think that consulting more mature, committed laypeople in the selection process would be a good thing. But opening up a confidential process to the public in the name of transparency would be a mistake. It would invite lobbying and also feed careerism in guys hoping to get on the list.

One of the big problems for me with today's technology is the damage it's done to the humanities. They're collapsing. Seminarians need a stronger exposure to the humanities because they transform the spirit and the imagination; they encourage the virtues. We don't do a good enough job with that. A priest needs to be reasonably well-read. I can't emphasize that enough. Guys need to understand and be able to communicate our history as a believing people, with its great Christian achievements, saints, and minds. And I also think it would be a disaster to end the requirement of celibacy. The priesthood would disappear as we know it. Celibate, genuinely masculine priests are a tremendous witness in a hypersexualized culture. Christian marriage and priestly celibacy go hand in hand. Good priests living their celibacy with confidence and joy are an example of self-discipline that encourages married couples to live out their own covenant faithfully.

❧ ❧ ❧

12. From a bishop, urban diocese

What's striking to me is the escalation of really toxic division and violence in the country: the name-calling, the refusal to engage in debate or talk about the merits of an issue. It's all *ad hominem* attacks, with people being slandered and punished and even losing their jobs because they're not sufficiently "woke". People don't trust the government anymore. They feel it's out of touch and destroying their lives. They see a political elite that's living very comfortably, while issuing all sorts of edicts that seem to be arbitrary. And that's dangerous. It encourages an appetite for rebellion. It's the stuff of which revolutions are made.

I've tried to work with public officials. They pay lip service to the value of faith and the role of religious leaders, but it never goes anywhere. We're heading into a dark time for the Church. We need bishops with more spiritual vision who can understand today's new environment for what it is. The political landscape has changed drastically, but as a Church, we still think we should interact with government officials collaboratively, even when we have disagreements. That's not realistic anymore. We need to relate to public authorities in a very different way, but the herd mentality among bishops can be astonishing. At the bishops' conference level, the group dynamics are such that a few powerful personalities can shift the whole momentum in a fruitless direction. So, I think Joseph Ratzinger's prediction from 50 years ago is coming to pass. We'll be a smaller Church. The process will happen more slowly in some of our ethnic groups that have a deeper Catholic culture. But we'll lose a lot of our institutions. The upside is that the people who stay will be stronger and more faithful.

I suppose what causes me the most anxiety is the question, "Does the Catholic Church even exist anymore?" Most of our people are effectively Protestants. The decline of people's belief in the Real Presence is a source of great distress. As bishops, we've been smeared and slandered in the media from both the ecclesial left and right. So we've basically lost our authority. Some days I worry that the real Catholic Church is just a remnant. So I put my hope in our young ... and in the laypeople and priests of the John Paul II and Benedict XVI generations; the people who remain faithful because they have an honest desire for spiritual depth, beautiful liturgy, and the fullness of the truth.

᠀ ᠀ ᠀

13. From a bishop, urban/rural diocese

It's easy to miss the good things happening in the Church. That's where we defeat ourselves. I'm involved in a lot of evangelizing efforts, and some people are doing the work really well. FOCUS, Augustine Institute: These are the obvious examples, but many others are getting terrific results. It's a big challenge though, because today's culture is so contrary to the Christian worldview. So, it's all about the parable of the sower and seed. Not all the seed falls on good ground, but some does, and it can be hugely fruitful. That's why more bishops need to regain their prophetic edge. John Paul II's pastoral style was, "Here's the flag, I'm going up the hill. Are you coming with me? Because it's the best thing you'll ever do, the greatest adventure you'll ever have." He had a compelling Christian humanism; versus Francis, who's a bit like, "I'm here to help. I know you're in trouble; let's talk about where you're at." Two very different styles, both legitimate. I just don't think the Francis approach works in our society right now.

I have good relations with our local authorities. I support our police and certainly don't fear them. But when it comes to the federal government, I do believe that we're dealing with a totalitarian attitude now. And it's going to force us to separate from the state more and more clearly. Our Catholic schools are very important to the Church, but government could easily shut them down with content regulations that would make teaching a genuinely Catholic curriculum impossible. It's just a matter of refusing our schools' accreditation. I don't know if it will happen, but I'm prepared for the worst. I talked recently with a mother whose daughter is very bright, very Catholic, and studying at one of the Ivy League universities. The daughter could go to any medical school she wants. But she's thinking very carefully about the branch of medicine she chooses, because she never wants to be forced to act against her faith. That's the sort of "soft" totalitarianism we'll see.

A big problem in the Church right now is our instinct to maintain institutions that absorb too many resources and prevent us from doing evangelization. Another is the way we pick bishops. We tend to select men with good administrative credentials, guys with seminary or chancery experience. And there's nothing wrong with those things. But what we really need is men deeply rooted in spiritual leadership; men with maturity and discernment who know the cultural terrain and want to convert it. And finally, a lesson I've learned is that theological and pastoral problems never go away by themselves. You need to deal with them promptly. Otherwise they get worse. Kicking the can down the road doesn't work.

ଅଙ୍କ ଅଙ୍କ ଅଙ୍କ

14. From a bishop, urban/rural diocese

I'm a lucky guy. I have a core of good priests, a great head of schools, and confidence that Christ asked me do this ministry. When I was made a bishop, a friend leaned over to me with a sardonic grin and said, "Remember, the only apostle who died a natural death was John." Dark humor—but I already knew the work would be difficult. In practice, though, it's been pure gift, and I've always had three priorities: formation of our young; strengthening our Catholic schools; and vocations to the priesthood and religious life. I'll never deviate from them. I'm very grateful for our permanent deacons and lay coworkers. They do a great job. But it's strong, good priests who'll put a divided Church back together again, and they need the help of solid religious.

I always stress that the qualities which make a man a good husband and father also make a good priest. A good husband is faithful to his wife. A good father protects and provides for his family, whatever the sacrifice. That's what I'm looking for in a priest: fidelity and selflessness, humility and generosity of heart. The central task of the priesthood is saving souls. And the things that tear a priest down are greed, lust, and ambition—all of them tied to a focus on the self, instead of an honest interior life of self-examination and prayer. In fact, that's been my biggest shock, looking around at some of my brother bishops: how ambition and personal friendships get in the way of what's needed for a bishop to be a real shepherd for his diocese. There's a human side to ecclesial life that can very easily become "Church Incorporated". And yet, on the other hand, I've also met many men who are good shepherds, and some who are truly great ones. Which shows you that in the end, despite sinful humanity, the Holy Spirit really does guide the Church.

In terms of our country, there's a deep well of frustration with the government among faithful Catholics in my diocese. These are decent people. We have a lot of farming communities. They believe in justice, law, order, and equality. But they watch rioters in our cities destroy things in the name of "social justice" without any consequences, and they're angry. And I understand why. I've never seen anything like today's cultural and political hostilities in my life.

Finally, there are elements of the current papacy that remind me of the Renaissance, and not in a healthy way. In my experience, God always provides for us, and I'm steadfast in that. But I wonder if some of today's cardinals have any real faith at all. So much of the stuff coming out of Rome in recent years seems to cause more confusion and division than clarity. Not one of the men who has entered our seminary since the election of Francis did so because of him. Not one.

∂∾ ∂∾ ∂∾

15. From a bishop, urban/rural diocese

Our parishes are pretty spread out, with many miles between some churches. But what has really impressed me is the fraternity of my priests across their different age groups. And also their generosity to their people and each other. Maybe that's because Catholics are a small minority here. The state's religious life is thin. There's a strong evangelical tradition, but the mainline Protestant churches are virtually extinct. We have workable relations with the civil authorities, but religion isn't a factor in our public affairs.

For me, it feels as though the American experiment is drawing to an end. The Founders created a republic. They put a big stress on the separation of powers, because it's impossible to have real freedom in a pure democracy. It always ends up in some form of tyranny. I also think the glue, the thing that holds our society together—the religious vision—has been ripped out of it. Even if the Founders themselves were not very religious, they recognized the value of religiosity to the culture and to the moral character of the people. None of our leaders right now is very bright. Donald Trump was nothing more than a transaction analyst. Joe Biden's faith stops at the rosary beads in his pocket. He captures some of the Church's social teaching, but our social teaching begins and is grounded in the right to life. You can't be "Catholic" halfway.

Meanwhile, the Church in this country has been thrown on its back, not just by the political environment, but also by the Holy See and what's going on in the Universal Church. Rome and the Church in the United States have always had a certain tension. The sex-abuse crisis aggravated it even more. And the failure of Rome to respond quickly to the issue on a universal level made it a serious crisis for the whole Church. This goes back 20 years, well before Francis. A lot of people blame our current problems on Pope Francis. I haven't sorted that out yet. But I sometimes feel that Francis is locked in a situation he doesn't understand and in which he can't successfully maneuver. He's not even a Westerner, if we mean by that a "European".

Pope Francis clearly believes in the Gospel. He sees it as central to any successful evangelizing. But he resists saying and doing things that could preemptively alienate people who might otherwise be drawn to the faith. I understand that motive. I like a lot of the content in his encyclical *Fratelli Tutti;* it has some beautiful ideas and phrases. Yet in the end it disintegrates into a kind a syncretism that creates a lot of difficulty. He's trying to work for a peaceful world across religious divides. But we'd be better off if Francis were simply more forthright about affirming who we are as Catholics, and what we believe.

ᘔ᙮ ᘔ᙮ ᘔ᙮

16. From a bishop, urban/rural diocese

I don't think any new bishop is really prepared for the parade of day-to-day decisions that need to be made until he starts doing the work. The clergy issues take a lot of time. In any diocese, a bishop's responsibility to his priests is paramount. But the number of issues involving clergy—most of them just routine stuff like personality conflicts and burnout—was a surprise.

Having said that, my relationship with our priests, deacons, and young seminarians is where I get a lot of my satisfaction. They're not perfect, and neither am I. But they're a great group of dedicated men with a lot of solidarity. I also really enjoy the time I spend out in the parishes with the people of the diocese, and having them to my home for dinners. I don't mind the office work too much, but it's not exactly life-giving.

We're mainly a rural diocese. Watching the demographic changes has been hard. Once upon a time, there was a whole network of little country and small town parishes scattered across the diocese. That was the backbone of our local Church and our culture. The structure of American agriculture is very different now, and the small family farm is more and more challenged. The number of people living in the countryside and actually engaged in farming has declined quite a bit. So, a lot of our small, rural parishes have either merged or closed outright. In an urban parish, people are part of a much larger group, but they're not as well known to each other. It's more impersonal, and I think that has a psychological effect on anyone who grew up in a rural community and knew everyone by name.

For what it's worth, since you ask, I think laypeople electing their bishops would be a very bad idea. It would turn the Church into a religious version of the American democratic system, and that would be a disaster. I also worry, and I've heard this same worry from half a dozen other bishops, about how bishops are selected today once a list of candidates gets to Rome. There's a feeling that one or two individuals—a particular cardinal, perhaps—manipulate Rome's perceptions and have an inordinate influence over what happens in this country. I don't know a single American bishop who's disloyal to the Holy See. But I do think some of the pope's advisers and collaborators undercut what we bishops are trying to do in the United States.

୬ ୬ ୬

17. From a bishop, urban diocese

Like a lot of cities, we had rioting and fires that did heavy damage to our poorer neighborhoods in 2020. This was during COVID and after the George Floyd killing. The people of our diocese were extraordinarily generous. They helped us provide a lot of support to families who lost their homes and businesses. But there was also plenty of really visceral anger, both toward the police and against the rioters. I think the events of 2020/2021 pushed people to greater extremes, whatever their political views are. Among our people, there's deep distrust of government now, and I'm not sure how the government can recover from it.

One of the unexpected things, and good things, we're experiencing is a boom in our more traditional parishes. Especially with young people and young families. It's happening in the parishes that offer the Extraordinary Form of the Mass, but also in those parishes that are true to the Ordinary Form, but maybe use more Latin and are thicker in Church traditions. And that's just the tip of the iceberg. Whatever video games might be doing to their brains, the Lord seems to be working in the hearts and capturing the attention of a lot of young people. Even at our cathedral, where the liturgies tend to be a little more "progressive" and the congregation is mainly singles and couples, not so much families, 60 percent of the people are younger than 40. It's fantastic. So there's a great hunger for beauty out there. The sacramental imagination is still alive. And if you feed that imagination—people's need for something sacred and true, something beautiful and greater than themselves—and combine it with active outreach and social ministry, the results are impressive.

It gives me a lot of hope. When you watch these young parents and children get all excited as they discover Jesus Christ in his
Church, you realize that the same message was preached 20 centuries
ago, and it still has enormous impact, despite all of the world's distractions and changes in culture and technology. The Lord continues
to do his work, and the work still bears fruit. We just need to be
nimbler in addressing the challenges that are coming our way. And
we need to be more willing to speak the truth ... even when it's not
welcome; even when it has a cost.

ॐ ॐ ॐ

18. From a bishop, urban diocese

Our state has a lot of conservative Protestants. The religious ethos
here is still strong. In other parts of the country the Church might
be declining, but here, we're growing. I could open up three new
Catholic parishes tomorrow if I had the resources. We have big numbers of candidates and catechumens coming into the Church each
year. Our diocese has also been very welcoming to immigrants and
refugees, and I'm proud of that. And the energy of our laypeople is
wonderful. Christ promised to stay with his Church, and we need to
believe his word. We all tend to live in the moment and focus on its
issues and problems. But whenever I get down or angry, I compare
the good that's happening here with the state of the Church in A.D.
1000. It was a debacle, a disaster beyond belief, and yet we came
through. So, I have a lot of hope.

I do still worry about the Church in the long run. When you look
at North Africa, it's hard to believe that it once had hundreds of Catholic dioceses and bishops. In some areas the Catholic Church may
simply die out in the years ahead. The Church will always survive
until the Lord returns, but there's no guarantee that she'll have any
big presence in the United States. Candidly, I don't know how things
will work out in this country. We have some really good bishops in
the national conference, but we're in an environment now where we
bishops need the courage to speak out more clearly and firmly.

Over the past decade, the Roman curia has focused much more
effectively on serving the needs of the local bishop. I give Pope Francis credit for that; and likewise for his efforts at reforming the Holy

See's finances. Those efforts are needed. But I think his manner of governance is actually quite ruthless. It weakens the authority of the papal office. He has a hard time delegating. His idea of obedience is very top-down and shaped by his Jesuit formation. He talks about accompaniment and listening, but then he relies on a very small group of advisers. All of this ends up being dangerous because of the ambiguity and friction it causes. So, I hope the cardinals will elect someone in the next conclave who'll just let the waves settle for a while. That's what we probably need.

᷑᷑ ᷑᷑ ᷑᷑

19. From a bishop, urban diocese

I grew up in an extraordinarily warm, liberating Catholic culture. That's gone. We can no longer count on the culture to support a Christian life. What we've got now in our country is, at best, a tolerance of religion as a personal hobby for superstitious weak people who cling to their childhood dreams. At worst, more and more, we're dealing with a real hatred, an outright bigotry, toward religious faith. Which is ironic, because there's never been a progressive reform movement in American history that wasn't birthed by religion. We're almost back in the days of the French Revolution. We have a gang of juiced-up Jacobins running society who really think the government should control everything.

I'm reminded of two good men. The first is John Tracy Ellis, who said that, in reality, there were *never* any "good old days" in the Church. We've always been a mix of success and disaster. The second is an African bishop who got up years ago at one of the synods and said, "Maybe you gentlemen from Europe and America didn't get the memo, but Constantine is dead. And so is his style of Church." The truth is, we're living on the fumes of a "used-to-be" Catholic culture and its institutional infrastructure. So, I could sit around and wring my hands and whine. Or I can say, "What's Jesus inviting us to do?" I think he's asking us to return—not to the 1950s, but to the 30s, and I mean to the A.D. 30s; as John Paul II said, to the shores of the Sea of Galilee. And that can be very painful because it disrupts how we imagine our world.

I do need to acknowledge Democratic Party leaders for a very shrewd, if deceitful, political strategy. It started in the Obama administration and carried over into the Biden White House. They no longer say, "We respect the views of the Catholic community, but unfortunately we plan to go in a different direction." That at least was honest. Instead, they now surround themselves with dissenting Catholics, who then argue that *they're* the real Church, not those out-of-touch bishops hung up on issues like sex. And that licenses a president, senators, and members of Congress, and anyone else, to claim that, yes, they disagree with their Church on some pivotal issues ... but that really doesn't affect their Catholic identity. Which then widens the fissures in the believing community, to the benefit of both party leadership and the dissenters. Yet it doesn't change the fact that, in the Catholic Church, *only* bishops have the authority to govern and teach in matters of faith. So, the results for loyal Catholics are purely destructive.

I never thought I'd put the prayer to St. Michael the Archangel on my medicine cabinet mirror. But I did. Now I pray it every morning when I shave. There is utter, raw evil in the world, and it's the strongest force in the universe. Save one.

2♥ 2♥ 2♥

20. From a bishop, urban diocese

COVID changed the way a lot of people think. During and after the pandemic we had an uptick of confessions in many of our parishes. A lot of people developed a deeper awareness of death and mortality. I'm not sure how many of them translated that into a healthy concern for the afterlife, or the real meaning of this one. But I'm amazed at how many suicides we've seen since 2020. It's been a soul-shaking time, and people are very aware of their vulnerability. It means that we need priests with the spiritual and intellectual skills to engage the culture, but also with a very deep human formation, men that can use their humanity as a bridge to other people.

That's a challenge because many of our seminarians and young priests themselves have wounded backgrounds. So, one of our tasks is helping them integrate their experiences in a wholesome way, and then helping them use those healed experiences as a means to reach, encourage, and evangelize others. It's interesting that a lot of our best candidates come from homeschooling families. We also get some very good candidates from our Catholic high schools. In my time, most seminarians were older, second-career type guys. But here, now, many of the men want to come right out of high school.

As for our people: One of the least-known documents of Vatican II is the Decree on the Apostolate of the Laity. It's profoundly beautiful, and reading it reminds me how badly we've neglected forming lay men and women for their mission in the world. We've muddied the water by mixing up terms like "ministry" and "apostolate". They're really not the same thing. But I think, in our diocese, that we've got a pretty strong young adult outreach. A couple of our priests have a real gift for the work. They bring young adults together in smaller communities to pray and socialize. There's a sports dimension, and a kind of informal matchmaking environment where people might meet a future spouse. But it's oriented around the idea of "vocation", with a focus on preparing people for the lay apostolate and what that actually means. It's made a big impact, and I'm proud of it. I hope we can expand it further.

I think we all need to realize, not just bishops but all of us, that we'll face a much less friendly climate in this country going forward. And I don't mean just from the federal government. Wealthy corporations have powerful tools at their disposal, and they're driving a lot of the woke message.

ᘔᕽ ᘔᕽ ᘔᕽ

21. From a bishop, urban diocese

Culturally, we're all in adrenaline mode right now. In a crisis, you don't usually spend your time making temperature checks. You tend to keep your eye on the horizon, look for creative solutions, and help the people around you stay calm. It's very difficult to pause, and maybe not wise to pause, and ask, "What's this mean for the rest of my life?" You just keep working. That's how I've spent most of my life as a bishop. I've had to live in that mode. So I don't think we'll fully understand the impact of things like the 2020/2021 COVID plague and our political antagonisms, and what they mean for the Church, for another

50 years. It usually takes that long to see how events really fit into a bigger picture. I mean, Vatican II ended in 1965, and we're still arguing about it.

COVID did make many more people aware of how fragile life is. They're a lot more conscious of their mortality. And for those who'll listen, there's a window in that for the Church to talk about faith as a pathway to meaning. American culture runs on a kind of unstated scientism. It's our unofficial state religion: When we're dead, that's it, because our lives don't really mean anything; but to keep going, we need to pretend that they do. The only way to handle that emptiness is to avoid ultimate questions. You see the result in a lot of funeral rituals. People want to celebrate the passing of a life, but they don't want to talk about an afterlife. That subject makes them uneasy. Most just avoid thinking about it too deeply.

People say that we need to retire the model of Christendom for the Church and think of ourselves as back in the Apostolic Age. That's true as far as it goes, but I think we need to draw our lessons, going forward, from all of our Christian history: the Church Fathers, the Renaissance, the post-Reformation period. I'm very much a coach and a shepherd, not a visionary. For vision I rely on the experiences of others and especially on the leadership of the popes and their pastoral letters. I understand why many people are thrilled with Pope Francis. He says a lot of good things, and I try to make good use of them. I do feel that his vision sometimes seems incomplete and naïve. The informal way he communicates isn't helpful. But I think these things will encourage bishops to take a more adult approach in their relationship with the Holy Father, instead of the child-father style of the past.

Finally, I strongly believe in the importance of priestly celibacy. It's a witness to the Kingdom of heaven, which we probably need more than ever. There's a temptation today to interpret the Church, her structures, and her issues sociologically. That's a dangerous mistake.

૱ ૱ ૱

22. From a bishop, urban diocese

I think it actually takes a lot more faith to be an atheist than a Christian, because you need to believe that everything just happened by extraordinary chance. And "believe" is the right word. Atheism, the serious kind, is a belief system just like a religion. You decide that there's no God. Then you build your life and reasoning and world-view on top of that. As Christians, we look at the beauty and order in the world, and we conclude that there's a divine intelligence bigger than ourselves. From that, we begin to understand that this Creator God pursues and desires friendship with us. He seeks a relationship with us, and we build from there. The trouble is that our society, as it stands right now, discourages deep thinking about anything, especially ultimate questions.

Plenty of people consider themselves "Christian" as a kind of cultural tradition. They might even have a sense that there's something after this world, but they don't really see the need for a Redeemer. It's just easier not to worry about that stuff until something like COVID comes along. Then they're afraid of dying. But they're more afraid of dying than anything that might come after it. So a lot of people today are living off the emotional and moral equity of a much stronger faith in the past, without thinking through what the Christian faith really teaches or requires. Our culture is very good at enabling that disinterest. In the end, though, it leads to a life that doesn't have any larger meaning. There's an opportunity in that emptiness for the Church to provide an alternative. But it takes intentional disciples, both lay-people and priests, to do the evangelization. That's not where most Catholics are at. And we need to get them there, because there's a real agenda now to make teaching Christian morality a hate crime, and a good part of the population might be willing to go along with that.

What concerns me most about American Catholics is that many of them haven't yet had a personal encounter with Jesus Christ. That only comes through a life of prayer. It's a central part of the Church's mission to facilitate that encounter. And of course we do it through the sacramental life, but also through preaching and teaching and personal witness. Ambiguity confuses. Clarity of teaching is essential. People follow a challenge, not a question mark. So my number one priority as a bishop is to do whatever I can to help that personal relationship with Jesus Christ to happen. My other priority is the family. So much of the moral chaos in our country right now is connected with gender and gay activism issues. So, building up the Christian family unit and good marriages has real urgency.

ズ ズ ズ

23. From a bishop, urban/rural diocese

I think the biggest impact on today's Catholic life is obvious. The effect of the 1960s sexual revolution on the Church and the world has been huge. It was pivotal in affecting the attitudes of both laypeople and priests in a detrimental way, leading to abuses that were manifested decades later. We're still under its cloud. Countering that spirit very powerfully was Paul VI's challenge in *Humanae Vitae*. But it was rejected at its publication by many Catholic theologians and clergy, who still dismiss it. The Church and the world, family life, and personal mores suffer today because that teaching was not embraced.

I'm no fan of the late Father Andrew Greeley, but I believe his research on Catholic schools as a sociologist is still relevant. Catholic culture was nurtured and sustained in the past by Catholic schools. It still is today. There's no comparable tool for providing a Catholic perspective on life to young people. We need to find a way to keep our schools going. With a hostile administration in Washington, and an increasingly secular government agenda, Catholic school education is more needed than ever.

As for the future: John Paul II stressed the need for a new evangelization—new, not in its message of salvation in Jesus Christ, but new in ardor, methods, and expressions. Paul VI had already, earlier, stressed evangelization as central to the Church's identity in *Evangelii Nuntiandi*. And Pope Francis has called all the baptized to be "missionary disciples" in *Evangelii Gaudium*. But these are just beautiful documents until we own their content in our personal thinking and behavior. Words are important, but actions make our intentions and language real.

Mother Angelica's excellent EWTN apostolate is now run by laypeople. Centers and resources led by laypeople help women with support for their unborn children. Alternatives to abortion now function in every diocese. So, I'd argue that a new evangelization is actually underway, despite all the obstacles. I just hope that today's surge in lay involvement will also lead to more vocations for the priesthood and religious life. We need the help of good priests and religious to make the Church firm in her doctrinal and moral teaching. She needs to recover a clear sense, not a fuzzy self-understanding, of who she is. Clarity in Church teaching is essential. We'll remain in our current spiritual morass unless the Church speaks clearly and persuasively.

And she speaks most persuasively by the example of her saints. We can be confident in the future to the extent that the Church produces saints as models for the rest of us. In the end, sanctity among our people is always the measure of the Church and her mission ... in the past, the present, and the future.

$$\approx \approx \approx$$

24. From a bishop, urban diocese

I have a lot of anxiety regarding the federal government and how it will impact the Church in the future on issues like family life, sexuality, education, the right to life, and religious liberty. Bishops will need to be more involved in the public arena. They'll need stronger voices and a willingness to push back against public authorities on matters of substance. The priests in my diocese have a very good grasp of what's happening. I have a youngish presbyterate, and the men tend to be warriors. They want to take on the culture and change it for the better. But the greatest counterweight to what's deforming our country will come from holy families; holy people living their faith without fear or embarrassment. And I see a lot of that. Things are getting really scary, and people now sense it. We've reached a point where just to say "I'm Catholic first" takes some real courage. Too many of us, both clergy and lay, have been naïve about where we fit in American culture. It's prevented us from thinking critically about the direction of the country. I see that even within the conference of bishops. But again, we're at a crossroads now, and each bishop will need to come to terms with reality.

I'm pleased that our men's groups across the diocese are very prevalent. Many of our parishes do evangelization really well, forming laypeople as intentional disciples. I think we do a pretty good job forming our seminarians to be ready for their priesthood intellectually, to preach and teach the Gospel. But they're also learning the need to touch people's hearts; that they need to prepare well and communicate their homilies in a way that inspires people. Above all, they need to develop an intimacy with Jesus Christ.

I'm a strong believer in Catholic schools. They're one of the most powerful forces in the Church. But they need to be thoroughly

Catholic or they're not worth the cost and effort. Which means we need to be very careful about whom we hire so that our Catholic identity penetrates every element of the curriculum. I do think we need better partnering with homeschool families. In the past there's been too much disconnect between Catholic schools and home-schooling. But homeschooling families, especially now, are the source of a lot of our vocations.

I think my biggest temptation is fear; the worry that we're becoming irrelevant as a Church. And there's a lot of dissonance, with different bishops in different dioceses saying different things, and thereby confusing everyday believers. But that's just the devil at work, and we need to fight him. What gives me hope is our seminarians. They're quality men, extremely well-formed, and they're on fire with the faith. And they're here to serve.

🙟 🙟 🙟

25. From a bishop, urban/rural diocese

The spike in anger and anxiety across the country since 2020 has been very obvious. The atmosphere now is different from anything in my lifetime. We're no longer arguing about how to get to a commonly shared goal. Now we have warring goals. Even in the USCCB, I'm worried that we've gone backwards regarding the relation of bishop to bishop. The tensions have become more pronounced. We've had a long period of bishops being named who were more theologically astute and ecclesially centered than socially centered. That has changed, and it's pulling us apart again, because if we don't speak to our people about the problem of public leaders who are Catholic in name only, we put a lot of souls at risk.

I've been impressed with the Roman curia under Pope Francis. They've been prompt and supportive, especially when I've needed help with doctrinal or clergy matters. On the downside, I'm concerned that the process of naming bishops isn't as carefully followed as it ought to be. Not as many persons are given the opportunity for input as should be. Appointments are being made that have been very surprising. Some new appointees seem to be completely unknown to their metropolitan archbishop or fellow bishops. It's as if no serious studies were done on them beforehand. If the process of Church law isn't followed, then you don't have checks and balances, and you're liable to end up in trouble later with a lot of regret and complications. Francis seems to have a coterie around him with an unhelpful ideology and agenda, and a very negative view of the United States.

In my own diocese, I focus on holy disciples, holy families, and holy vocations. That's the tripod of any new evangelization. We have more faithful laypeople involved here in the oversight of the diocese than ever before. They're very good at what they do, and they're inspiring in their fidelity. As for the future: I try to avoid language like "strategic planning" because that's the most dreaded expression in the lexicon of diocesan-speak. For most priests and people, what they actually hear is this: "They're going to close us." We do need to plan at the diocesan and parish levels in an intentional way. But it needs to be done in a framework of new evangelizing—and not just with those pious-sounding words, but in a real spirit of renewed mission. Of course, that's a lot easier said than done. But it does need to be done.

My hope in all of today's confusion comes in front of the tabernacle every morning. My hope is in the Eucharist. The late Cardinal John O'Connor, a great man, used to say, "Lord, help me get out of the way and just let you do your work." I've never forgotten his words. I pray them every day.

ॐ ॐ ॐ

26. From a bishop, urban/rural diocese

I was raised Catholic. I kept my faith throughout my time in the military and then into my university days. But a bunch of things happened in my sophomore year. I found a good prayer group in a local parish. I began to feel that my faith was like a beautiful car that didn't have enough gas in it, and I wanted something more. Things just started to switch on. I had an experience of God that made him very real to me, and my faith came alive in a way that it hadn't been before. I still remember going to Mass for the first time after that. We were praying the Gloria, and I was just taken up in that moment. God was intensely present. Everything came alive for me: Scripture, the sacraments, all of it. I hadn't made any long-term life decisions, so I just put myself radically in the hands of the Holy Spirit. It sounds naïve maybe, but here we are. That's how it happened.

I think the way we currently form young Catholics often vaccinates them *against* actually believing once they're out in the big world. That needs to change. We need to lead them to a personal encounter with God, where they let him grab hold of their lives and do wonderful things through them. We're not doing that anywhere near adequately. I see this a lot on college campuses, including the Catholic ones. The students might go to Sunday Mass or volunteer at the social justice center, but the faith doesn't really penetrate and transform their lives. Part of it is our history. We had a pioneer Church until not too long ago. The kind of persons you need for a pioneer Church are missionaries, evangelists, people willing to be proactive. In a marriage, you marry your wife rather than some other woman because you love her more than anybody else. Love makes us do extraordinary, unselfish, all-consuming things. The Church in this country was founded by people who loved the Lord in exactly that fashion. But around 1900, the Church started getting established. We weren't pioneers anymore. We became settlers. And when you settle the land, you need a different skill set. The trouble is, when you focus too much on settling, you can forget why you started in the first place. You lose that pioneer, evangelizing spirit. That's where we're at now.

I respect my brother bishops. They're nearly all good, faithful men. Maybe 10 percent of the guys have bad ideas, and another 20 percent or 30 percent are mainly well-meaning, managerial specialists. But the political environment in the United States today is forcing all of us to wake up to the new realities. Men who were wishy-washy and could hide from some of the hot issues before ... well, nobody can hide anymore. Our culture doesn't want the Church hanging around unless we bless and agree with it. That won't happen, not in the long run, because our culture has nothing transcendent to offer; nothing that gives real hope or purpose to our lives. And God, whatever the weaknesses of his Church, *does* have that "something more", something higher and greater, to offer.

𝒶𝒷 𝒶𝒷 𝒶𝒷

27. From a bishop, urban diocese

Silence is where spiritual depth and creative evangelization are born. In that regard, I'm amazed at some of my seminarians. I've got some outstanding guys who are mature, responsible, and capable of dealing with the culture; exceptional young men anchored in the interior life. They don't have any illusions about what they're getting into. As for ongoing formation *after* guys are ordained, that's another matter. In that, we have something of a crisis. I think we've assumed, as bishops, that getting all our priests together in a hotel for three days of talks once a year will do the trick. Maybe for some, but for many others, probably not.

As for me: My dad served in World War II. He saw a lot of suffering and death. His war experience and the questions it raised about meaning led both him and my mother into the Church. So, that's part of my background. And I had a great priest-mentor in college. He was a wonderful listener with a humble demeanor. But he was as demanding as any sports coach in his spiritual direction. I suppose he was training me to be a priest. And one of the things I learned from him was not to let people damage the mission of the Church by being timid in my ministry, or using a false sense of charity as an alibi for a lack of courage, or excusing bad actions and ideas.

A problem I've often seen, among seminarians and priests alike, is envy. Another is that priests say they want more support from the chancery, but then they also want you to stay out of their business. So, I place a lot of stress on building up priestly fraternity, trust, and intergenerational charity; not just with those words, but with their substance. I encourage guys to form regional rectories where it's possible. Conceptually, a lot of priests will support the idea. Then they'll resist it individually. But if the men are willing, it can create some good synergy and mutual support.

Finally, on the matter of reform: The Sacrament of Penance is the engine not just of Church renewal but of social healing. St. Oscar Romero is an icon of ecumenical and interfaith social justice and peace. He's a man admired by atheists, agnostics, and believers alike. But we should never forget that he was always fundamentally a *pastor*. He understood the power of repentance and forgiveness; he treasured the Sacrament of Penance in his own life; and he promoted it as a key to societal reform.

CHAPTER THREE

The Road Less Traveled

A Report from the Vineyard and Its Workers

What's a parish? It's a stable community of the faithful, constituted in a local area, and headed by a parish priest. That's all it is. It's not the buildings or even the staff, other than the parish priest. It's a network of Christian relationality that comes together in a particular place to worship. The parish isn't a sacrament factory. If it becomes one, the relational aspects wither, and the whole thing becomes impersonal.

—Rev. Eric Banecker, pastor

Bishops may be the pastors and shepherds of their dioceses, but for many Catholics the "diocese", a word borrowed from the administrative divisions of the late Roman Empire, is a remote institution with little direct impact on their daily lives. For the average practicing Catholic, the pastor who really matters is the priest who leads his or her local parish. That's where the action is. That's where the Christian life begins and ends. And the quality of the local pastor—his energy, ability, and availability to his people—shapes the health or stagnation of the parish. As the French Trappist Dom Jean-Baptiste Chautard wrote in his classic text, *The Soul of the Apostolate*: "If the priest is a saint, the people will be fervent; if the priest is fervent, the people will be pious; if the priest is pious, the people will at least be decent; if the priest is only decent, the people will be godless. The spiritual generation is always one degree less intense in its life than the one who begets it in Christ."

The priests I knew as a young boy were great men. They had a huge influence on the course of my life. I remember and pray for them still. Likewise, the priests I worked with throughout my career were nearly all admirable men. The priesthood is a gift, and the good news for the Church is that Catholics tend to love and respect their priests, no matter what their skills or personalities. As a result, "despite the trials and stressors of their lives, U.S. priests enjoy higher than average levels of well-being" and a full 77 percent of priests "can be categorized as flourishing". In the words of one diocesan priest, "I feel remarkably fulfilled in my life ... I mean, just being able to minister to people, being able to love them. Being able to be Christ for them ... it's just such a beautiful life."

Such were the results of a national survey of priests released in 2022 by The Catholic Project at Catholic University of America, *Well-being, Trust, and Policy in a Time of Crisis*. And yet the same study noted that "priests, among their various sources of social support, rank their bishop the lowest." Only 49 percent of diocesan priests expressed confidence in their bishop, and barely 24 percent felt confident in the leadership and decision-making of the U.S. bishops as a whole. Much of this can be traced to the clergy abuse scandal erupting in 2001/2002 and its handling by Church leaders. To this day, many priests feel vulnerable to false accusations and worry about being abandoned by their bishop. This in turn accounts for the fact that while nearly three-quarters of bishops see themselves as a coworker, father, and brother to their priests, less than a third of their priests feel the same.

The trust gap is significant. Which means that in the wake of the abuse crisis, and tasked with working at ground level in a culture that's often unfriendly, the perseverance of priests, and the permanent deacons and religious who assist them, is remarkable ... and their voices in the following interviews make for essential listening.

᠁ ᠁ ᠁

Rev. Eric Banecker, young pastor, inner-city parish

The 2020/2021 COVID pandemic was something of a watershed for the Church in the United States. How did it affect your ministry?

BANECKER: It was interesting because I straddled two parishes during that time. When we went into lockdown, I was an associate at St. P's, a middle-class, suburban parish. Two weeks after we emerged from lockdown, I became the administrator and then the pastor at St. F's, an inner-city parish. So I saw both ends of the pastoral spectrum. Each had its own perspective.

How would you compare them?

BANECKER: Completely different. St. P's is filled with people who, quite frankly, moved out of the city and away from its problems two generations ago, probably about 3,200 families; 325 students in the school, most of them Catholic; a strong Catholic culture. St. F's is a small, urban parish with a very large school—larger than St. P's— and students who are 70 percent non-Catholic. The neighborhood's demographic skews younger than St. P's, and we have about 200 parish households actually on the books. I do 12 or so funerals a year here, and probably three-quarters of them are for African-Americans. I did about 30 baptisms last year, and 75 percent of them were for Caucasians. So the parish is still largely African-American, but the neighborhood is gentrifying.

Has that impacted parish finances?

BANECKER: Our collections are up. We may be one of the few parishes in the city where that's happened. Our people, both African-American and newcomers, are generous. Families are moving into the area because it's safer than some of the other neighborhoods in the city, and houses are still affordable.

How did COVID mortality rates affect the spiritual life of your parishioners?

BANECKER: As human beings, we're very, very good at numbing ourselves to the most important questions of our existence. People like to say that there are no atheists in foxholes. It isn't true. There are plenty of materialists in foxholes; people who have no sense of anything beyond material reality. We've done a terrible job of inculcating in children a sense of wonder about the universe. We teach them everything that can be investigated and studied under a microscope, but then they grow up and don't have the language, or the habits, for wondering about reality or even their own mortality. If you don't know how to ask the really fundamental questions, or if you're scared to ask them, then you'll numb yourself with Netflix or drugs or whatever else comes to hand.

Technology is only going to accelerate that materialist outlook; would that be accurate to say?

BANECKER: There's nothing inevitable about any of this. If you look at the Catholic landscape right now, the groups and organizations that are doing well all have a couple of things in common. First, they're focused on beauty; the beauty of the Christian life well lived. And second, they're relational; they build relationships, friendships, networks of good people supporting each other. So yes, for the overall culture, technology may make things worse. But for Catholic organizations skilled at swimming against that tide, there's a tremendous opportunity out there. Technology isn't somehow inherently evil.

In terms of structures, what will the Church look like in the next few decades?

BANECKER: What's a parish? It's a stable community of the faithful, constituted in a local area, and headed by a parish priest. That's all it is. It's not the buildings or even the staff, other than the parish priest. It's a network of Christian relationality that comes together in a particular place to worship. The parish isn't a sacrament factory. If it becomes one, the relational aspect thing becomes impersonal. Which has happened again and again. You have parishes in some dioceses with 4,000 households officially on the books, but only 100 people, a surviving remnant, coming to Mass on Sundays. And yet they still do the things they used to do when they were a large, urban sacrament factory. Instead of evangelization, which is the very thing we're supposed to be doing at all times, they still advertise for the St. Patty's party. It's like, folks, that's over. It's done. We need a radical rethink about our structures.

What about seminary formation? You were ordained a priest in 2018. What do you remember as the particular strengths or inadequacies in your seminary training, once you got into the field?

BANECKER: The strengths were a great fraternal spirit and an orthodox faculty of good, balanced men, really intelligent instructors.
There was a lot of healthy camaraderie. And some of the best faculty
were laywomen who really inspired us and taught us how to think
about our ministry today. As for deficits? I think the seminary, in my
time, made many good-faith attempts to prepare us to assume the
leadership of institutions earlier than in past generations. Meanwhile
though, the seminary was wrestling with financial questions about its
own survival. And that wrestling is serious and true at every level of
the Church, all the way up to the Vatican. So, in a sense, seminary
was preparing us for an era that had already passed. Right now, for a
lot of pastors, it's like the Wild West out there; you really just have
to throw everything against the wall and see what sticks.

*It's hardwired into the American Catholic mentality that we need to assimi-
late; to succeed; to prove that we belong in this (formerly) Protestant country.
So, the Church tends to cooperate gladly with government and support public
institutions because, you know, we're good citizens ... But how viable is that
going forward in the current environment?*

BANECKER: Augustine would say that the purpose of the state is to
maintain peace. And that's a good thing. We can't just exempt ourselves from public life. But—and this is important—if we want peace,
we need to work for justice. And, quite frankly, if we continue going
down the current road of injustices that are either state-sponsored or
state-permitted, we won't have peace for much longer.

*We live in a culture that's obsessed with sex; a culture that sees priestly cel-
ibacy as weird, if not behaviorally damaging. Can celibacy as a discipline of
the Western Church survive?*

BANECKER: Celibacy is a gift to the Church; it can and should survive. It's a charism. It's not doctrinally necessary, but it's no accident
that all of the great Christian missionary movements came out of the
Western Church, not the Eastern Church. If I'm married with two or
four or six kids, I don't have the freedom to give all of myself to the
Church and her people. It would be profoundly unjust to expect a
married man with children to spend the kind of time that I do in and

around the parish. Plus, candidly, along with the sacrifice there's a lot of freedom and happiness in celibacy, especially as priests age.

You've made the point in past conversations that celibacy actually enhances the ability of the priest to be a father to his parish and its people. The priest is not just a sacramental functionary, but a real father; yet that touches on another peculiar twist of American culture: a dysfunctional attitude toward fatherhood.

BANECKER: Right, I think the rise of the LGBTQ movement can be traced, at least in part, to the failure of fathers to model a mature, unselfish masculinity, and to teach their children about healthy and virtuous sexuality. If men want to lead and be respected, they need to act in a way that earns it. A person's sexual issues can have all sorts of complicated roots. But by and large, I think in a lot of cases, there's a disconnect between the child and his experience of his earthly father.

Last question, if we can turn to the lay vocation for a moment: How would you describe the difference between what you do as a priest and what I do as a layman?

BANECKER: The mission of the laity is the same mission as the clergy's. It's to be a saint. At a fundamental level, laypeople, religious, and clergy, men and women—all of us in the Church—have equal dignity before God by virtue of our baptism. We do have different tasks. The priest acts *in persona Christi*: he represents Christ to his people; he mediates for them in the celebration of the Eucharist, and then by extension, in the pastoral life and governance of the Church. But any sensible father knows that he can't manage the family alone. And so a good priest will cultivate the talents of laypeople and help them serve the mission of the Church in ways suited to their abilities. That can include work in Church structures, but mainly the lay vocation is *in* the world and *to* the world, *for the sake* of the world.

Vatican II never meant to "clericalize" the laity. The Council sought to show laypeople that they have a unique and irreplaceable role in the mission of the Church: the role of sanctifying the world through their families, their workplaces, and their friends.

᠆᠆᠆

Rev. Andrew Brownholtz, veteran pastor, suburban parish

The 2020/2021 COVID lockdown was obviously a major national event. How did it affect your parish? I'm interested in COVID's material impact on parish survival; but more importantly, on how it influenced the emotional and spiritual state of your people.

BROWNHOLTZ: After the mask mandate was lifted, it was slow bringing people back to church. But after a few months we were back to normal. Our parishioners continued to support the parish, as well as giving generous donations to our local community throughout the lockdown. We were able to collect and distribute more than $100,000 to needy individuals, regardless of their religious affiliation. We also saw an uptick in confessions; they were more real and sincere, probably because so many people were dying. We're still pretty busy with confessions on Saturdays.

In your experience, with all the technology and distractions today, do people have a genuine grasp of the supernatural? Is their sense of an afterlife any different today from when you were a first ordained?

BROWNHOLTZ: I've been ordained 20 years. The abuse scandal hit six months into my priesthood. That damaged the credibility of the Church, making it harder for many people to believe what she taught. All the technology and distractions haven't made it any easier over the years. I don't think people really have a grasp of the supernatural.

How did the scandal affect you as a newly ordained priest? You didn't sign up for a disaster.

BROWNHOLTZ: I'm very grateful that I lived with three other, older priests at the time. They were good men, very encouraging, and they helped me get through those difficult times.

You were ordained at what age?

BROWNHOLTZ: I was 34.

What drew you to the priesthood?

BROWNHOLTZ: My upbringing. My parents had seven children, and they did a great job. We were a one-income type of family. We didn't know we were poor. I also had an aunt and an uncle with vocations, and I admired them, giving their lives over to the Church.

What do you suppose the Church will look like in the United States in 20 years?

BROWNHOLTZ: Without vocations, it could look pretty bleak. The hierarchy will probably look the same, but the style of leadership may be different, with leaner staffs.

How well did your seminary training prepare you for your actual pastoral service?

BROWNHOLTZ: The seminary did a great job in helping us to understand our theology, our responsibilities, and leading others to know who Jesus is. Our parish apostolates were the most useful part of our training. The seminary also formed us well in the identity of being celibate; but it wasn't until I started living alone that I understood what that meant. Being celibate and living alone, a priest needs to cultivate strong friendships with both priests and laity to help him stay balanced and grounded.

Maybe a deficit was in not preparing us adequately to form pastoral relationships with parishioners. I think being more mature when I entered the seminary and having had professional relationships prior to entering helped me.

How do you rate the prospects for formal Catholic education over the next 20 years?

BROWNHOLTZ: The schools in more affluent parishes have the best chance of surviving. A lot of great diocesan stewardship has gone into supporting Catholic schools in large cities, but I don't know if they can keep their Catholic identity without local parish support. We have a strong Catholic identity in our parish, and that spills over into the school.

Do you think celibacy will survive as an essential element of priestly life in the West?

BROWNHOLTZ: I don't know, but I entered the seminary with the assumption that I'd be celibate for the rest of my priesthood.

How would it affect pastoral service to the people if that discipline were changed?

BROWNHOLTZ: If you have a family, that takes priority; your job's important, but your family comes first. In priestly life, we were taught that our parish duties take priority over personal matters. If something comes up in the parish, it should be your first concern. A married priesthood would change what priests could provide for their people.

What do laypeople typically not understand about the burdens and issues of priestly life?

BROWNHOLTZ: Running a small corporation—like this or any parish, even with a good staff—can really wear on you. People sometimes don't understand that as a priest, you need at least *some* life outside of the parish in order to continue to be effective.

Do you feel adequately supported by diocesan offices?

BROWNHOLTZ: If I need help, I can always call downtown. My parish has a school and a cemetery. Both have benefitted from the diocesan human resource and legal departments at times when the issue is outside the scope of the parish staff.

I suspect that most laypeople don't realize that, under canon law, pastors actually have significant rights and a lot of autonomy. They can't just be shoved around.

BROWNHOLTZ: At present, we do have a lot of rights and autonomy in our diocese. But other dioceses are instituting guidelines such as six-year terms for pastors, and I could see those types of measures being put into place to remind a priest of the promises he made at ordination.

As a pastor, how do you balance parish management versus worship and pastoral witness?

BROWNHOLTZ: You need a dedicated prayer life, confession on a regular basis, and a good spiritual director.

Are you ever embarrassed to wear your clerical garb in public? How did the abuse crisis affect your morale and the morale of your fellow priests?

BROWNHOLTZ: The only time I felt embarrassed was in 2001 when the abuse scandal began to hit. I was newly ordained, and someone yelled something at me in an elevator when I was making a hospital visit. So I started taking the stairs because I felt uncomfortable. Priestly morale was very low for years. I lost a lot of my classmates, and good priest friends who left the priesthood in disgust and are now married with kids. Morale seems to be on an upswing now. I now take the elevator and feel more comfortable. I have more than 20 years of experience to answer any remark.

What are your greatest worries, and also your greatest sources of hope and confidence, about the future of the Church?

BROWNHOLTZ: Going back a number of years, there was a group of priests who were upset with the way priests were blamed and treated. They wanted to challenge the archbishop and organize as a union. And I was approached by them. But I said no. I promised obedience to my archbishop. I trust that the same Holy Spirit who guided me into the priesthood at 34 is going to help me continue to grow and to lead me in my priestly life, whatever the frustrations.

So, I'd say that reliance on the Holy Spirit gives you some healthy perspective. The Church has grown, gone down, and grown again. Right now, maybe we're at a stalemate. But I'm encouraged by the young guys I've been allowed to work with. The seminary sends me seminarians every Thursday, and they come for the summer and live here for an experience of parish life. And it's great for me to see that what attracted them to the seminary and priesthood is the same ingredients that had such an impact on me. Some of these seminarians have great parents; some don't have a perfect family or even the semblance of one. But their prayer life is strong and sincere, and the Holy Spirit is clearly guiding them.

Last question: If you could change one or two things about how the Church is organized or lived in order to set a real Catholic renewal in motion, what would those changes be?

BROWNHOLTZ: I don't know; there would need to be changes in attitude, and maybe in structure. I wouldn't want to copy a Protestant model, but we might try larger congregational parishes, staffed by multiple priests. Maybe our auxiliary bishops could pastor different parishes as well. It might help to bring back some of the priests, even if they're married, who left active ministry in disgust during the abuse crisis, but who are still faithful to the Church in many ways. They could become weekend helpers, not supported with a salary from the diocese, and keep their current job to support their family ... It would take some thinking outside the box.

"Thinking outside the box." I suspect that's the heart of the matter.

ᘒᕀ ᘒᕀ ᘒᕀ

Rev. Philip Larrey, professor and author,
Pontifical Lateran University

You served for a time in the United States. From where you now teach in Rome, what do you see as the key problems facing the Church/Christian faith today in the developed nations, and also as a global entity?

LARREY: Indifference towards the faith, due to secularization. Also, the lack of belief in an afterlife; Christianity doesn't make sense without a profound eschatological point of view.

Based on your observation and experience, to what degree are the episcopal selection, priestly formation, and Catholic education processes part of today's ecclesial problems?

LARREY: Those are three very separate contexts. The selection of bishops is usually handled quite well. Priestly formation is constantly being tweaked and reevaluated, but the numbers are way down. Catholic education varies greatly across the globe, but most Catholics don't feel the need to study their faith and learn about its richness.

To what degree does today's Church leadership understand the challenges facing the Church? If renewal is possible, how might it happen?

LARREY: It all depends on the leader in question. Some leaders are enlightened, some are not. Some are able to assess their situation very well, but they lack the courage and vision to do much about it. In the West, finance seems to be the number one priority, and a wealthy Church is not necessarily a good or holy one. Renewal generally comes from the faithful, not from the leadership, except on rare occasions with men like St. Charles Borromeo.

You've worked in and around Church-related educational bureaucracies and theological/philosophical faculties for many years. What's the state of their health, and why?

LARREY: This also depends on the place you're speaking about. I wonder if we're adequately teaching how to apply the richness of the Church's philosophical and theological tradition to our context today. Are we able to translate the truths of the Church in a way that people understand? I'm not at all sure we've mastered how to speak the language of our culture.

If you see practical sources of hope, what are they, and why?

LARREY: Holy priests, who are present to the faithful. Groups which are dynamic and energizing. Hope is a theological virtue, and too often in short supply.

In your view, what are the most negative and most positive factors/trends/ forces shaping emergent Western culture? Disparities in wealth and education? Sexual habits? Science and technology? In his book Homo Deus *the philosopher/futurist Yuval Noah Harari paints a pretty bleak picture of technology's eventual effect on religious belief and biblical anthropology.*

LARREY: I've read *Homo Deus*, and I use it in my seminar on digital transformation here at Lateran University. Harari speaks about "Data-ism", which he says is a kind of religion, and he may be right; a "Silicon Valley religion", because it deals with most of the classical themes which religion covers: our origin, our destiny, what gives life meaning, the sense of transcendence. He says we should trust algorithms more than our own judgment. At the same time, I think he deliberately tries to shock us about the future so we'll alter our present course.

Positive forces include a greater awareness of our need to take care of creation as stewards, not lords; greater awareness of the dignity of each human being; longer life expectancy; the growing trend toward equality between men and women in the workplace; and an increase of spirituality, although not through organized religion.

Negative forces would be the thriving arms industry and the business of war; market forces as the most decisive factor shaping social trends; human trafficking; fake news and deep political fakes undermining popular trust; gender theory and the confusion it creates; widespread acceptance of abortion and euthanasia; ambiguous norms of sexual behavior in the West; breakdown of the family; and the difficulty of transmitting values.

Is the Church completely out of the game? Is there something she can do to influence significantly the cultural course of the next two or three decades?

LARREY: The Church in Europe has little to no practical influence on the decisions people take on a daily basis. There are more practicing Catholics in India than there are in Italy, although Catholics represent only 1.5 percent of the population there, and 92 percent of the population in Italy. Most Catholics in the West are only nominally Catholic, and most practicing Catholics see Mass attendance as a formality. And since the institutional Church has difficulty attracting young people, the next two or three decades are going to be worse than now.

Are seminaries preparing priestly candidates for the real work and challenges they'll face in a rapidly changing pastoral environment, especially in developed nations?

LARREY: Some seminaries are better than others at this. The late Cardinal Jean-Marie Lustiger in Paris had a great idea in terms of making seminary training more practical—i.e., largely done within parish structures; it became known as "the Paris Model", but it hasn't seen continuity, and it depends on the support of pastors. Some bishops keep a list of the best parishes to send the newly ordained, because a man's first experience of priestly life is often the most important. In developed nations, the central focus of seminary life is no longer on academic training; it's now more holistic. The downside is that psychology can at times replace genuine spirituality, because the difficulties facing young priests often include disillusionment; loneliness; burn-out; getting along with their pastors; affective frustration; egocentrism; and desiring the attention and affirmation of parishioners too keenly. Not sure how this could be changed, but it does need to change.

In your pastoral experience, have you felt a closeness to and support from your bishop and his staff? Do you as a priest, and they as leadership, share the same priorities?

LARREY: No. Very few priests trust their bishops, because they—the priests—are often seen as potential liabilities. Bishops are no longer father figures for priests, but rather heads of a bureaucratic machine. Priorities are very different indeed.

Do administrative affairs take up most of your time and energy; how much of your life is management versus worship and witness? How would you change that?

LARREY: For ordinary pastors, "management versus worship and witness" is a real issue. Serving on a pontifical faculty, my own life is taken up with reading, writing, and teaching.

Are you embarrassed to wear clerical garb in public? Has the abuse crisis touched you in a particular way? Do you think that some innocent clergy members suffered unjustly?

LARREY: In general, yes, I'm often embarrassed to wear the collar in public. The clergy sexual abuse crisis has been devastating, and was handled poorly on many levels. I do think some innocent clergy members suffered unjustly, but I also think that many of the accused were guilty in one way or another. The climate that has been created will remain with us for many years to come. In the majority of cases of those found guilty, it was about sexual attraction to male teenagers. The percentage of homosexual priests in the West is much higher than in the general population, although numbers differ from country to country.

Aside from the actual, enormous damage done to abused individuals, the media in general used the crisis to demonize the Catholic priesthood as a whole. It also resulted in draining the financial resources of the Church, especially in English-speaking countries.

What about the issue of celibacy? Do you experience a lack of intimacy otherwise desired? If so, how would you address that?

LARREY: Good question. I'm now 59 years old, so celibacy is less of an issue than before. Many psychologists speak about a lack of intimacy in the life of a priest, but I'm not sure they understand what this actually means. It continues to be a sacrifice.

Do you sense that, for mainstream Catholics in America, the practice of the faith is based more on nostalgia and cultural habits rather than authentic, missionary discipleship? If so, how would you address that?

LARREY: Yes, and priests need to learn how to engage the faithful more genuinely. Most Catholics don't practice their faith in a vibrant way. Young people generally don't get involved in their parish communities. And yet, young people *do* have a million questions surrounding themes which can be explored through the Catholic tradition: What happens when we die? Do we have an immortal soul? How can I attain happiness in my life? Is Jesus Christ truly the "Son of God"? Are we the result of Darwinian evolution or created by God? What's my obligation to my fellow human beings? Is there a divine will that I should fulfill? And many more. I tend to look at this issue from an intellectual point of view, being in academia. But I do think young people are searching, and unfortunately they don't perceive the priest as someone relevant and worth engaging.

❧ ❧ ❧

Rev. Mr. Michael Cibenko, permanent deacon, suburban parish

You spent most of your life as a layman, in a job—police work—that involved a lot of the uglier problems of humanity. Now you're a permanent deacon. So in your context of the parish "trenches", what practical issues do you see as decisive over the next 20 years for the renewal of the Church in the United States?

CIBENKO: We need to work on today first. When I was in law enforcement, the key questions we always asked ourselves were very basic: What's the mission? What's my purpose? What can I learn from the *past* without repeating it? What can I do *today* to improve the future? I see a lot of confusion about all those things in the Church right now.

How does that confusion express itself in a practical way, on a parish level? You're in the parish every day; you see people in every kind of situation.

CIBENKO: People are better catechized by the surrounding secular environment than they are by their Church. Parents may send their kids to a Catholic school, but then they question, or argue with, or don't really care what the Church actually teaches. So the mission of the parish, teaching the truth of Jesus Christ, gets blurred.

If you were to change one or two things to start a process of gradual renewal, what would they be?

CIBENKO: Preaching the need for confession. Regular, personal confession. Stressing the importance of worship every Sunday. And getting people to understand that the Eucharist is more than just a piece of bread, but really the Body and Blood of Jesus.

Very few people in law enforcement are naïve about human nature. A cop knows that even people who claim to be religious can be thoroughly nasty and veteran sinners. Given that knowledge, what drew you to the diaconate? Someone on the outside looking in might think you're a glutton for punishment.

CIBENKO: I've always felt that we're created in the image of God. So, that was my little seed of religion. But I was never aware that I was growing in my faith. Over the years I had three different people tell me that I should be a deacon. I always said, "No way." I didn't have the time. I had no desire for the diaconate. None. In fact, I didn't really know what a deacon was or what he did. But the issue just kept coming up.

How many years ago was that, Mike?

CIBENKO: I was ordained in 2012, but I started wrestling with the idea long before that.

And is this life, your diaconal work, better or worse (or both), than what you expected?

CIBENKO: Harder, in the sense that I need really to know the Gospel and my faith, and I was never a great student. But I love it, because I've grown more and more. And I feel the peace and contentment of being where Jesus wants me. The priesthood is a totally different calling. I'm just here to assist. I'm here to help the priest, and be a bridge between him and his people.

So what does a permanent deacon do that a priest can't?

CIBENKO: Most of us permanent deacons are married. In the Roman rite, priests are celibate, and sometimes people feel that priests, for that reason, can't understand them. Or they put the priest on a pedestal as somehow holier than themselves, and that creates a distance between them. Deacons are just closer to the lay experience, so maybe they're easier to approach. But again, the greatest value of a deacon is to assist the priest and help him bring people to God.

Over the years, I've noticed a pattern of Catholic men getting to a certain age, like in their late 40s, and seeking a deeper relationship with God. And sometimes they assume that the permanent diaconate is the natural next step up from the lay state, a kind of layman-plus. But the diaconate strikes me as its own unique vocation, not for everyone, and quite distinct from lay life.

CIBENKO: I need to think about those words, because as you were speaking, I was trying to relate them to myself. Quite frankly, the diaconal life is a challenge. It's not a job. It's a ministry. If you're called to it, it's a joy and a blessing; if not, you won't be successful. Or happy.

How many years were you active as a cop?

CIBENKO: I did 23 years; I retired as a police lieutenant. I worked for the Port Authority in New York and New Jersey. I was there for the 1993 Trade Center bombing. Later, when 9/11 happened, I was already retired. But I went back and offered my services that day, and volunteered for three weeks. And I was really moved, because I saw such a need for Jesus Christ in the men who were working the wreckage, and who needed someone to talk to. I became that individual, even though I wasn't in the ministry. And I guess it was then that I realized I had a calling. I just seemed to fall into it.

Why did they come to you?

CIBENKO: I would ask them why. It was because I'd worked as a cop for years. They had confidence that they could come to me, and I'd listen to what they went through each day and what was going on in their heads. I felt like the Holy Spirit was guiding me to these people, so I had to learn how to help them.

In your experience, is the permanent diaconate properly understood and valued by priests?

CIBENKO: Yes. Most priests really do appreciate the work of their deacons. You run into priests who are arrogant or lazy, but they're not the standard. I'm encouraged these days by the new young men I meet in the seminary; they're willing to learn from you.

From your point of view as a deacon, what are the biggest mistakes bishops and priests make in working with and understanding laypeople?

CIBENKO: I don't put them all in the same boat. I know priests and bishops who clearly *do* understand their people. With others, there's a disconnect. Sometimes bishops live in another realm; they forget who they are and where they're from.

What, in your experience, makes a parish succeed or fail? A good pastor is key, obviously. But are there other essential factors that contribute to the success or failure of a parish?

CIBENKO: Good preaching. Good preaching that speaks the truth. Good preaching is powerful.

If you were to isolate the key elements of the lay vocation, what would they be?

CIBENKO: Laypeople are meant to be examples of holiness in the everyday world. That's their calling. There's no "one model" of the lay vocation. Each one of us has special gifts that we've been given by God. It's our job to acknowledge and develop those gifts, and then use them for the benefit of others.

I suspect the default position for many laypeople might be, "Mike, you're the deacon, you're the official Church guy, you take care of the religious stuff; we're gonna go home and watch the game." Getting people to reflect, deeply and seriously, on what God wants from them can be very difficult with adults, especially in this culture, which is just a 24/7 catechesis in noise and toys.

CIBENKO: People need to understand that we can't delegate away the Christian instruction of our children to others, or ignore our own responsibility for Christian witness. The domestic church— our families—is where we learn, or don't learn, how to live a good Christian life. And as the years go by, we'll get the results that we earn by our actions.

๛ ๛ ๛

Rev. Mr. Christopher Roberts, permanent deacon, author, president of a classical high school

Let's imagine that your fairy godmother or godfather (or godperson) hands you a magic wand to fix the problems you see in the Church. What would you do with it? Where would you start?

ROBERTS: I'd start with eight or nine things. I'd enhance our Novus Ordo Masses with more beauty and dignity. I'd support more classical schools and "catechists of the Good Shepherd". I'd do more straight talk to parents about technology. It's not enough to focus on internet bullying and pornography. We need to help our children develop interior silence and a capacity for interior prayer. Being constantly online makes all of us, but especially our kids, even more vulnerable to libidinal and market forces. And I don't think we talk enough about Gnosticism. That sounds strange, but Gnosticism is at the root of all the negative Big Idea movements of the modern world—the belief that some special brand of purely human knowledge will provide us with redemption. People in the pews aren't stupid. If we talk about an issue in a pastoral way, they'll get the message.

We need more bishops who are heroes; men with some backbone. We should reward gumption. We should stop using labels like left-wing and right-wing and focus on being "full catechism Catholics". We need to reconnect social action with transcendent mystery, activism with contemplation, and social justice with personal sexual morality. I'd try to find ways for the Church to create some cognitive dissonance, gestures that capture the imagination, like showing up at events and in places that just don't compute. Evangelicals are really good at engaging the green movement and the hip, secular young: opening coffee bars, creating little urban farms and local house churches, that sort of thing. Where's the Catholic Church? She's invisible. But orthodox faith and cultural savvy can easily go together.

I'd be firmer in dealing with BS: the nonsense like clown mask liturgies, or Father James Martin dancing around on LGBTQ issues. And while we're on the subject of BS, I'd cancel any staff meetings and pastors that are just incapable of talking culturally and theologically about what's happening in the parish, instead of the upcoming calendar. Staff meetings can be their own form of insidious, soul-destroying penance. We need to talk about real things in real ways. And finally, I'd sponsor fewer programs and conferences with celebrity Catholic speakers, and have more fasting, prayer, and study. A thousand Catholics on their knees outside the cathedral, fasting, would be much better than a thousand Catholics in the auditorium of some Catholic high school, listening to a celebrity speaker.

That's more than nine things.

ROBERTS: I could go on a long time.

You're the son of a respected Baptist pastor, a scholar, and an author who was once on an academic track; so how did you end up a Catholic deacon?

ROBERTS: The seedbed was my childhood. When I was growing up, my dad and my family modeled a happy, congregational life. Our church congregation really was an extended family. So, in effect I had 10 adopted brothers and sisters, 10 adopted aunts and uncles, 10 adopted grandparents. We had a vivid domestic church that was oriented toward the wider Church, and I saw it well lived. Congregational leadership and service were in my imagination as a good way to live. So, when I did become a Catholic, the priest who received me into the Church in graduate school in London suggested that I should become a permanent deacon. He was from West Africa, and he said, "Come to Ghana, and we'll make you a deacon tomorrow." But I needed to get used to being a Catholic first. Then, when I came back to the States, after a couple years of being active in the Church, my pastor suggested the same thing. It really mattered that two different priests suggested it, because it meant that the idea wasn't coming from me. I wasn't raising my hand saying, oh, I want to do this, like I was applying for some prestigious career bump. It was coming from the outside. It was an invitation.

How is your life different now from being a layperson?

ROBERTS: I'm vowed to saying the Liturgy of the Hours every day. If I don't say morning and evening prayer, I have to take it to confession. I'm one of the people responsible for making sure that the public, continuous prayer of the Church happens. And even if I'm saying the Liturgy of the Hours by myself, I'm saying it because I promised publicly that I'd be part of ensuring that our prayer without ceasing happens. So, I assist at the altar. I preach. I do baptisms. I regularly do benediction at the classical high school where I serve as president; those kinds of liturgical experiences have real grace in them. And there's things I was doing as a layman, like theological writing and teaching, that I now do in a way that's more hardwired into the Church's liturgy. So, there's added grace in that.

Is there anything disappointing or unexpectedly hard in what you're doing now as a deacon?

ROBERTS: It's harder in the sense—you tried to warn me, and I knew this intellectually, but now I really see it—that theological conversation doesn't happen in the Church's bureaucracy and leadership structures, and entrepreneurial gumption is not only *not* rewarded, but is regarded with a level of suspicion that's just stunning to me. And here's another nugget. I remember, in the process of getting reassigned from one parish to another, having a conversation with the diocesan clergy office. And I asked them, "Doesn't anybody in the diocese want to do an exit interview with me? Doesn't anybody want to know what I've seen and experienced?" The guy in charge said, "No, I've spent my life in bureaucratic hierarchies, and I'm telling you, Chris, that you don't want to get more of a reputation than you already have for spouting off." I'm paraphrasing, but not by much.

This was just a month after the [former Cardinal Theodore] Mc-Carrick report. So, I said, "I'm not accusing anybody of McCarrick-like crimes. I'm not accusing anybody of sexual or financial immorality. But I *will* say that the common denominator between the McCarrick report and what I'm now experiencing, as I get transferred from one parish to another, is an indifference to pastoral excellence." Nobody wants to talk about how to do missionary, evangelizing work better. It doesn't take gross immorality to replicate the McCarrick mess. All it takes is lethargic mediocrity.

Two things. Were you adequately trained for realities in the field by your seminary training? And, in your experience and observation, are deacons properly valued by the priests they work with?

ROBERTS: So, seminary formation. The best thing about it was the fraternity with my classmates. It was the best extended men's prayer community I've ever been a part of. The worst thing about the seminary's culture was that, on a bad day, it was belittling and emasculating. There was little attempt to engage us as mature men. My classmates would often complain that we were being treated like we were 20 years old. It's as if there were a template for formation; that whether you were 40 or 20, they were determined to do it the same way.

Whenever I get a fundraising letter from the diocese, I'm addressed as Dr. Roberts. Whenever I get a letter from the seminary or the diocese asking me to do something as a deacon or a student, I'm addressed as Mr. Roberts. The diocese knows how to respect professional accomplishments when they want money. But when they're actually trying to work with me, pastorally, evangelically, it's like all that stuff is invisible. There's no engagement with your history or skills. So, overall, the seminary's training was adequate; but homiletics, in particular, was a real disappointment. There was some effort to place Scripture readings in ecclesial and theological perspective, but the real emphasis was on speaking for five to eight minutes, and being done. Homiletics felt like it had too little evangelical imagination.

How has your diaconal service impacted your marriage and family?

ROBERTS: Even if we had all the good priests we would ever need—and I pray that someday we will—a permanent deacon and his family are bridges to the world in ways that a priest simply can't be. My neighbors see me walk out of the house wearing a clerical collar in the morning. We're a presence of the Church on our city block in an active, public way. Seeing my family live a parish-oriented life raises the bar for other parishioners. They can see what it looks like to have a domestic church oriented toward the parish. My kids know the Liturgy of the Hours. They know that we're not consumers at church; we're not "parish shoppers", and that has witness value.

On the downside, the diocese doesn't take family and children adequately into account when making diaconal assignments. And if you raise kid and family issues, they get grumpy and complain that, well, you got yourself into this, and you should've thought ahead.

What are your thoughts on married priests?

ROBERTS: They're similar to my thoughts on women priests. Even if a married priesthood were a good thing—which I doubt—we're the wrong culture to pursue it. We're so confused about sex and gender as a society, that I just don't trust our ability to think sanely. If we believe that a "he" can become a "she", then we're too confused to have any standing to discern this question for the universal Church. I'd much rather see us have a creative discussion about celibacy, and how to do it right, before we start doing goofy stuff, like married priests.

What are the biggest mistakes you see priests and bishops making as they work with laypeople?

ROBERTS: They either expect and need the layperson to be syco-phantic, or alternatively, they're intimidated, because that person is a lawyer or a wealthy businessman.

One last question: How would you describe the lay vocation?

ROBERTS: All forms of Christian life have a cross in them somewhere. "Empowerment" rhetoric is misleading because it doesn't get us thinking about the cross. Any model of lay leadership that doesn't first train people in being sacrificial is a mistake. Laypeople need to be formed and trained so that they can be docile to the Spirit and resistant to today's culture. That's the key to the lay vocation. And if laypeople don't have a sense of being countercultural, then they're worse than useless. Committed laypeople should get off their bot-toms and do things without waiting for the bishops. There's a lot that the official, administrative Church can do to support good apostolic efforts. If you have enough formed, active, sacrificial, and tithing laypeople, then administrative authority will naturally bend to their needs. But attempting to solve the "lay vocation" through bureau-cratic structures without the cross and countercultural formation is the equivalent of a dog chasing its tail. It doesn't work.

ᘒᕲ ᘒᕲ ᘒᕲ

Sister Gabrielle Mary Braccio, R.S.M., religious superior, bishop's liaison for diocesan consecrated life

I'll start with a question that I've asked nearly everyone: What practical issue or issues would be central for the renewal of the Church in the United States?

BRACCIO: I'd have to say family life. That's my number one thought about this. Family life is the foundation for everything we do in the world. It's the foundation for vocation, the foundation for the

Church. And our society has been trying to annihilate family life; literally to obliterate it.

Were you born Catholic?

BRACCIO: I'm a cradle Catholic, but always converting. My dad died when I was 11. My mom was a practicing Catholic and a good woman; but she had some struggles in her life. So, we were kind of in and out and around the Church.

Who was decisive in deepening your faith? Obviously your mother was very important.

BRACCIO: As I got older, it was probably my brother. Mainly because he left the faith. He was floating all over Europe and the United States, searching in his own heart of hearts for truth. So, a friend of his brought him to a Benedictine monastery, and it had a big effect on him. You might have heard of it: Regina Laudis in Connecticut. So, my brother said to me, "I want to take you to Regina Laudis." I was adventurous. I grew up in Atlantic City. I went with him one Labor Day weekend. I hadn't traveled much at that age. We were traveling at night, and I had no idea where we were going. So, then I got to the monastery, and I probably would have left that night if I had known how to get away. But I met the Sisters there, and they were very dear. I became friends with a couple of them. And they were influential in helping me to go deeper into my faith.

As a teenager you just do "the scene" with your friends, but by my early 20s I thought, "This is absurd." No one wanted to make a commitment in life; to marriage or anything else. So I remember one day, I was walking on the beach, just talking out loud. I said, "Lord, there must be more to life than what I'm living." I had no idea where he would lead me. But he began opening doors. I'd never thought of religious life, not even an inkling. I wanted to get married, have children, and all that. But the Lord kept leading me. It's not that I didn't fight it. I did. But that's how it all began.

I've been in religious life now for 43 years with the Religious Sisters of Mercy of Alma, Michigan. They were re-founded in 1973 as part of the post–Vatican II reform. They were a very loving community. And very direct. They were *committed*; committed to the

mission of the Church, and it didn't make any difference what walk
of life you were from. I wasn't educated. I was a beautician. I swore
I'd never go back to school again. And here I was entering this community, and Mother Mary Quentin [Sheridan] said, "What are you
going to do?" I said, "Well, I can do hair. I could cut everybody's
hair, and I love to cook." So I did that, but Mother said, "You've got
to study." So I went into nursing.

*Mother Mary Quentin is a very impressive woman; an extraordinary leader.
But that leads me to the next question. The Alma community was founded
at a very strange, very confused, time in the Church. Why did some communities of religious women disintegrate while others didn't; they all took much
the same vows.*

BRACCIO: Some of our Sisters who lived in the old form of religious
life say that things had to change. Certain things needed to change.
But in the process, many communities lost their identity. They went
to extremes. They went from rigor to falling apart, with Sisters living
outside the community and no common life.

Was religious life harder than you imagined when you began?

BRACCIO: My first three years of religious life were really exciting. I
loved it. Then with first vows, those years were very difficult. You
mentally attach to certain places and people. I had to get acclimated
to the fact that I could be reassigned anywhere we had a convent, and
that wasn't always easy for me. But over time, I've come to know
most of our Sisters because we're not that large a community, maybe
about 110 women, which I appreciate because we have real relationships with each other. And we can always speak with our Mothers
in the community; they're never distant from us, even if we're miles
away. They're always available for us.

*The Church hasn't always valued religious life. The clergy is male, and its
ordained men have the responsibility of leadership. But they've had a spotty
record at times in the treatment of women's religious communities and laypeople, taking them for granted.*

BRACCIO: I think Vatican II corrected a lot of that. But I do understand where many of the alienated women religious were coming

from. Again, some things needed to change. But religious life isn't a matter of demanding our rights. And sometimes I just have to laugh. I have no problem serving a bishop or priest at table, or opening the door for them, that sort of thing. But some women religious look at me like I'm crazy. And even a bishop or priest will sometimes be embarrassed that I'm serving him. It has nothing to do with embarrassment; it's simply a loving respect for the office they hold. Mother Catherine McAuley, the foundress of the Sisters of Mercy, respected bishops and priests. She, too, would be of service to them. It's a beautiful thing to open the door for your grandmother, or your grandfather, or to serve them; it's not so very different in the Church, to respect those in office or those who are older.

I do wonder if many bishops and priests really understand what religious life is. I oversee an Office for Consecrated Life in a diocese. Religious life is an element of consecrated life, but they're not identical. In a sense, we're all "consecrated" if we're baptized. Secular Institutes and Societies of Apostolic Life are wonderful vocations, but they're not the same as a religious order with a specific charism and a vowed, common life.

Why do you think women's religious vocations are relatively sparse now?

BRACCIO: Obedience is not a high value in America. Women religious say they want to be treated as adults; well, obviously, so do I. I'm the superior in my local community. But when I need something for myself, I go to my superior general, who oversees the superiors in our overall community. I ask her permission, just like the Sisters here will ask my permission. There's nothing childish about that; if anything, it's reassuring; it's responsible. I don't see a lot of women in today's America as being very happy. They're always struggling to be something else. At one of the recent Holy Thursdays here at our cathedral, 10 or so women were outside, picketing for women's ordination. All I could do was smile at them. I thought, "You wouldn't be happy, even if you *were* ordained."

Issues like women's ordination strike me as a kind of fixation on power.

BRACCIO: There's that. I think they believe they can do things better. They look at the clergy abuse scandal and say that all-male bishops and priests have failed us. I can understand their anger. But if they have such trouble with men, why are they acting and thinking like them? They've lost the touch of the feminine.

So, if you yourself had 24 hours of unlimited power, how would you go about "fixing" the Church? What would you do? Where would you start?

BRACCIO: Well, going back to your first question, family life and how parents rear their children are essential to the life and future of the Church. And we need priests and religious who are truly dedicated, willing to give their lives to their ministry at all hours of the day or night. I mean, if we say yes to our vocation as a priest or a religious, then we need to mean it all the way, and not waffle. In practice, that's too often not the case. If we don't take our callings seriously enough, there's no way we can evangelize or be true Gospel witnesses.

Have you ever doubted your vocation in a serious way?

BRACCIO: Oh yes. When things got tough, a couple of times. I just wanted to leave; the tension was too high. But I had a great superior. She said, "You're speaking out of emotion, out of passion." And she was right. I started working with one of our other Sisters, about the meaning of obedience, and I loved it. I was so grateful. I had my struggles. I had the freedom to leave. And I could have walked away. But when you make this kind of a commitment, it's really because you're looking for a love that's everlasting. And to walk away from that because things are getting tough ... well, I just couldn't do it.

Last question: Is there something important I haven't asked; something you need to add?

BRACCIO: I keep coming back to that passage in Scripture about laying down your life for another. That's the nature of love. So, I suppose new life in the Church starts right there, in laying down your life for others. That's the cost. That's where it starts.

ஜ ஜ ஜ

Miss Kerry Kober, consecrated virgin; bishop's secretary

As an adult, Kerry, you chose the consecrated life. What factors led you to that?

KOBER: I had always been attracted to religious life and to things of God. I knew I couldn't be a nun because I wasn't unselfish enough. I didn't want to be a nurse or a teacher, and I couldn't give myself totally to a religious community. So, I didn't know what to do until I heard about consecrated virginity. It was a state of life in the early Church that Vatican II restored. So, I started reading about it. It was the niche I needed as an adult; a way to tell our Lord how much I love him.

What has it meant to you over the years? How long have you been consecrated?

KOBER: I was consecrated in 1999. It gave me an anchor in the Lord, no matter what was happening, through prayer and daily Mass.

If someone were to ask, "I don't see why consecrated life and religious community life are important today. They may have been useful 500 years ago, but why do we need them now, when so much emphasis seems to be on the laity?", how would you respond?

KOBER: Making a public consecration of the self to service in the Church is a form of prayer for others. It's also a recognition of the nature of the Church; a proof that the Church isn't "mine" or "yours". She belongs to Jesus Christ for the sake of everyone in the Church.

As a consecrated woman working directly for a bishop, you saw the practical side of ecclesial life and most of its issues from the inside. In your own view, what are the main problems facing the Church in the United States?

KOBER: So many people are consumed today by entertainment and distractions, or by political passions that don't really give them meaning and can't finally satisfy them. I don't know how to address those problems with persons who lack any sense of the eternal, any opening to the metaphysical; people who can't imagine the reality of things they can't touch or see. So they can't understand the high stakes that are involved in every life, including their own. They either don't believe they'll die and be judged, or they just don't think about it.

You handled very sensitive correspondence for a bishop, who later became a metropolitan archbishop, for quite a long time.

KOBER: I started with then–Bishop Charles Chaput in 1994. I retired when he retired as archbishop in 2020, but I continue to work part-time for him.

Without violating any confidences, when you reflect on your experience, does U.S. Church leadership really understand the nature and scope of the problems facing American Catholic life today?

KOBER: The bishop I worked for certainly knows, and so do many others. But too many bishops don't. The USCCB, for example, often struck me as a bureaucracy just like Congress. It reminded me of Congress, with differing political parties. Some of the staff often had preconceived ideas that seemed to shape conference documents. That was frustrating for at least some of the bishops. And many of the bishops, while they were good men, just weren't strong.

How much dictation did Archbishop Chaput routinely do in a day? I remember him as pretty relentless in responding personally to emails and letters as they came in.

KOBER: It was all day long. I was typing all day long. And it was always a mix. Some of his dictation was administrative; some was responding to people who were angry or insulting or afraid or asking for advice. But from the very beginning, the content of his responses and the tone of his voice were always charitable. Strong but compassionate.

He told me once that he spent three to five hours a day responding to people.

KOBER: When email became common, yes.

I don't think most people understood the centrality of your work to his ministry. You were stuck in that tiny office, invisible. But you really helped him accomplish what he wanted: to connect with individuals immediately and personally. He was never remote from people, and that remoteness seems to be a pervasive complaint about leadership today, and not just in the Church.

KOBER: When the *New York Times* interviewed the archbishop during the 2004 election campaign, mainly about the Communion issue, he got a huge number of emails, nearly all of them from Democrats and most of them angry. He answered all of them, with charity.

There were more than 900 emails. I remember because I stopped counting at 900. But the work you did those days was unbelievable. So, based on your experiences like that, what do ordinary Catholics not understand about the life and duties of a bishop?

KOBER: They don't understand that, if a bishop takes his vocation seriously, it's seven days a week, all day long, with appointments or duties or problems. Then at night, it's events and church functions, talks, confessions, and spiritual direction. And then add the constant hate mail and media criticism. It never stops.

Over time, you've served in three very different dioceses. What were the surprises about the Church when you began working directly for a bishop?

KOBER: The different streams of theology; and also the conflict. The level of conflict in the Church was a surprise. Rapid City was a happy place; there were problems, but the nature of the diocese meant that the bishop could be a good father. Denver was bigger and more complicated, but financially sound and exciting. Philadelphia had a lot of very serious problems; the one bright side was its orthodoxy, the faithfulness of its priests.

What gave you the most joy about your work over the years? And what caused you the most distress?

KOBER: The archbishop spent a lot of time explaining things to people when they would write in with questions about the faith. That was a blessing because I learned so much as I typed. And it was a joy to work hard, because he did. The difficult part was the unjust media criticism; the attacks and complaints.

What did you learn about the nature of the Church from all the years of your service?

KOBER: The Church connected me to a family that's not just my parish or my diocese, but worldwide and headed by Jesus Christ.

How would you begin the process of reviving the Church in this country?

KOBER: I would start with the seminaries, because good priests help make good people. Parishioners need to be more active in inviting other people to come with them to church. And we need more bishops like St. John Fisher, especially now.

Last question: When you look at the pastoral terrain of the Catholic Church in the United States right now, what are your sources of hope?

KOBER: The work of the Augustine Institute and the National Catholic Bioethics Center, the revival of Scripture study in a lot of parishes, those sorts of things. The more time and resources that are spent on frontline, person-to-person education of everyday Catholics about their faith, the faster the Church will regain the strength of her mission.

You've seen a lot of good, but also a lot of unpleasant things in the Church over your career.

KOBER: The problems are nothing compared to the good; nothing compared to the truth in the Church. God loves us, and he didn't have to do that after we fell. He could have let us go, but he didn't. God put us here for a purpose, out of love; and I've always felt that we're working, and serving, and fighting to thank him for his ongoing presence and consolation.

જ *જ* *જ*

Postscript: Letter from a veteran priest and friend

You ask why I love the Church. First off, we'd need to clarify what we mean by "Church".

I don't care much for the institutional dimension of the Church, even though I realize it's necessary. The Church as an institution has allowed her to survive down the centuries, conserving and protecting Western culture from extinction. I'd never give my life for an institution like Ford Motor Company or the Bank of America, but for God and for his people, yes, I would. But while it's important, the *structure* of the Church should never be a priority. It's the Spirit that counts, and the intention of the people who make up the Mystical Body of Christ.

I know we can't go back to the primitive Church of the first century, because times have changed. But we should constantly check our priorities and make sure that we're spending our time, energy, and inspiration on those facets of the Church which are the most important. If all we do is look for money, and hope to sway political power in favor of the structure—buildings, land, stocks, etc.—then we're missing the point. I don't feel particularly attracted to maintaining and supporting the institutional dimension of the Church, and this at times has alienated me from the hierarchy, especially those who care mainly about those things.

Secondly, we need to clarify what we mean by "love". It's a vague term. Some people say that Catholic priests don't get married because they're married to the Church. I don't like this metaphor; I think it's inappropriate. I don't feel married to the Church: Marriage is something that happens between a man and a woman who become one body in their intimacy and life together. I suppose I "love" the Church inasmuch as I'm giving my life in service to the Church, whether that be at a parish—I celebrated my birthday recently, and a pastor friend threw a great lunch for me after Mass with more than a hundred in attendance; it was fantastic, with all the presents, cake, and affection of so many people—or with other priests whom I consider my brothers. I feel motivated to do what I do because of the value that the Church represents and because she's ultimately a work of God.

The historical configuration of the Church changes in different contexts throughout time, and the way she's configured today is

probably outdated and dysfunctional, but the hierarchy within the
Church won't change anything until the current model is completely
destroyed, and then we'll have no choice but to switch models. In
1974, Avery Dulles wrote his great work, *Models of the Church*, and
though nearly 50 years have passed, his reflections are still very relevant today.

The human dimension of the Church is filled with corruption,
sin, and deceit, as you'd expect from anything human. But the divine
dimension of the Church is much more important. If Christ doesn't
come back and end the whole thing tomorrow, it's worth continuing
to fight for the ultimate victory. We still have time.

So, do I love the Church? Yes, because I've always found in her
the presence of Jesus Christ, both in the Eucharist and in the faithful members of the Church. And I'm willing to offer my life for
the good of the Church. This is also one of the main points that
Joseph Ratzinger makes in his classic treatise *Introduction to Christianity*, another book written decades ago, but as relevant today as it
was then. Archbishop Rino Fisichella, one the finest minds in the
Church today, always stresses that the Christian faith is *not* "a religion
of the book" (meaning a sacred text), but rather "a religion of a person, Jesus Christ". Without a deep, personal relationship with Jesus,
membership in the Church has little meaning. It becomes reduced to
a mere formality, or an experience of community, which isn't a bad
thing, but it's an evasion of the true nature of Christianity. Evelyn
Waugh, G. K. Chesterton, and C. S. Lewis have all tried to convince
us of this truth, with greater or lesser success; these were very influential authors for me growing up, before entering seminary.

Navigating life today, including life in the Church, can be a
constant challenge to one's faith, because of the politics, struggles
for power, corruption, homosexuality, and misguided use of time,
energy, and resources. But I knew that going into my ministry. As
you know, Augustine says where there's sin, there's also grace, and
I'm banking on that.

Keep in touch, and God bless.

Name withheld

CHAPTER FOUR

The Machinery and Its Fixing

After You Hit the Iceberg

I remember the day when one of the staff walked in and said, "Dave, I've been looking at our financials audited by Price Waterhouse, and I think they're all wrong." So, he showed me, and he was right. So, I had to go to the bank, where we already had tens of millions of dollars in loans outstanding, and say, "Uh, guys, we need to restate our financials for the last three years ... and they're not off by a little; they're off by $20 million or $30 million or whatever." It just kept getting worse.

—David Holden
Interim CFO, Archdiocese of Philadelphia

In July 2011, Denver's Archbishop Charles Chaput was named as the new archbishop of Philadelphia. He was installed in September. It was an unlikely appointment. Bishops rarely move cross-country from west to east, and rarely from a relatively small metropolitan see to one of the storied dioceses of the United States, the home of two saints and the birthplace of the American parish school system. Chaput had no facility in languages beyond English and some basic Spanish. He had no Roman experience. He had no doctorate. Nor was he a canonist, a former seminary rector, or a former diocesan vicar general—all standard routes to the episcopate.

What he did have was a reputation for strong leadership and administrative skill. He was also quite comfortable making unpopular but necessary decisions, and then making sure they happened. For the Church in Philadelphia at the time—facing multiple sex-abuse civil lawsuits, criminal investigations and criminal cases against priests, a history of budget deficits, a $300+ million debt, broken priestly morale, anger in the pews, a $1 million theft by its former chief financial officer, and intense media and legislative hostility—he was exactly what the doctor ordered.

While still in Denver, Chaput commissioned a 90-day professional review of the Philadelphia Archdiocese to begin as soon as he was installed. David Holden, Denver's CFO, and attorney Scott Browning, a partner in the Lewis Roca law firm, completed the audit on-site in Philadelphia later that fall. They then developed a plan to deal with the problems and supervised the hiring of a new archdiocesan CFO, Timothy O'Shaughnessy, and a new general counsel. I staffed the overall process, and my interviews with Holden, Browning, and O'Shaughnessy, as well as Matthew O'Brien, president of a Philadelphia investment advisory firm, follow below.

The implementation of the Holden-Browning plan revealed that the Philadelphia Archdiocese suffered from confusion in its legal structures; improper use and management of funds; trauma and poor work ethic among various staff; widespread institutional distrust; incompetent or over-controlling decision-makers; a silo mentality from administrators; and habitual avoidance of urgent problems. Over the next eight years, all of these problems were addressed and either eliminated or sharply reduced.

The point is simply this. Philadelphia in 2011 was an extreme case of many discrete mistakes, bad assumptions, and ignored problems over time, congealing into one big catastrophe. But it's hardly the only or last example of poor Church management. And in an age of limited resources and intense public scrutiny, the price of flawed stewardship and weak Church leadership is exceedingly high.

ख ख ख

David Holden, former CFO, Archdiocese of Denver

You spent the first 14 years of your career in one of the nation's largest accounting firms, then served as chief financial officer for a sports and entertainment corporation, and eventually ended up working with, and counseling, a variety of bishops and diocesan staffs.

HOLDEN: I had extensive experience with four dioceses, each different in size and challenges, and in different parts of the country. I also had limited exposure to two other dioceses. I did the annual review of their financial statements for their metropolitan archbishop.

What makes for a pattern of diocesan financial success?

HOLDEN: A willingness to admit mistakes, disclose financial challenges, and tell the truth. The leadership of the bishop is crucial. He needs good communication skills with his brother priests and his people. He also needs a capable moderator of the curia, a good finance officer, and an experienced, candid finance council. Another factor is the bishop's senior staff. They need to collaborate. They need to respect one another, even when they disagree. And the bishop needs to solicit and really listen to their honest opinions. He can't take an autocratic approach to his governance.

What makes for a pattern of failure?

HOLDEN: A bishop's inexperience in making hard decisions and working with advisory bodies. Or alternatively, relying on just one or two trusted advisers. Ignoring problems, hoping they'll go away— they don't. Conflicts of interest within management and the finance council. Lack of transparency in financial disclosures. Taking the easy way out to avoid conflicts or bad news, rather than telling the truth and dealing with painful issues head on.

Overall, based on your experience, what are the biggest strengths and weaknesses in today's diocesan structures and leadership?

HOLDEN: For my wife, Joanie, and me, my work for the Church only strengthened our faith. The bishops I worked with closely were all good men. So were the dozens of priests I met and helped. I have no "bad" memories of working for the Church; there were complicated and difficult things, but I always worked with a great group of people.

That's what I remember most. I got to work with dedicated people who were doing something for the greater good. People within the

Church with strongly differing opinions and practices never hurt our faith in any way. It gave us a broader perspective on the challenges ahead. Also, I'm a competitive person. I hate to fail. In the secular business world, you're always looking for the next promotion, the next career step. When you're a CFO in the Church, there's no new title to seek, and it was a perfect fit because it's a consuming job, and it left me free to serve the bishop, the moderator of the curia, and the members of the finance council with my best efforts.

Having said that, the Church is no different from corporate America or Washington in the way that politics plays a very important role in the Church's internal life. Existing practices of promotion to leadership positions in the local, national, and worldwide Church need to be challenged to ensure that the best priests are placed in key positions.

The clergy I worked with were nearly all trustworthy, committed men. But too often I heard a priest or even a bishop say he was never trained for the financial leadership role of running a parish or diocese. It's understandable; that's not why a man gets ordained. But it's not an excuse. It can lead to delegating things he shouldn't; failing to take personal responsibility for the financial health of his parish or diocese; failing to hold staff accountable for meeting their job expectations, delivering timely work product, or doing the necessary work to make prudent decisions. There are plenty of opportunities today for clergy to get the financial and leadership training they need.

Another problem is a lack of strong lay leadership in diocesan financial governing bodies and a seeming willingness for otherwise experienced lay business professionals to check their credentials at the door and acquiesce to whatever the bishop or pastor wants. There's a history of weak financial management and expertise in many dioceses and an apathetic attitude by staff toward improving things. "This is the way we've always done it" is a favorite song of both clergy and staff.

At the national level, I served on the USCCB's Accounting/ Finance Committee from about 2008 to 2014. I was grateful for the opportunity, but I never felt our work was taken seriously by the broader bishops' conference. I'm not sure most diocesan CFOs were even aware of the work product that the committee, through the conference, provided to assist them. That may have changed. I hope it has.

One experience stays with me, though. After completing my assignments for the Archdiocese of Philadelphia, I thought it would be wise to share some observations of my experiences with my fellow members of the USCCB committee. This was in 2012 or 2013, and the chairman of the committee supported such a presentation. We met in Dallas. I got permission from Archbishop Charles Chaput to brief the group on the financial analysis I'd done for him when he was transferred [in 2011] to Philadelphia. The former archdiocesan CFO had embezzled $1 million, and that was just the smallest of the problems, which were a governance, financial, legal, and organizational disaster. So, I gave a briefing on it for about half an hour. A bishop was in the audience—he's now in Rome—and at the end of my comments, he seemed to dismiss the whole presentation. He told me, "We knew all about that garbage", or something to that effect. Of course that wasn't possible; but even if it had been, the bishop's attitude was just stunning. He couldn't have cared less. To this day, I regret not challenging him, and trying to better understand his intentions.

What were your personal satisfactions and frustrations?

HOLDEN: There were a couple of projects I just couldn't complete before retiring because of time and resources. And I wish I'd taken more time with my staff to help them grow in their careers as financial stewards in the Church. There was always a new task or challenge that got in the way, or that I prioritized over my staff's development.

Denver was a well-run archdiocese when I arrived. So I could concentrate on tweaking and improving the financial governance standards, getting our parishes incorporated, building on a good foundation. Philadelphia was the opposite. The Denver Archdiocese loaned me to Philadelphia for eight months in 2011–2012. I did the financial analysis for the new archbishop, laid out the financial restructuring plan, helped the team that hired the new CFO [Tim O'Shaughnessy], and enjoyed watching him succeed. I also helped with the hiring of new CFOs in the Toledo and Lincoln Dioceses.

Do any bishops stand out in your experience?

HOLDEN: Sure, several. Bishop Daniel Thomas, when I worked with him in Toledo, was very dedicated, very alert to learning how to be a better leader. He was an excellent communicator; he understood the power of communicating well and in the right way. I had a lot of respect for Bishop James Conley in Lincoln; his diocese had some big challenges. There were others; men like Archbishop José Gomez, whom I knew from his time as an auxiliary in Denver. And Archbishop Chaput, in Denver and Philadelphia, was exceptional. Even with the worst news, he was at peace. He never flinched. He was honest, very smart, and he could work and communicate on a practical leadership level better than most of the corporate CEOs I dealt with over the decades. And he was humble. He never let ego drive his decisions.

Looking back on your years of Church service, any other thoughts?

HOLDEN: We need better leadership within the Vatican bureaucracy and U.S. Church so that they truly stand as world-class examples of Christian governance and best practices. If the Church, from an institutional perspective, continues to lose credibility, our moral culture will continue to weaken. The ongoing financial scandals in Rome and the arrogance of those involved reflect a culture and management philosophy that are so radically different from how we're taught to manage business in the United States; it's embarrassing to me.

In my lifetime, the Church has always seemed to accept criticism and dishonest portrayals of its fundamental beliefs from Hollywood and the press without really fighting back, except on some local levels. The Jewish and Muslim communities take a much different approach. Our current culture seems to be steamrolling over the teachings of the Church, and our response is negligible at best.

I'm proud of my faith. I sincerely believe that it's "the way, the truth, and the life". I felt so good about the Church and her mission during the pontificate of St. John Paul. During his time as pope, the voice and actions of the Church seemed to matter. Clearly the clergy scandal has been a terrible stain, and it's a wound we continue to live with. But the pendulum has swung so strongly under Pope Francis that I worry about where the Church is heading. So many things seem to be confusing and lacking in honesty; to be wrong and getting worse. At the same time, I know that there are many laypeople and clergy who seem to admire the current Church leadership and its style. So, I've come to realize that I need to focus my efforts on being right with God through daily prayer and the sacraments, and not worry about the institutional Church.

ح‍ح ح‍ح ح‍ح

Timothy O'Shaughnessy, former CFO,
Archdiocese of Philadelphia

I interviewed Dave Holden for this chapter, Tim, and his memories were very useful and very positive. Of course, he's been out of the diocesan machinery long enough that he may not remember some of the more challenging moments.

O'SHAUGHNESSY: I'm not sure I'm there yet. You'll probably see that in the next few minutes.

We've talked in the past about the difficulty of right-sizing Catholic institutions as Catholic resources and numbers contract.

O'SHAUGHNESSY: It's harder and takes longer than people expect. We all love our local childhood parishes and schools, and the nostalgia and memories attached to those places are all good. When you're facing massive financial problems though, you need to be objective with your thinking. We all tend sometimes to be too emotionally attached to this or that organization or building or school. But the people in charge need to have the resolve to make the hard decisions. It's good too when the boards and committees supporting a diocese are staffed with diverse groups willing to have the challenging conversations.

The problems occur at both the parish and diocesan levels.

O'SHAUGHNESSY: Yes. We had big challenges in Philadelphia, but I think our boards and committees were well functioning. We could always do better with diversity; there need to be more women and people of color involved. I do think we made a good effort, but there's a lot more work to be done.

You served as a CFO and in other senior executive positions in large secular enterprises both before and after your diocesan service. Based on your experiences, what are the practical issues you see in revivifying the Catholic Church in the United States?

O'SHAUGHNESSY: Well, I can speak on the financial issues. The Philadelphia Archdiocese ignored its financial situation for a long time. Other big dioceses did the same thing. The lay pension plan was underfunded by more than $150 million. The priests' pension plan was literally empty and needed $90 million to be fully funded. It was "pay as you go". In hindsight, we grappled with the financial issues well. Dioceses must be honest and deal with their financial realities, and I think we did that.

But why do you suppose that doesn't happen?

O'SHAUGHNESSY: There needs to be more fortitude at the leadership level to deal with financial problems. Sometimes it's easier just to run a deficit and push off the problem for as long as you can. In Philadelphia, I'm not sure anybody ever pulled it all together to say, "Wait a minute, we're almost bankrupt here except for publicly declaring it."

You were formed in a business environment where you either performed or you were fired. I wonder if sometimes bishops neglect dealing with the finances because that's not what they were ordained for. And then they hire CFOs who just don't have the force of personality, or the background of professional experience, to say, "Look, we have a problem, and we need to fix it. And if you don't want to do that, I can't be here."

O'SHAUGHNESSY: Well, it was true for us in Philly. And I imagine it's true elsewhere. You can't keep kicking the can down the road. For us, we *saw* the end of the road, right? We had balance sheet problems of more than $300 million and a recurring operating deficit of almost $20 million. You need fortitude to deal with that, and we did. Archbishop Chaput was absolutely the right guy for Philadelphia at the time.

I remember sitting in an archdiocesan office after the CFO position was offered to me in 2012, and on the table in front of me was a list of disasters as long as my arm. The pensions were a wreck. There was no cemetery perpetual-care fund. The budgets were upside down. The internal parish loan fund was basically bankrupt. We faced multiple lawsuits. The banks wouldn't lend to us. I don't usually get shaken, but this was worse than I could have imagined. So, the archbishop walked in and asked me what I thought, and if I was going to take the job. I said something like, "Archbishop, this is so screwed up that you'll pretty much need to let me do whatever I need to do to fix this." I wasn't that blunt. But he put his hand on my shoulder, and he said to me (and this is a quote), "If blood needs to be shed, including my own, blood will be shed. You do whatever you need to do to fix this." If I hadn't sensed that level of resolve, I wouldn't have taken the job. A water pistol wasn't going to put out the fire.

But really, in retrospect, you're the only guy who could have gotten it done. What were the biggest surprises once you were actually on the job?

O'SHAUGHNESSY: I'm not the only guy who could have gotten it done. But I did feel some obligation to help, and knowing that the archbishop was resolved to fix things meant a lot. Sometimes when you're in a bad situation, for a while, it seems that you're the only one who knows it. At the archdiocese, I didn't have to convince anybody that we had very serious problems. Everyone already knew it. So actually in that first year, the senior people all had good focus. We were a well-functioning senior staff. We knew that if we didn't do big things, and big things quickly, we wouldn't have a chance. So, we started right away to work on leasing out the management of our cemeteries, selling our nursing homes, cutting offices and programs, reducing staff, that sort of thing. It was painful. The nursing homes were a great ministry, and in particular, that decision was probably the hardest for me personally. But if we'd had the nursing homes during the COVID pandemic, with our very limited resources, it would've been very difficult.

There were also staff and clergy who were ambivalent or territorial about the whole thing.

O'SHAUGHNESSY: No doubt. But I never discounted their commitment to the good work they were doing

That leads to another issue, though. How much bureaucratic "silo-ing" did you find in your diocesan service?

O'SHAUGHNESSY: Oh, it was prevalent; and probably natural because of the way the Church organizes around its ministries. And it's probably still there.

Does that parallel your previous professional experience?

O'SHAUGHNESSY: Organizations often have silos; different functions, different businesses. At times, people can be parochial about what they're responsible for and not see the importance of the greater enterprise. That's not just a Church issue. But leaders must make decisions that are best for the enterprise.

What about the professional quality of the people you worked with, diocesan versus secular staffs?

O'SHAUGHNESSY: In my time at the archdiocese, we were a house on fire, and sometimes veteran staff tended to reminisce about "the good old days". But I worked with a lot of good people there, a good level of talent, and a higher degree of competency than I expected going in. I was really pleased with the people that I worked with in Philadelphia.

Looking back, what's your biggest satisfaction, having worked in a diocesan environment?

O'SHAUGHNESSY: We improved the balance sheet by literally a quarter billion dollars. We eliminated the operating deficit. I take satisfaction in that.

And what are the biggest mistakes a diocese or parish typically makes?

O'SHAUGHNESSY: Living beyond its means and not even realizing it. And then having trouble dialing things back. Getting too big when times are good and assuming they'll always be good. Borrowing too much money. Not setting resources aside or building endowments for the lean times.

How did your service at the diocese affect your family, your home life?

O'SHAUGHNESSY: For a while, it was really hard. This stuff just consumes you.

Spouses really go for that.

O'SHAUGHNESSY: Well, I don't want to do "mission impossible" jobs anymore. They take a lot out of you and the people who love you.

Is there anything I haven't asked about from your diocesan experience that you think is important to mention?

O'SHAUGHNESSY: I worry about the one or two generations coming up behind us. They're impacted by social media and all the noise out there in ways we never were. And so much of it is trash. I also think that some of the hard issues that concern the Church today don't matter at all to our kids, and probably their kids. That's something that needs grappling with. And I don't know what the right answer is.

❧ ❧ ❧

Scott Browning, partner, Lewis Roca

As an attorney you've helped a wide range of religious and nonprofit organizations, nationally and internationally, over a long period of time.

BROWNING: I've represented the Catholic Church in various ways for more than 30 years. I've also worked with Protestant and Jewish organizations, the Sikhs, the LDS Church, the Boy Scouts, U.S.

Olympics, private schools, boarding schools, and other nonprofit and youth-serving organizations. In a diocesan and religious order environment, I typically work directly with the bishop or religious superior, and then collaborate with his advisers and councils. But I've also worked with parishes, Catholic foundations, and Catholic Charities.

What has been your specific legal focus?

BROWNING: In the context of the Catholic Church, I've addressed all aspects of the Church's ministry, including religious freedom issues, real estate transactions, parish incorporation, internal diocesan structural work, tax issues, reorganizing foundations, and other business and accounting work. Because of the historic sexual abuse problems, I've also advised on those difficult issues.

To what degree do Catholic bishops understand the nature and scope of the challenges now facing the Church? And has that changed over time?

BROWNING: It depends on the leader and the issue. When I first got involved with the Church—and that was quite a while ago now—the experience with Church administrators was very different from my work with companies like ESPN and AT&T. Secular corporations routinely use lawyers for counsel, legal defense, and objective advice. Bishops, though, tended to rely on a very small group of consultors, who were almost always priests. And it was clear in those early days that Church leaders weren't typically seeking outside advice. Today bishops have gotten better about understanding the challenges they face and who can help them. But many Church administrators still need to grow in allowing outsiders in to help them. And again, it depends on the bishop. Even now in the Church, when a crisis comes up, there's often a reflexive instinct to make far-reaching decisions internally. That can lead to real difficulty.

Bishops can end up isolated. Some are brilliant about getting into parishes to meet and understand people. Others live a life in the chancery. A lot of reality has been forced on bishops by the abuse scandal. They've been deposed and attacked by plaintiffs' attorneys. They've been brought into courts. Vilified in the press. They've been questioned by people who aren't their friends but enemies. And that's a real learning environment. It's a shame they've had to live through it. But it's definitely a learning environment.

In your experience, is the sexual abuse problem somehow unique to the Catholic Church?

BROWNING: I've represented more than a dozen religious faiths on the sexual abuse problem; hundreds of hours for each of those faiths, along with helping secular youth-serving organizations on the same issue. There's no question that the scale of the Catholic problem mirrors the scale of the Catholic Church, which is a very big organization. And it's clear that the Church had a serious historical problem. But society has the same problem. I don't think the scale is any bigger in the Catholic Church than it is for the Boy Scouts, for example. I was an Eagle Scout, and a sadness and irony for me is that when the Boy Scouts filed for bankruptcy, after a lot of due diligence, they thought they'd face about 1,700 claims. As we speak, it's been widely publicized that the Scouts face more than 80,000 claims and are scheduled to pay $2.46 billion to alleged victims in their national bankruptcy. In the press every day are reports of sexual abuse in sports, in colleges, and in many other organizations. So no, the abuse issue isn't unique to the Catholic Church.

I'd add that the Catholic Church and faith-based organizations are clearly hunted on a whole range of issues by the secular media. And the abuse scandal gives the press a tool to do that. In the areas of the country where I've worked, I've seen instances where public school abuse issues are far broader, and even plaintiffs' lawyers will tell you that the sex-abuse issue is worse in many public school jurisdictions. Yet the media are virtually silent about it. In my view, that's deliberate.

What are the biggest mistakes Catholic institutions make in preventing crises like abuse or financial scandals?

BROWNING: Well again, it's not just a Catholic problem. Nonprofit organizations in general, but particularly faith-based organizations, tend to have a common focus on mission. They put less attention into potential lawsuits and risk management. There's an understandable

desire to spend money on the organization's mission, not on antic-
ipating problems in litigation; even basic things like fixing cracks
in the sidewalk or a broken guardrail are often seen as a burden to
address. The nonprofit environment is instinctively reactive. People may say in a meeting, "Let's get that fixed before someone gets
hurt" or "Let's spend time on a policy to manage that issue." But it
often takes more time in nonprofits than in the corporate world to
focus their attention and resources on "non-mission" items. That's
because nonprofit managers' initial reaction is often that they don't
want to spend time and money on such things, compared to what
they see as their central purpose, which is helping others. And typically, the administrators didn't join the nonprofit to deal with tedious
risk management issues.

That's the case in many faith entities and nonprofits I've worked
with. In a secular business, if there's a crack in the sidewalk, they rush
to fix it and prevent a slip-and-fall claim. There's a lot of work done
on policies and compliance. In the nonprofit context, it takes extra
effort by the leaders to avoid being reactive. It's possible to overcome
these challenges with discernment and hard work. And a good example of this is the Church's work in the last two-plus decades to protect
children and young adults. In the United States, the Church now is
very proactive; it has some of the most detailed policies and practices
in the nation to create safe environments, and outside auditors check
compliance. It's a model for other organizations on how to tackle
difficult challenges with resources, training, detailed policies, and full
compliance—to avoid any problems to the fullest extent possible.

*You've faced some of the best, and very tough, plaintiffs' attorneys in the
country. What's their appropriate role?*

BROWNING: Honest personal injury lawyers do provide a service.
When people get sick from groundwater that a corporation poi-
soned, or they need breathing machines from asbestos lung damage,
plaintiffs' attorneys get them the help they deserve. That's important.
And these lawyers can go to their graves feeling really good about the
outcome. The fact that they also took 40 or 50 cents of every dollar
awarded to the victims when they settled a case ... that's a problem.
I have a plaintiffs' lawyer friend worth $300 million who retired in

his 40s. That money came from 40 to 50 percent of every asbestos settlement he worked on in the United States. The plaintiffs' lawyers suing nonprofits have made billions of dollars otherwise meant to help victims. I'm a defense lawyer, and we're accused of our own challenges and problems. We're certainly far from perfect. But just like carpenters, when we do an hour of work, we charge for an hour of work. We're not paid some percentage of a settlement. In the sexual abuse crisis, there's been a massive incentive for plaintiffs' lawyers to create or exaggerate claims, because they have a personal financial stake in it. It's become big business. Even Wall Street is involved, with hedge funds putting millions of dollars into generating claims, and then taking a cut of the plaintiff law firms' enormous legal fees.

What's the percentage of Church sexual misconduct and abuse claims that have some legitimate substance?

BROWNING: In the early days of the clergy abuse scandal—and it's now well established that the vast majority of these cases are based on incidents 40 and more years ago—a lot of the cases were very serious, and that's incredibly sad. In the court filings from 20 to 30 years ago, there were few instances of fraud; my estimate would be nine out of 10 or more claims had real substance and were being brought by legitimate survivors of abuse. This is supported by the public research that's been done. Today a lot more of the cases are, at a minimum, exaggerated, sometimes simply because of memory issues and the passage of time. And there are many clear examples, in many different contexts and lawsuits, of people who are just desperately seeking money. So, the amount of fraud and exaggeration has gone up over time. That's the pattern in many personal injury and so-called "toxic tort" areas of the law.

What would fair legislation look like governing sexual abuse cases from the past?

BROWNING: The older the claim is, the less likely you'll get to the truth in the civil legal system. Every judge, lawyer, and policeman understands that reality. With memory changing and evidence degrading over time, there's no way to get to reliable truth after

five or 10 or 20 years. Laws that reach back and revive claims that
are decades old simply are not good for anyone involved, from the
employer accused of being a bad employer decades ago to the survi-
vor. This is the view of many academics, experts, and even victims'
advocates who work in this area. The lesson from experts who focus
on healing, restorative justice, and helping survivors is that legislation
should focus on healing, and the burden should be shared by anyone
who caused the harm and by the society that wants people to be
healthy. Money should go to helping survivors based on their healing
needs, which means punitive damages aren't appropriate in historical
claims. Instead, this money is best used to heal survivors of abuse and
create safe environments in organizations. And you want to encourage people to come forward quickly if they're a victim—to help
the authorities stop the perpetrator—not wait decades to file a civil case
when the perpetrator is often dead. Good legislation would involve
some sort of crime victims' fund; not running the program through
government, but setting up systems to help victims with real dollars
for real issues; not letting plaintiffs' attorneys pick apart the Olympics
or the Boy Scouts, for example, and take money that should go to the
victims. These days, autonomous reparations programs have become
my mantra. They've been successful all over the country.

*You've been exceptional in your service to the Church. But you're not Cath-
olic; on some level, you're on the outside looking in. After all this time, what
are your impressions of the Church, and have they changed over the years?*

BROWNING: Well, I'm a Methodist, as you know. But I've worked
with Catholics more than any other faith, including my own. Being
around the hundreds of good Catholics I've met, including many
good churchmen in our own country and elsewhere, has made me
a better and more spiritual person. So, I feel a deep affinity for the
Catholic Church, the core Church that does amazing work, and I
have profound respect for the Catholics who sacrifice every day to
do that work. I think Catholics are harder on themselves than anyone
else I've worked with.

My maternal great-great-grandfather was a Methodist minister, a
circuit-riding minister, in Bulgaria. And my mother's entire family
there was wiped out by the Communists because of their faith. I never

imagined that we'd be in a world where hatred of religion would be an American issue. That just couldn't happen in the United States. And yet, the government now systematically tries to weaken faith communities. It interferes with people's right to worship and believe, and to live those beliefs. And the secular media often collaborate in these efforts, assailing or demeaning religious believers. Catholics and all people of faith can't afford to be deluded. They need to stand up and push back. Otherwise, the result will be very dangerous.

ॐ ॐ ॐ

Matthew O'Brien, president, O'Brien Greene & Co., Inc.

To begin with a couple of facts: You lead an investment advisory firm. You also cofounded and chair a Catholic institute at one of the Ivy League schools, the University of Pennsylvania.

O'BRIEN: Right. The firm serves a number of religious entities, but the majority of our clients are families and secular nonprofits or businesses. At Penn, I'm involved with the Collegium Institute for Catholic Thought and Culture.

You're a financial professional, but also a committed layman, husband, and father with young children. What's your sense of the health of the Church in the United States?

O'BRIEN: At the moment, it's culturally and politically spent. It doesn't have much influence at all. If you look at its official forms of outreach, USCCB statements and initiatives, they're almost wholly derivative. They're off-brand Catholic versions of what other people are thinking and doing anyway. The Church is ineffectual because it's listless and bitterly divided. Most Catholics are indistinguishable from other Americans. And if you're indistinguishable from something, you can't influence it, because you *are* it.

On the other hand, there's a subset of Catholics who do want to live their faith seriously, who do try to live the evangelical counsels, who do reach for sanctity. Can they influence the broader culture? Probably not in the short run. There's too few of them. But they can influence the life of the Church by helping it reclaim its true identity, centering its focus on Jesus Christ and the pursuit of holiness. If that happens, the Church could have a positive influence on the culture. It's the only way.

To what degree do U.S. Church leaders understand the nature of the problems they face?

O'BRIEN: In my experience, not many of them really "get it". And among those that do, too few seem willing to do or capable of doing much that's very different from anyone else. It's strange. The American spirit is instinctively entrepreneurial. It's open to moving fast, breaking stuff, trying new things, and then trying again. That spirit is almost absent from the Church's legacy institutions, and it leads to suffocation and decay. I'm not suggesting that the Church is hidebound by traditionalism. Far from it. Genuinely traditional expressions of solidarity within the Church would be healthily disruptive. Instead, we get an ethos of managed decline that feels like we're living in the human resources division of a bloated conglomerate. Some of our sclerotic institutional structures should just be reimagined or blown up entirely. They need reordering toward Christ.

The Catholic education system, for example, needs a deep rethink. I had a conversation a few years ago with the rector of one of the country's major seminaries. He mentioned, just in passing, that more than half of his seminarians came from homeschooling families. I have no idea if that's a general pattern. But the interesting thing is that none, or very few, of his seminarians had any background in Catholic schools. The implications of that just didn't seem to register with the rector or the diocesan educational establishment.

People in the Church have an inability just to be honest about the way things are—like the prevalence of homosexuality as a factor in the clergy abuse crisis; or the complete implosion of so many women's religious communities now headed for extinction—and the result is a high level of delusion. Even Church leaders who acknowledge this impending extinction of religious communities sometimes rationalize it as an "achievement" of Vatican II's emphasis upon lay piety ... which is absurd, because lay and religious or clerical piety are complementary parts of an organic whole, not competing alternatives.

I want to turn to finances, but first this question: Vatican II put a new empha-
sis on the importance of the lay apostolate. How do you think about your own
vocation as a lay Catholic?

O'BRIEN: That's a great question, because I've changed my view on
this. I've become more sympathetic with some of the grumpy trads.
My observation is that when families are open to having a fair number of kids, the base rate of seriousness and sacrifice about the faith
among those people is a lot higher than that of many of today's bishops and priests. I have a friend, an accomplished medical doctor, who
entered the priesthood after his wife died. He was shocked by the
culture of laziness among his fellow diocesan priests.

Elizabeth Anscombe, the Catholic philosopher, wrote an indig-
nant essay in the 1970s against the idea that anyone would call marriage a vocation. When I read it as a student, I thought, "This
is ridiculous." But now, reading it in retrospect, I think she was
saying that if everything in ordinary life is a vocation, then nothing
is. Too much focus on the vocation of the laity can undermine the
uniquely important vocations of priests and religious, and we need
a lot more of the good kind of both. Good families, open to new
life, produce them. Whether we call that a vocation is less important than the results.

Starting in 2018 you researched and published a number of articles on prob-
lems in Church financial matters. In 2019 you wrote, "The sex-abuse scandal
rocking the Catholic Church is not just about sex. Nor is it just about cleri-
calism. It's also about money." How is it about money?

O'BRIEN: It's about money in different ways. Most abuse perpe-
trators in the Church have been gay men. That's simply a fact,
ratified by the *New York Times*/John Jay College study from some
years ago. In addition to the confusion in their sexual lives, many
tend to be comfort-seeking and acquisitive, and being members
of a relatively poor institution, some form of corruption is a way of
getting the money they need. I was once told by an attorney
friend of mine, who had been involved in numerous diocesan sex-
abuse investigations, that a pattern emerges which repeats itself in
otherwise disparate abuse cases: the use of pornography, same-sex

attraction, and financial misappropriation. Of course, another factor is ambition. The Church always needs funding for its ministries, and a rainmaker who solves money problems can move up the ladder more quickly; think former Cardinal Ted McCarrick and others like him.

As a financial analyst, what got you focused on the abuse scandal?

O'BRIEN: The 2018 Pennsylvania grand jury report that included information about priests from my own high school; the McCarrick connection to the U.S.-based Papal Foundation; and a general sense of how poorly financial matters were often handled in the Church.

How much of the problem in Church finance is a matter of corruption, and how much a matter of inadequate competence, clericalism, departmental territoriality, etc.?

O'BRIEN: All of the above, depending on the specific circumstances. In this country, probably more of the latter than the former. I think the postconciliar turmoil of the 1970s and 1980s had a big impact on the clergy talent pool, and that has worked its way out in a crisis of talent and achievement across Catholic culture. I saw it personally in a religious order that was a client of ours. The high-competence people left, died, or retired, and the quality of the remaining leaders was eroded. They weren't very intelligent, sometimes struggled to show up on time for things, or to complete what they said they would do. If you have people like that running the operation, things just gradually start falling apart.

What about the financial condition of the Vatican?

O'BRIEN: The Vatican swims and breathes in an Italian environment. There are many very well-run Italian businesses and markets, but there's also a cultural tolerance for fraud and self-dealing. The statute of limitations for financial crimes is very short. Some CEOs of major publicly listed companies in Italy, right now as we speak, have been found guilty of felonies involving tax evasion and fraud. Such infractions would be career-ending for an executive in the United States, but in Italy they're largely inconsequential to professional advancement at the highest levels.

That reminds me: In 2015, during Cardinal George Pell's time running the Secretariat of the Economy, he had Danny Casey, his senior aide, brief me on the state of Vatican finances. Casey had found a lot of internal confusion, loose procedures, a curial cardinal with a secret €10 million account that he hadn't reported, etc. Pope Francis, at least in his early years, seemed determined to clean things up. Has that actually happened?

O'BRIEN: What Francis has done with the finances is similar to his actions in other areas: He is inconsistent, works in fits and starts, drives the reform, and then seems to undermine it. Back in 2017 there was a lot of applause for his efforts to internationalize the Vatican's financial bureaucracy with reputable and independent professionals, and it was initially true. By early 2022, the efforts had largely stalled or even been reversed. A lot of the Vatican's wealth is tied up in real estate that is badly mismanaged and produces much less income than it should. And keep in mind that the Vatican's annual operating budget is less than the yearly budget of a university like Harvard or Notre Dame. There's not a lot of room for mismanagement. Yet it's been going on for decades; and it directly impacts mission.

Presumably the Church in the United States does a better job, at least better than the Vatican.

O'BRIEN: Sure, some dioceses and parishes are run very well. The Chicago Archdiocese is respected; it's a tight ship administratively, staffed by high-quality people, or so I'm told. There are others.

You're still young with a long career ahead of you, including your family's life in the Church. It can be tempting to worry about the future.

O'BRIEN: The only appropriate view, I suppose, is expressed by that bumper sticker you sometimes see on Boomer-driven Volvo station wagons: "If you're not completely appalled, you haven't been paying attention." If that's a sensible attitude toward flaws in the Church, it's even more so the right attitude toward humanity in general. We're a compromised, sinful lot who need salvation. And yet, from what I see, there's also a lot of good happening at the local level in the Church; a lot more than 10 or 15 years ago, and this means the Holy Spirit is still at work. There's a lot of problems, but also a lot of good things.

So, hope is the key. It's hope that transforms pessimism into mirthful detachment.

CHAPTER FIVE

Here Comes Everybody

The Formators and Their Thoughts

I live very much in the lay space, so I don't spend much time criticizing what the Church should or shouldn't do beyond paying attention to the integrity of the liturgy, the sacraments, and the care of the needy, like widows and orphans. I think we're all called, in our own ways, to be saints. And if we're really invested in developing personal sanctity in our practical circumstances here and now, then the Holy Spirit will use us, each of us differently, to accomplish good things.

—from a wife, mother, and legal scholar

"Here comes everybody" refers to the Catholic Church, as the Irish author James Joyce once described her. Or so people often assume; but the story may be apocryphal. In 1923, Joyce wrote an initial sketch for his novel *Finnegan's Wake* and titled it *Here Comes Everybody*. The title actually comes from the initials, HCE, of Humphrey Chimpden Earwicker, a character in *Finnegan's Wake*. But, whatever Joyce said or meant or didn't about the Church, she really *is* for everybody. And in the Catholic world, well over 90 percent of "everybody" belongs to the laity, men and women from every imaginable background.

In its Decree on the Apostolate of the Laity, *Apostolicam Actuositatem*, Vatican II stressed, "Since the laity, in accordance with their state of life, live in the midst of the world and its concerns, they are called by God to exercise their apostolate in the world like leaven, with the ardor of the spirit of Christ." And then, "On all Christians therefore is laid the preeminent responsibility of working to make the divine message of salvation known and accepted by all men throughout the world" (nos. 2–3).

Readers will note that not "everybody" is represented in the comments below. The ethnicity of those who speak in this chapter is suitably diverse: Latino, Latina, African-American, Asian, and generic Euro. But the focus is mainly, and quite deliberately, on parents, educators (especially of college-age adults, the years when crucial life decisions are made), and those engaged in public witness. The reason why is simple. They shape the future in a uniquely powerful way.

2♥ 2♥ 2♥

1. From a wife, mother, and university professor

I've always loved the Church. I love her because I was raised in her care. When I remember myself as a child in my home parish, I can still smell the wood and the incense, and see the candles flickering on the altar. And I knew vividly, even then, that the church building itself was *mine,* and that the Church was like a mother watching over me. She was serene and loving; a completely surrounding and eternal presence. So, I've never been terribly disillusioned about the Church. I've always felt God's personal presence in the buildings, the sacraments, and the friendship of holy people. These things have kept me sane.

The lukewarm spirit in so much of the Church today does bother me. Too much time is spent on administration. Too little goes to helping people come to grips with the meaning and message of Jesus. And there's too much Catholic cowardice in the face of today's "isms" that are poisonous for human beings and hateful toward God. Getting cozy with the world is a dangerous thing. One of my fantasies is having more bishops with smaller dioceses, so their Catholic believers and institutions could really feel their bishop's pastoral presence. We need fewer "things"—like buildings, etc.—to maintain, and more time for evangelization, community prayer, sharing experiences of God, and living out the evangelical counsels. In other words, we need less to lose in the way of money and things, which then might increase our courage to take on bad ideas more bravely. We also need to rethink our social service efforts. Some of our large hospitals and universities, and even some of our charities, are basically Catholic "zombies".They have the shell of a Catholic entity, but their reward structures are tied to worldly objectives, not religious goals.

At the same time, especially in the face of so many pressures, we have a lot of reasons for hope. There's huge energy in many of our parishes. Lay-driven, bottom-up Christian initiatives are everywhere. A lot of them are very effective. I've seen a sharp uptick in students who want to work on religious liberty and free speech issues. They're very aware of today's threats against both of those constitutional rights. A lot of good things about our country still work well, despite all the moaning and mudslinging. And finally, being an academic, I take intense pride in the intellectual brilliance of the Church and the gifted converts who continue to find a home in her. There's a wonderful irony, and a delicious justice, in the fact that if the anticlerical *philosophes* of the French Revolution returned to earth today, they'd find that the single greatest defender of human reason is ... the Catholic Church.

೫ ೫ ೫

2. From a wife, mother, policy expert, and author

As much as some of our Catholic leaders talk about the importance of inclusion, that's not going to solve our problems. People don't leave the Church, and they don't fail to join the Church, because they feel "excluded". It's because they don't see anything in her that compels their interest. The culture has deadened their souls. And we're not helping people to see that only a spiritual answer, not a material one, can address their loneliness and crisis of meaning. We're stuck in a kind of "managed decline" mode. A lot of our younger priests are really good men. That's a sign of hope. And one of the best things about traveling in my work is meeting a lot of ordinary Catholics who are engaged in their parishes. They're generous. They volunteer. They have a strong faith. But they're also disappointed in many of their bishops for what they see as ambiguity, or compromised principles, or a lack of courage.

So many of our current issues come down to a confusion about sex and gender. We've lost our cultural memory that sex has something to do with reproduction; with self-giving, intimacy, and sustained relationship. And here's the irony: In the name of liberation, the biggest losers are women. We've been formed by today's culture to reject our femininity; to repudiate the core fact that we're created for motherhood, whether that's spiritual or physical. I see this when I talk with younger women. Motherhood is simply a category of things that they might someday do, as opposed to an intrinsic dimension of their identity. In the current environment, you're either a sexual object, or a breeding object, or you're a sterile, wannabe man competing on male terms. And the fact that women don't know who they are, is a reason why so many men no longer know who *they* are, either.

Technology plays a big part in all of this. Starting with the birth control pill, and then with abortion, surrogacy, and egg freezing, technology has focused on dominating the things that are uniquely good about being female. Technology is also closely linked to today's gender dysphoria, because having first confused young women about who they are, the culture now enables them to cut off their breasts, take hormones, and transform themselves into "males". But even here, the promise of technology is a cheat because men can now become "female" and beat real women in athletic contests, while invading their private spaces. So women have effectively disappeared. Women have been erased because the social category of "woman" is no longer tethered to the reality of being born female with a female body and all that it entails.

Fast forward all of this 20 years, and imagine what we'll be facing. We need leaders who will stand up and say, "I'm *unwilling* to live with lies, and I'm willing to die for what's true." If you don't have that passion in your heart as a priest or bishop, you should get out and go home. The same applies for anyone who claims to be a believer.

ᴥ ᴥ ᴥ

3. From a wife, theologian, and ministry executive

The most urgent need Catholics face is a renewal of our baptismal vocation, and tied to that is addressing the issue of clericalism. Clericalism has two faces. It's both the laity sitting back and expecting the clergy to do everything. And then, obviously, there's the clerical hierarchy, which assumes and sometimes misuses its authority. I don't think we've yet seen the kind of genuine, clergy-and-lay collaboration that Vatican II talked about. And saying that surfaces another need, which involves teaching best management practices to current and future Church leaders. Priests and religious need to learn how to hire the right lay expertise, which would then free them up for the more particular elements of their vocation—in the case of clergy, the sacraments and pastoral guidance. A lot of priests are overwhelmed by what they're expected to do in terms of administration. They haven't been adequately trained, and many don't have a natural administrative skill set.

I've served in all sorts of Church and Church-related positions, so I've seen a lot of today's institutional dysfunction, especially going back to 2001–2002. And yet I feel very committed. When people ask me, "Why do you still work for the Church?", I say, well, because I want to stay and fight to make her better. I'd never give up on the Church as my mother and teacher. It's our obligation, all of us, to help the Church be the Church that our Lord and the faithful deserve; the Church that the world needs. And frankly, I find that very often the problems and dysfunctions in Church life come less from bad intentions, and more from a lack of formation, especially in basic leadership and relational skills. Over the last few years, I've had a number of priests ask me if I would just teach a course on emotional affectivity. That's astonishing. I've never heard priests be so realistic about their challenges. They're looking for resources, and they're asking very practical questions: "How can I live my life and my priesthood more fruitfully? How can I do my job better? How can I serve my people better?" In my experience that's a significant change, and a very good one.

Laypeople do need to understand that the lay and clergy vocations differ in important ways. Some natural boundaries exist, and they need to be respected. And here's a final fact that seems to be compulsively neglected today: Lay leadership is primarily *exercised in the world,* not in ecclesial positions. There's a whole world out there. It's foolish to argue and complain about "power in the Church" while we relinquish our baptismal power to shape society at large.

ﻦﻦﻦ

4. From a single laywoman and ministry leader

My love for the Church has everything to do with the Eucharist
and the institution that follows from it, all the way down through
an ancient tradition that I believe is faithful. I don't care that her
people are broken and flawed. I expect that. It's the human side of
things. But the supernatural side of the Church is real. And it's true.
Over and over again, that's been proven to me. My father is a very
scriptural man. When I was growing up, he always talked to us about
the Bible. We read it together and prayed the Rosary as a family.
My parents wanted their children to be successful in the world, but
they wanted us to be faithful people first. For them and for us, there
was nothing more important than encountering Jesus Christ. So, as
an adult I have a confessor, and prayer partners, and other forms of
accountability. But I was raised praying all the time. Prayer is your
bridge to walking with God at every moment. If you don't have a
strong, distinct prayer life, you can too easily identify your work with
your prayer. And then, sooner or later, you stop believing.

We underestimate our strengths. The Church in the United States
is much less corrupt with much more freedom and many more
resources than in many other places. And there are many more opportunities for lay leadership, including women's leadership, in the American Church. We need to acknowledge and take pride in that. I've
been astounded at the faith and energy that many young people have,
and the diversity of people who are hungry for religious answers. We
have some great legal openings to protect the Church if we step into
them. Every single diocese that once had adoption and foster care
ministries should be working to take those spaces back from the state.
Everywhere the administrative state loses an inch of its overreach, we
should be rushing in to take back that space. And we have some great
new bishops, even if some of them inherit houses built on sand.

I do think lay leaders have deferred too much to clerics for formation, rather than taking that work on themselves. And Catholics have
lagged in their engagement on the religious liberty front, compared
to Evangelicals. The Church continues to try to make deals with
government authorities that are fundamentally unfriendly. That's
a mistake. I also think that one of our biggest problems is money.
We're a very rich Church, and we've started living that way. Pope

Francis is exactly right when he talks about the need for us to recover a spirit of sacrifice and poverty. Sometimes he articulates it poorly. But what he says is true. In the end, there are always plenty of reasons to be depressed about the world and the Church. The devil hasn't changed. But I do feel that the angels and saints of our current generation are very different from the past, and very much the ones we need. And they fill me with hope.

5. *From a wife, mother, author, and legal scholar*

What's our common faith as Americans? Well, it used to be the Constitution with its ideals of liberty and equality. And those are obviously good things. But the meaning of those ideals, once God has been removed from the picture, is very much contested. They're now typically defined downward toward our lower appetites. One of the results has been a kind of hyper-sexualization of the culture, especially through technology, leading finally to today's gender and identity confusions. When we lose our identity as God's children, we look for a substitute in all sorts of different places, some of them really toxic. So, for me, it seems that the Church has a massive opportunity to provide an attractive alternative.

I live very much in the lay space, so I don't spend much time criticizing what the Church should or shouldn't do beyond paying attention to the integrity of the liturgy, the sacraments, and the care of the needy, like widows and orphans. I think we're all called, in our own ways, to be saints. And if we're really invested in developing personal sanctity in our practical circumstances here and now, then the Holy Spirit will use us, each of us differently, to accomplish good things. In my case, I have a background in women's studies, and I remember discussing gender equality after *Roe v. Wade* with pro-choice women scholars. This was before the *Dobbs* decision. I had five kids at that stage—now seven—and I was reading a lot of feminist legal literature. I felt like God was giving me insights that these other women couldn't see. So, that put me on my current course. Without going into detail, I had a lot of family issues growing up, and suicides by two of my friends. By the time I was 17, I was a bundle of anxiety and depression, a real existential wreck. So, when I came back to the Church, I was fully on my knees, fully invested—like, "God, I'll do whatever you want for me. Whatever it is, I'll do it."

I think one of the dangers for Catholics right now is the nature of our political engagement. We need to leaven society with the Gospel through politics and law. That's clear. But too often we do it in isolation from our pursuit of personal sanctity. We need to do our politics and law propelled by, and as an expression of, our relationship with Jesus Christ. He needs to be constantly at the heart of our efforts. If we take the truths of our faith and turn them into just another political program, it defeats the whole enterprise. And that worries me. I have a lot of hope, though. Maybe it's just born of grace. It's funny because, despite all the problems in the world, I'm really excited about this time we live in. I just think there's an enormous number of good things percolating under the surface, and the mainstream media don't know about it. It's not even on their radar. And that must make God smile.

༄ ༄ ༄

6. From a wife, homeschooling mother, and graduate student

The Church's 2020–2021 response to COVID was a "nail in the coffin" moment for me. It's easy to look back, knowing what we know now, and say what was or wasn't prudent. But it was clear to me and many of my friends at the time, that the tenor of the messaging about the pandemic from most Catholic chanceries was bad. So, I contacted a priest friend. I said, "Let's make a little comparison." I sent him a letter about the pandemic from our local ordinary, and in contrast, I sent along some parallel messaging from the metropolitan of the Russian Orthodox Church in New York City. The metropolitan made clear that while elderly people should pray from home, the Divine Liturgy would continue in churches for as long as possible. That's what I expected to hear from my own Church leadership. But that's not what I heard. Instead, I got letters from the chancery reminding me how to wash my hands properly. They read like they had been written by a secular NGO and vetted by an aggressive legal team.

The cavalier way in which Catholics were treated was frustrating. Aquinas is very clear that "spiritual communion" is not as efficacious as actually, physically, receiving the Sacrament. In my diocese, we were told that even private Masses, no matter how small, wouldn't be allowed. And I know from our priest friends that this was devastating. Can you imagine being a father and then, in a crisis, being told that you can't love and feed your children?

I know too, from bishops I admire, that Rome, in the current pontificate, does not have their backs. So, if I could ask Pope Francis one question, it would be this: Why is it that my friends who like the traditional Latin Mass and homeschool their 10 kids are the source of division in the Church, but not somebody like a Joe Biden? Here's a man who shows his Catholic card when convenient, but then simultaneously advocates for transgender "rights" and the expansion of abortion access. He's also made himself an enemy of religious liberty, so why isn't *Biden* getting a smackdown? Francis has a flippant, off-the-cuff manner that creates ambiguity and undermines the teaching of his predecessors. I'd be grateful if he'd just stop talking so loosely to the press on his airplane trips.

ཨ ཨ ཨ

7. *From a wife, mother, and university professor*

I'd rate the health of our higher-education institutions, at least in the United States, at about five on a scale of 10. It's not exclusively a narrative of decline, but the overarching story isn't promising. The level of stress on students today is astonishing compared to when I was in high school, college, and graduate studies. They end up being cogs in a machine. I think their anxieties come from an intense pressure for status and prestige, the technological transformation of their lives, and today's enhanced state of sexual confusion. It's exhausting. Plus, there's a strange inability of young people to connect in any kind of traditional, organic way. I just had a student in my office who's in his early 20s. He has never held a young woman's hand. He's never had a first kiss. The lack of basic skills at an interpersonal level among a lot of young adults is just stunning. As part of a discussion of contemporary culture recently, I mentioned in one of my classes that young people need to go on dates ... and only two of my students had done so.

And these are students at a major urban university.

Students are desperate for real relationships, real friendships, real romantic connections that lead in a dotted line to family life, instead of just hooking up. There's an epidemic of loneliness, and I see it every day. My afternoon office hours are booked with students wanting to talk about their love lives. Young adult sex culture is a complete mess, leading to all sorts of personal wounds. But the real problem is even more consequential. It's the long-term damage done to family structure and domestic life. Far more women are attending college now than men, and no one's paying attention to the implications. Mothers will be working, and fathers—assuming they're around, and not just drones—will be at home. The pool of educated women will grow, and the pool of suitable husbands will shrink. Think that one through.

At least some heads of elite universities have begun to understand that the radical professionalization of contemporary higher education has left no room for any kind of moral or ethical vocabulary; that such a vacuum has a cost; and so they're trying to find ways to address it. In the meantime though, the vocabulary that dominates the typical college campus is closer to an emotional fever than reasoned discourse. It's a witch hunt, frankly. I had lunch a few months ago with a former student, a recent alumnus, who is now working in the tech industry. He told me he was surprised that I hadn't already been "canceled". And I suppose I'm surprised too. It's just that God does exist. So, I still have a job.

ॐ ॐ ॐ

8. From a wife, mother, and theologian

In my experience, higher-ed institutions are in very poor shape. And that includes most Catholic universities. There's little real education happening, along with a remarkable lack of wisdom, courage, and memory. They've abandoned the mission of conveying truth. As a result, they're fundamentally transactional, antimetaphysical, and presumptive of the claims of scientism. They're "capitalist" in the worst sense. Even our private universities are little more than corporations, eager to meet the needs of their consumers. There's also an extraordinary stress on novelty and new knowledge, which makes sense for the natural sciences, but it's a terrible model for the humanities. The humanities are about the constant reinvestigation of what's eternally true, the highest qualities of character in culture and society, not what's novel or "new". And that's how we end up with today's crackpot academic theories and ideologies, because people are struggling to gain attention, to win tenure, instead of investigating and building on the truth of things already lived and learned. It's the worst possible approach for theology in particular.

If education is for the purpose of encountering truth and becoming a fully rounded, mature human being, then—dare I say it?—we actually need to hear *more* from "dead white males", rather than less. We need *more* immersion in classical texts and great thinkers from the past, not less. Most of the students I teach these days have no experience of anything written before the events of 1968. That's insane. It's a bubble confining them to an extremely limited historical horizon and stunting their view of reality. The most alarming thing in my work is that so many of my students have no intellectual curiosity at all. That sounds excessive and terrible, but unfortunately it's true. They're at university to jump through the appropriate hoops in order to get a piece of paper, so they can get a job and move on with the rest of their lives. There's no appetite for truth or knowledge for its own sake or a sustained interest in anything. Their college years are simply a matter of credentialism.

America as a nation is essentially antitraditional, individualistic, and atomistic. So, it's logical, in a weird way, that the dominant spirit now on so many university campuses is progressive; "progressive" in the politically diseased sense of *transgressive*, the idea that life is about breaking rules and boundaries so that you can recreate yourself according to your own desires. Everything is about desire and power, not intellect and submission to the needs of others. In such an environment, the Church doesn't need to be our "companion", as trendy as accompaniment might be at the moment. The Church needs to *lead*, which means that we need more leaders who are credible: bishops and priests who are men of genuine substance. And since there's an obvious crisis of male identity in Western societies, one of our most urgent priorities right now needs to be the formation of good Christian ... men.

ॐ ॐ ॐ

9. From a wife, social scientist, and university professor

I've spent most of my career in secular institutions. A point that often gets overlooked is the demographics of higher education compared to 50 years ago, with many more women, and many more racial and ethnic minorities enrolled. That's one reason why so many schools abandoned a core curriculum of philosophy, literature, history, and theology. It was a misguided decision, meant to respond to diversity, but grounded on a shallow understanding of what the classics and humanities can teach us ... as if somehow the classics and human- ities only speak to their own time period and don't have anything to say to diversity. So, what is happening now is that most students go through a secular college or even, frankly, most Catholic colleges, and they get no philosophical, theological, or human coherence in what they study. This is why so many students experience fragmenta- tion, anxiety, and despair. It's because they don't see a way in which personal identity connects to a community of memory, which is what education is supposed to help young people do. So, no surprise, my students' biggest struggles involve intimacy and commitment.

It's clear to me that when students are fragmented and unhappy, they can be riled up to think that by latching onto this or that large cause of justice, it's somehow going to give their life meaning. But if you don't deal with the core of the problem, which is that they don't have intimacy, and they don't have a commitment to things higher than mere politics, then they don't live in a way that builds order from the ground up. All of that effusive energy for social justice soon collapses. We've seen this historically with Marxist movements in Latin America and in Europe. And what worries me is that the dislocation which students feel today can be weaponized to promote a seeming social-justice cause which actually just creates damaged people and a lot of noise, and then dissipates. When that happens, society is not better off. The students aren't better off. And it simply deepens a pervasive atmosphere of meaninglessness. So, there's a kind of negative cycle between the mental health crisis and the social crisis. The one feeds the other. What we need to do is reverse that process.

For me personally, I had a Catholic background, so I was able to draw from saints and mystics about the interior life. That kept me sane. And it helped me to guide students in their desire for social change and political progress. One of the ongoing problems for the Church in the United States is that, in her everyday practice, middle-class assimilation with all of its mediocrity has displaced a genuinely Catholic culture of family. The early Church was a Church of high festivals and great holy days; a Church of martyrs, saints, and pilgrimages. That's what we need to recover.

₂₀ ₂₀ ₂₀

10. From a wife, mother, and legal scholar

A bishop who doesn't have at least one or two women in cabinet leadership positions is shooting himself in the foot. It's not a feminist thing or an "equal representation" thing. It's a matter of practical wisdom. He's losing an entirely different perspective on issues and problems, because women will tell you things privately that men won't, or don't even see. Women love the Church. They don't want to see her embarrassed or made to look stupid. Which means they don't want their bishop to seem like an "emperor with no clothes". The one caveat I would add is that a woman in senior diocesan service needs to be well-grounded in the faith. The motive can't be "I'm doing this because someday I want to be a priest" or to exercise what little power you might get. Once you start thinking in power terms, it ruins the whole apostolic aspect of your work.

The biggest problem in today's Church is an abysmal lack of catechesis. I think our Catholic population is one of the most poorly educated in history when it comes to what the Church teaches. And I don't mean an ignorance of obscure details in moral theology. I mean an inability to name the four Gospels and the seven Sacraments; a blank stare when asked the definition of the Immaculate Conception; or a lack of understanding that the Eucharist is the actual Body and Blood of Jesus. We have parents who were so badly educated in the 1970s and 1980s that they don't know how to form their own kids. And this lack of formation has had tragic, trickle-down staffing and mission consequences for all the institutions that have been the backbone of the Church in this country: our hospitals, schools, social service ministries, and so on. Uncatechized people might be very good persons who truly love our Lord; they might attend Mass every Sunday. But they don't know how to defend the Church and her institutions, because they were never taught in the first place.

When I served in a diocese, my bishop routinely asked his senior staff, "If God didn't exist, would we do anything differently around here?" It was a shrewd question. It made people focus. Is the Catholic Church just another social service agency, or is she something different and more? In certain Church positions you need people who are fiercely committed to the whole Catholic mission. Otherwise things go off the rails. I attended a religious liberty law training week with the Alliance Defending Freedom (ADF) awhile back. ADF has both Catholic and Protestant employees and does great religious freedom work. But before I was accepted into the program, I had to sign a statement affirming that I believed and professed the Nicene Creed—and they took compliance with that statement very seriously. I wasn't offended. On the contrary, I thought it was great. It reminded me that in the Catholic Church, we too often *don't* hire for mission, and we should. Everyone would benefit as a result.

ஜ ஜ ஜ

11. From a husband, father, and lay ministry leader

One of the urgent needs in the Church right now is a healthy masculine Christianity; a male leadership marked by faith and courage, but avoiding today's "Bronze Age", Nietzschean nonsense. Hypermasculinity is immature in its own way. It's onto something, but it's immature. What puts a lot of men off is the perception that Church life now is overly feminized and too therapeutic. Men and women are different. So is the way they experience and express their faith. Men don't talk about the status of their relationships or the nature of their wounds. Men do things together. And *then* they come into relationship and friendship.

So, for example, Catholic guys just getting together to smoke cigars, hang out, and shoot the breeze is good. But it's not enough. It can also be a superficial, stylistic response to what's really an inability to articulate a male spirituality. We need to recover the Christian tradition for men. Emotivism doesn't work with men. Jesus Christ didn't lead with his "woundedness". He led with a task. A demanding task. And the men who followed him reshaped the world, because there's a very particular joy in pursuing a very high ideal with brothers who share complete transparency.

We're living in a strange time, a Gnostic age, a crisis of truth. When Church leaders and advisers close to the pope claim that we should change or soften the Church's teaching on homosexuality, for example, that's the moment for serious Christian men to draw the line. We're past being "pastoral" on important matters of belief. A false understanding of prudence and obedience in Church life doesn't serve the truth. The Church is *built* on the truth. That's the heart of what she offers humanity. That's the grounding of her authority. And without men to defend the truth, the house collapses.

I suppose, in a way, this is the best time to be a Christian. I like the clarity. The world is pushing us back on to the Gospel, and that's a gift, because most people really aren't materialists. They just believe the wrong things. Do they hunger for justice? Do they feel broken? Excellent. Jesus Christ came to die for them. So, being elaborately clever about evangelization isn't what we need right now. We need to preach the Gospel with clarity, confidence, energy, and joy. We need to live, and to be, a new Acts of the Apostles.

ஐ ஐ ஐ

12. From a husband, father, and theologian

I've been teaching theology on Catholic campuses, at all levels from undergraduate to Ph.D., for many years. There's definitely more work involved in reaching undergrads today than in the past. A lot more of the students identify as agnostic. My colleagues and I see our introductory courses as a way of making students take a second, more serious look at religious questions they thought they had outgrown. And we've had a lot of success. Quite a few of our students continue their university studies with majors or minors in theology.

Young people today tend to view the Church as less than the sum of her controversies. They have no real experience of faith. That's what I try to give them. If you teach nothing but historical criticism, the who and how of compiling the Book of Genesis from different materials and traditions, they get nothing but the idea that some compiler in the wayback of history threw together a mildly interesting text. But if you show them how the Bible presents a much more sophisticated series of contemplations on issues they think they've already figured out; if you show them the absolute control of theme and character woven from start to finish in Genesis, or Exodus, or the Gospels, then you start to win them over. Theology needs to provide a framework for the central mysteries of faith; what they are and how deeply satisfying they are. If you can achieve that, young people will give the Church the benefit of the doubt on other issues. The doctrine of the Trinity, when properly presented, is profoundly beautiful and attractive. You can't have the statement "God is love" without the Trinity.

This is why the discipline of "religious studies" is never a substitute for theology. They are two different creatures. They have very different dynamics. It's true that the methodologies of religious studies are employed in theology departments, but theology has a *telos*, a purpose, a higher goal. There's no "there" there in religious studies. As a discipline, it's intrinsically fragmenting because the idea of religion itself—what religion is or isn't—is open to argument.

We need bishops willing actually to engage with laypeople and give them co-responsibility for the work of the Church. Rhetoric and theatrics about "synodality" won't get the job done. In the end, the Gospel is true. There are many, many ordinary laypeople who feel that very deeply. They're willing to evangelize in an organized way or on their own, and they won't go away. So, we need to tap into that spirit if we want a renewal of the Church. Because that's where the real energy lies.

ᘓ ᘓ ᘓ

13. From a husband, father, and author

My entry into the Church wasn't because of any quality of the Church herself. It was more just a recognition that the Church of Rome is the primary substance of Christianity in the West. And when I lost confidence, as I did, in mainline Protestantism being able to sustain apostolic Christianity, I became Catholic by default. Is she now still the same Church? Well, I had pretty low expectations, because I taught at a Catholic university. I was fully aware of what was going on in the Church. I was conscious of all those clergy who were bargaining away the Church's inheritance for the mess of pottage that's credibility in contemporary culture. Academia has been destroyed by postmodernism. The problem with "progressivism" in Christian circles is not that it goes too far, but that it goes in exactly the wrong direction. It's not a matter of good sentiments gone wrong; it's actually morally reprehensible.

But I should say the Church has far exceeded my expectations. So, my faith hasn't changed an iota. The Church gave me the sacred reality of the Mass, which is very palpable. The typical Catholic congregation, no matter where you are on the ideological spectrum, liberal or conservative, takes the Sacrifice of the Mass seriously. I may be rankled by some of the irregularities in the way the Mass is celebrated, but it's real Christianity. I never doubt that this is the real thing. The Francis pontificate has had no negative effect on my spiritual life. If you have a sound historical view, you might anguish over the lost opportunities of the current papacy and see Francis as a stumbling block. But personally I've not had a moment's regret. Like I said, I became a Catholic with very low expectations.

In terms of problems facing the Church: I think the big one is self-inflicted fear. It's a vicious circle. Fear diminishes the vitality of the Church's witness, which then deprives people of the fullness of faith, which then further saps Christian vitality. There's a huge degree of bourgeois financial anxiety among laypeople, and a fear of being canceled, or outside the main action, or marginalized among our Catholic leaders. We need to stop wringing our hands about what we can't do anymore and focus on what we *can* do.

Priestly formation in the United States is far better than it was a generation ago. The seminaries are stronger, and the young men studying for the priesthood are much clearer about their vocation and its challenges than at any time in the recent past. That's a big "good news" area for us. And sure, we want double the seminarians we have now. But the ones we do have are pretty solid. We need consciously to reorient ourselves away from a model of "Christendom" toward being a creative, motivated minority. The collapse of marriage in this country happened against the actual wishes of most people. That can be turned around, at least in part, with the right leaders. But we need bishops willing to be controversial when needed, and unwilling to be bureaucratic and mediocre. We need to think counterrevolutionary thoughts, not "stabilizing" thoughts.

In the end, good leadership requires leaders sensitive to the fact that we have souls, not just appetites. That's why our technocratic class is so smart and so stupid at the same time. We're only really free if we commit ourselves in faith to something greater than ourselves. We need to give ourselves away in love. Otherwise we're too easily put in bondage by our fears.

ᔕ ᔕ ᔕ

14. From a husband, father, and senior Church staffer

What's the biggest problem facing the Church in the United States? I'd say "secularism", but that's just a catch-all word for a tangle of other problems: scientism, technology-worship, unthinking consumerism, and a globalist mentality among our leaders that lacks any hint of transcendence or spiritual dimension; that neglects any visceral allegiance to the nation and the people they're meant to serve. There's a widening gap between the people who have power and the rest of us. As for the state of the Church herself: It all depends on what you think her mission is. If the mission of the Church is to maintain the institution in its material form, the ministries, the schools, the programs we have—then OK, we're giving that our best efforts. But we should be training our people like we train for war. We should be forming a countercultural resistance, and we're not. Are we actually forming *evangelizers*? It doesn't seem so. The "new evangelization" is a very positive idea, but it's morphed into a kind of jingle that doesn't have any substance in the way persons actually go about their lives.

For me the issue is Jesus Christ. Do we believe his Gospel has the power to change our lives and the world? Too often I don't think we do. I certainly believe it, but I'm not sure we're set up to proclaim it or persuasively live it. I work every day with people who maintain a machine. I'm a Church bureaucrat myself. My colleagues are all good persons. But if we measure ourselves against the goal of bringing souls to Jesus Christ and transforming people with the Gospel, well, we just don't do it—and this, at a time when many Church leaders seem clueless and walking into the abyss when it comes to understanding the nature and scope of the challenges heading our way. Again, we need a countercultural Gospel; a whole new intellectual and practical approach to our problems.

What gives me hope is mainly the lay movements in the Church. I just don't see the will to renew the institution, in its current form, from the bureaucratic inside. Many of the guys in the younger generation of our priests are outstanding men and more "conservative" in matters of faith; but too many are also too comfortable, and intensely clerical, when they need to be the opposite. Regular confession, silent Adoration, and reading the New Testament in sequence, a little each day: These are the things that sustain my faith. They're transformative experiences. And it lifts my spirit that many people seem to be recovering a sense that human beings are made for freedom … in part, ironically, because the culture is becoming totalitarian. I just wish the "Francis effect" served more of the solutions we need, rather than the challenges we face.

ᘓ ᘓ ᘓ

15. From a husband, father, and religion journalist

I consume an enormous amount of media. My kids have actually begged me to cut back over the past several years, because it tends to put me in a bad mood. One of our great dangers culturally is that journalism has migrated from news to opinion. Sometimes it's intentional, but a lot of it is just the immediacy of a news industry driven by social media. Before web-based media, with newspapers, you had some time to think about things. Now, the *New York Times* or *Washington Post* has to assume that you've already heard a story three or four times by the time you read it in print. So, that pushes them to load on the analysis, which can quickly become opinion. This feeds a corrosion of our trust in the news media, because people see them as part of our ideological polarization. There has also been a decline in professional standards; a decline in editing. And that's especially true with the role of the copy editor, the guy who checks facts and puts the brakes on the opinionating.

We're at a weird moment when Twitter is where journalists and intellectuals go to get their ideas. But they do. And the irony is that none of my kids do Twitter. They do Instagram. They're totally into image-based communications, which adds to my worries because it suggests we're heading into a postliterate world shaped by advertising, not reasoning. And it's affecting everyone. I'm finding it harder and harder to read longer pieces. People in general have less patience, less tolerance.

Some 200 counties in the United States now have no newspaper at all, which means that there's less local surveillance of what local governments are doing in terms of corruption and bad decisions. It also means people know less about their immediate communities. And as bishops kill off their own news media, a similar trend takes place in the Church. But the Church doesn't serve her people well in doing that. There's a great need for Catholics to know their faith, given all the challenges the world poses. Intellectual and spiritual formation is essential. But I don't think America's bishops really have a media strategy, which means that more and more Catholic "news deserts" are popping up that parallel the secular news terrain.

We need a renewal of preaching. That's the only antidote we have to what's going on in social media. It's why *The Joy of the Gospel*, Pope Francis' first apostolic exhortation, had such a huge impact on me; the stress he put on good homilies. He has a way of speaking to people that's real and understandable. I hear that feedback all the time. It's one of the big things that attracts people to Francis.

ᘔ᙭ ᘔ᙭ ᘔ᙭

16. *From a husband, father, and social critic*

If Christianity is true, which I firmly believe it to be, then there's really no alternative to the Catholic Church. My conversion was unique in that I wasn't disaffected from my Protestant tradition. I didn't leave it because I hated it. I left *in spite of the fact* that I still loved it. And in some ways, I had to be dragged into the Catholic

Church, even though I knew a decade beforehand that I needed to be Catholic. I wanted to die as a Catholic. I just wasn't sure I wanted to live as one. But at the end of the day, I knew that the Catholic Church alone stood for both the fullness of the faith and also for what's true about nature, what's true about being human, in a way that churches that had broken from Rome did not. And I still believe that.

However disaffected I might sometimes be, there's nowhere else to go. So, I won't be leaving. And yet, in a strange way, I'm also grateful for the people I've known who *have* left the Church because they were angry with her. Try as they might, the Church is so deeply embedded in them that they can't get rid of her. If nothing else, having been raised Catholic has given them something precious, a lifelong struggle with belief and meaning, that can't be erased. At the very least, I want to give that to my kids. I'll give them a Church that won't leave them alone; that won't leave their consciences alone.

We need to understand that there's a pious kind of "Catholic atheism" that doesn't recognize itself. An eclipse of God can occur even within the Church; an eclipse whose shadow is so perfect and dark that we don't see it. We're too often not aware of the extent to which we think and act as if God didn't exist, even if we formally acknowledge him. And when we live in our daily routines as if God doesn't exist, God gets called in secondarily, as a kind of fire brigade from the outside, in all sorts of pious ways. But that's not discipleship. We have an unrealistic optimism in Catholic thought about today's world and its brave new possibilities. And it won't end well.

The current champions of progress in the Church like to hail a "paradigm shift" in Catholic thinking. But what exactly does that mean? Fundamentally, it means nothing more than a change of subject. It's neither a refutation of, nor an answer to, the serious problems we face. It's just an assertion that we're not going to talk or think any more about unpopular teachings on issues like human sexuality. It's tantamount to refounding the Catholic faith for our own convenience. And ultimately it's a repudiation of both the authority of the Church and the substance of Vatican II.

❧ ❧ ❧

17. From a priest religious and college professor

I'm on a Catholic campus, but for most of my students, their Christianity is a mixed picture. It's an ethical system they've inherited from their parents. Some of these kids have gone to decent Catholic high schools. But even there, teaching the faith has taken an ethical approach. They've done a service trip, they've built homes for the poor in Peru or Colombia, but mainly they're focused on doing well professionally after graduation, and then moving ahead quickly in society. We do have a constituency of kids who take part in regular Scripture study groups. Probably about 20 percent of our students are intense about their Catholic faith. Another 50 percent or so attend Mass in the dorms on Sunday night. And then there's another group of about 20 percent, maybe even 25 percent, who no longer bother. Yes, we're a "Catholic" institution ... but we gave them a good financial aid package, and we were the highest-ranked school they could get into. So they decided to show up here.

Among the faculty it's about the same. Maybe a quarter of the faculty are committed Catholics. We do have a group of non-Catholic faculty, some dedicated Protestants and Jews, who take their faith seriously. And that's a very good thing. But there's also a large group of quite secular faculty. So I doubt there's much campus reflection on the afterlife or the transcendent. Even within my religious community here, we rarely talk about eternity or the struggle against evil. The language of spiritual battle just isn't present. And campus preaching is mainly about being a good person; in other words, more of the ethical thing.

There's a lot of talk, though, about how we can make campus a more welcoming and inclusive place for gay students. Sometimes I can't bear to listen to it. Church teaching on sexual morality, even at otherwise Catholic schools, will inevitably come under increasing pressure. It would be unusual now for a priest in my religious community to teach anything on campus like, "Marriage is only between a man and a woman, and get that through your heads." The atmosphere is thick with sentimental support for same-sex couples. It's nuts. But that's where we are.

&

18. From a husband and long-time public official

People complain all the time about the condition of our public institutions and political environment, but it depends on what we measure them against. Compared to the rest of the world, their health, I
would say, is pretty good. Compared to their condition historically in
our own country, I'd say they're on a downward slant. Whether the
founding was badly flawed in some way, or whether it predestined
our current circumstances, I don't know; but the fact remains that we
can't go back and have a do-over. The government's done a lot of
things wrong, but we generally get what the American people want.

I think cultural forces have gotten us where we are. Our mores
and appetites at the level of ordinary people have changed, and a lot
of that change is driven by the power of mass entertainment, which
has had a damaging effect on families, and broken families are at the
root of so much of what has gone wrong. Government can't fix that.
We need to rebuild the culture from the bottom up, and that's a
long-term project without many short-term victories. We could start
by recognizing that America is about the individual and his or her
freedom, sure; but that can't be our highest priority. The individual
has duties and responsibilities to others, or society falls apart. We've
lost that awareness.

I think our biggest *political* problems are four: The administrative
state keeps growing; our civic education is poor; party activists shape
party policy far more deeply than the average Democratic or Republican voter; and we have bad leaders. Who was the last president
who qualified as a good national leader? I'd argue it was Bill Clinton.
Whatever his deficits, he did know how to compromise. He understood that he couldn't get everything he wanted and had to find ways
to a common agreement on disputed issues. Compare that to a Joe
Biden or a Donald Trump. Compare that to our political atmosphere
now. We're not like other countries. We don't have a common ethnic identity to hold us together. We're a nation built on an idea, and I
think our leaders, our elites, have stopped believing in the idea, and
the ideals, that shaped us.

The result is pretty clear. Our political life is more ideological now
and much more bitter because of it. And our political divisions have
entered and split the Church, crippling her ability to speak with a

unified voice. We need more faithful leadership in the Church and from the Church, but I'm not counting on that. I see more hope in our Catholic grassroots.

୬୦ ୬୦ ୬୦

19. From a husband, father, and university professor

Many of the problems in our current political institutions and environment are the product of bad jurisprudence and bad decisions made by our elites 50 years ago. It's true that we became a kind of *de facto* empire after the Second World War, the period from 1946 to 1991. In the Soviet era, I don't know that we had any other choice. But the subsequent humanitarian peacekeeping and regime-change mentalities of Clinton and the two Bushes involved a lot of flawed thinking rooted originally in the liberal internationalism of Woodrow Wilson's foreign policy. I think that's a bad general approach, coupled with very bad implementation. So, we did things that were unwise to do, and then we did them very badly.

I'm not "antidemocracy", but global democracy is not the be-all and end-all of America's vital interests. An unthinking commitment to democratizing the planet is just another raw appetite of those in our political class. When the *Washington Post* says "democracy dies in darkness"—and that's the newspaper's official slogan—it's as if the real pathologies that often go along with democracy never occurred to the editors.

As for today's disputes about the nation's founding: The Founders, nearly all them, were men of faith and reason. They were largely Protestants, and faith and reason were still harmonious for them. The Declaration of Independence is a statement of natural rights, coming from the natural law, which in turn comes from the Creator. There's a theological framework to the whole project. God created us in a certain way, and for the Founders, human flourishing depends on living in accordance with that framework. But since the time of the founding, we've had Kant, Darwin, Marx, and Freud, leading to a war between men who can recognize that a natural moral law exists, and others who don't believe any such law exists, and therefore human beings are their own gods. The Founders' constitutionalism is all about putting restraints on people's freedom. Once you go down the path of freedom, you need to restrain its excesses. And that's because too much freedom leads to fragmentation, and fragmentation inevitably leads to a centralization of power in the national government. Which is why today, we the people really *aren't* sovereign. We now live in a sort of technocratic oligarchy, with the congealing of vast wealth in a very small group of people.

The Church should be a leader in confronting all this. But the takeaway from the 2020–2021 COVID pandemic is that the Church was compliant when she should have been courageous. The Eucharist is too important to let the government *ever* shut it down by closing access to churches. In practical effect, through its overeager cooperation with authorities, the Church taught that the Mass is optional and the Eucharist isn't really essential. That's the lasting lesson of COVID. Church leadership completely failed.

ट ट ट

20. *From a husband, father, and university professor*

I've been thinking a lot lately about the 1960s, the way they presaged today's crisis of legitimacy in everything from government to religion to our mass media and universities; all of the institutions that society needs to function well in service to the common good. What I sense among my students, Catholic or otherwise, is a deep confusion, and often a pessimism, about the future of the country; but also a genuine curiosity about how we got into our current jam.

A central question in any era is, what makes a good ruling class? There's always an elite in every society. It's an inescapable fact of life. The illness eating away at the liberal democracies of the West today is people's suspicion that our elites have no interest in ruling on behalf of the common good. Barbara Tuchman, the historian, wrote that Europe's old aristocracy lost its legitimacy when people realized that their rulers had abandoned a sense of *noblesse oblige*; had lost a concern for the common good. We're in a very similar situation today. One of the hallmarks of the progressive era was, and still is, a belief that the common sense of everyday humans is unreliable and an obstacle to progress. "Progress" thus depends on a clergy-like knowledge class that can manipulate the various levers of power to forestall or reduce the dangerous influence of ordinary people.

This results in an atmosphere of constant conflict. It doesn't matter who wins a national election now. The losing side will always call the results unfair. And it didn't start with the 2020 election or the January 6, 2021, Capitol riot. The [Democratic] losers in 2016 attacked the legitimacy of the winner from the moment the results were in, and we had four straight years of relentless undermining from the political and cultural left. Add to that our mass media that slant stories in whatever way they like, and an economy that ruthlessly sorts winners from losers, and the result is a society-wide environment of anxiety.

We need to recover the idea of a mixed constitution that can balance the leadership of elites with the common sense of ordinary people. We need to rethink our institutions to foster that kind of genuinely shared public life. Is that possible? It's certainly hard. But I'm given immense hope by some of the talented and keenly engaged young people that I encounter in my teaching. They don't want to revive the 1980s. They don't want to go back to the 1950s. They're aware that we need a radical reassessment of the nature of our current political regime and the sources of its crisis of legitimacy; "radical" in the sense of a search for the roots. They're a minority, these young people. But a small, creative, committed minority can shake the world.

CHAPTER SIX

Special People

What "Special" Means

I'm not really comfortable with that word "suffering" because it suggests somebody who's bleeding or beaten down. There's an element in every part of every day that's very difficult. But that same difficulty has opened up an entirely new technicolor world that I was never aware of. . . . I feel content, I feel at peace, I feel entertained. I feel loved. I feel all of those things. And despite the fact that this other part of my life can be difficult, I'd choose this basket of goods any time, over anything and anybody else.

—Ursula Hennessey

"Special needs" is an interesting expression. The two words describe a generic world of needs and disabilities without capturing the lived experience of any of them. At the level of flesh and blood, the greatest need of persons with "special needs"—the orphan, the infirm, the chronically disabled—is other people willing to love them. And in a culture of methodically cultivated selfishness, that can be too big a burden for many to bear. Ninety percent of unborn children with Down syndrome, to take an especially ugly example, are now killed in the womb. The humanity of our species, the unique, miraculous thing that makes us more than just another form of dumb animal, is sustained by the special people who give their lives to the special needs of others.

Writing about his daughter Magdalena in *First Things* in 2021, Matthew Hennessey, an author and deputy op-ed editor at the *Wall Street Journal*, noted that

Magdalena loves potatoes. Doesn't matter what kind. . . .

It's good to love something in this life, [because] the list of things she doesn't love at the moment is long. She doesn't love loud noises or broken promises. She doesn't love waiting. Most people suffer from mild to moderate impatience, but most people don't break down in tears and screaming when the shower takes a minute or two to warm up.

Magdalena doesn't love rice. If she sees rice on her dinner plate, she'll flip the dish across the room.

But the main thing Magdalena doesn't love is laughter. For Magdalena, laughter is the worst sound in the world. She panics and shrieks. It's worse than nails on a chalkboard. It's like a bad dream. Laughter is the sound of Magdalena's nightmares.

Magdalena has Down syndrome. The condition can manifest itself in a wide range of ways, some mild, some intense. Magdalena's problems, and their impact on family life, can be intense. Yet the Hennesseys love her as deeply as they love their other four children. And they're far from alone. Julie and Bill McGurn (a *Wall Street Journal* columnist) adopted all three of their children as infants from China; now grown, they're impressive young women. Kate and J.D. Flynn (the cofounder of *The Pillar* news service) likewise have three children. Two are adopted. Both have Down syndrome. And again, none of the three couples is alone. Each belongs to an unseen world of hope; a world of ordinary, special people. People who welcome new life and revere it, whatever the risks.

Which becomes clear in the interviews below.

ཨ ཨ ཨ

Ursula and Matthew Hennessey, New York

How long have you been married?

URSULA: Twenty years.

Were you practicing your faith when you met? Did that factor in any way in your relationship?

URSULA: No. It had zero impact. And I feel terrible about it. I'd grown up with very serious Catholic parents and gone to church my whole life. But Matthew wasn't active at all.

MATT: My parents stopped taking us to Mass when I was a teen. They moved left in their politics over time. My mother felt she'd had a very restrictive upbringing in terms of her relationship with the Church, and some of that rubbed off onto me. I remember around the time of John Paul II's death, there was a big article in the *New York Times* about all of the possible successors. And I said to Ursula over coffee, "Look at all these fat bozos who want to be pope." And she was horrified. She said, "You're so sacrilegious. I can't believe I'm going to marry you."

Apparently she did though.

URSULA: Maybe that should have been a red flag for me. But it wasn't. We eloped.

MATT: It was after our 10th anniversary that we finally married in the Church and got the sacraments.

What changed?

MATT: When Clara, our oldest, was born, we started going to Mass. I remember Ursula's brothers conspiring to force us to get her baptized. Today she's 18. When Clara was born, everything got rearranged in my head. It was strange. I felt like a different person; like I was settling in to who I was supposed to be. And Ursula was certainly ready to start going back to Mass.

URSULA: For me, it was Magdalena's birth that was the pivotal moment in our faith and in our life.

It's Magdalena, not Clara, who has Down syndrome, correct?

URSULA: Right. At the prenatal diagnosis, there was a strong push to abort, and I didn't want that. But I also didn't want to be a mother to this child. I hated the idea of an abortion, but I still didn't want this situation to be happening to me. It was Matthew who said, "It's not her fault, she doesn't know." Matthew saying that helped me see her as a person. It gave me a great feeling of maternity. And I needed that. It didn't take away the grief. I was still feeling sorry for myself, and sorry for our older daughter. And that lasted a year or more; a real self-pity party about what this child would never be, the problems our family would face.

After Magdalena was born, I remember taking her out in a stroller in New York City and being almost ashamed when people would look at her. I hated that about myself. But I think that experience of total humility brings you down to the baseline of what it means to be a parent. It made a revolution in my head and heart about what it meant to be a Christian, a mom, a Catholic.

When you look back over your life with Magdalena, it must have had an impact on your marriage and your other kids. What's the family ecology like?

URSULA: It certainly strengthened our marriage. I'd like to say that it's strengthened our family life. That's my view of it now. But we don't really know. Magdalena can be very difficult to be around. I'd love to say that our other children have stronger pro-life views because of her, but I'm not sure that I can, because I can't really speak for them on a matter like this.

MATT: The jury's still out. That's the scary thing about this whole journey. I just pray that we're doing everything right.

URSULA: One thing I resent a bit is people's impression that having a child with special needs brings a warm, fuzzy feeling to the house all the time. My one worry at night is about the way we handle the really hard moments, of which there are plenty. I know that we don't respond well every time. So how is that viewed by our other kids? If we're all going for a family hike, and Magdalena refuses to do anything, we all need to come home. We try our best, but we don't often have family talks about the difficult things that have happened year after year, week after week.

I think you need to trust in the fact that you and Matt love each other, you're doing your best, and your kids see that and will learn from the good in your example. And even if they resent the difficulties now, they'll understand when they're older. If you just succeed in loving each other and loving them well, that's a big win.

MATT: A lot of people who don't have experience with someone like Magdalena will cross the street rather than deal with anything out of the ordinary or uncomfortable. At the very least, our children won't be frightened or horrified at the prospect of someone struggling with physical or mental disabilities the way I was when I was a kid.

You're married, you have children, you also have the special circumstance of a child with unique needs. How does the Church fit into your family life?

MATT: Magdalena is 16 now. She reads, she's very verbal, she speaks clearly, she enjoys doing math, she has a great personality, she can be funny and charming. But she's also very physical, like a bull in a China shop. When she was younger we had to keep a close eye on her because she would reach out and pull strangers' hair. She's just very headstrong and temperamental. Before the pandemic, we had her at the point where she would attend Mass peacefully without being disruptive. The COVID lockdown wiped that out; it was really brutal for us in that regard. We're back to square one. We can't yet trust her to take Communion without spitting it out, and she resists going to Mass.

Do you have a network of friends who can support you?

URSULA: We have a lot of friends, good friends, but very few who really understand our situation and its limits.

The questions I sent you in advance about mainstream culture, the direction of the country, what the Church will look like in 20 years . . . they seem pretty irrelevant. You don't ask such questions of people who are struggling to keep their noses above water.

URSULA: They were great questions. I want the Church to succeed. I get angry when the *New York Times* gloats about some alleged

Catholic failure; it drives me absolutely insane. But I can't really be part of the solution. Given our circumstances, we're bystanders watching. And we're totally at peace with that.

So what gives you joy in all this? You've come back to the Church; your faith obviously means a lot to you or we wouldn't be having this conversation. Something must make the life you share an expression of love and joy, what is it?

MATT: Ursula. Ursula gives me joy.

URSULA: We love each other a lot. We also like each other a lot. And we love our kids; we have great kids, every one of them. And I love the Mass. I learn things from the Scripture readings. I have a great husband. I have a great family. I'm OK with the routines of the day. I'm tired of the laundry, and I complain about it to Matt; and he complains about the dishes to me. And then we move on with the next day.

That seems to be a key to the lay vocation: just being faithful to each other, and trying to live your faith and share it with others, either through words or everyday witness.

URSULA: I think we appear happy to other people because we are; we're happily married with beautiful kids. I feel like personal witness is probably the most useful thing we can do. Just the simple habits of going to Mass every Sunday and learning more about our faith: These things matter.

How do you make sense of the suffering involved in your circumstances?

URSULA: I'm not really comfortable with that word "suffering" because it suggests somebody who's bleeding or beaten down. There's an element in every part of every day that's very difficult. But that same difficulty has opened up an entirely new technicolor world that I was never aware of. And I can accept the difficulties with great joy. I don't know if it's a glimpse of heaven, but having children, raising new lives, watching them find meaning in their faith, which they do; that seems to me like a pretty good life.

MATT: I believe in God. I believe he has a plan for us. I don't know what it is, but he won't let us down. I feel sad for people who are looking for someone to love, because I don't know what Ursula and I did to deserve our life together. But I believe that God cares about our lives. He knows what we're going through. So, if it's hard today ... well, maybe tomorrow will be better.

Is there anything you want to add that I haven't asked you?

MATT: I don't want people to hear our story, as we've told it to you, and to think, "Well, *we* could never do that." The fear I always have is that someone would hear me talk about the challenges in raising Magdalena and choose to have an abortion rather than the baby. I want the world to see what's good about raising Magdalena; to know that she's beautiful, and lovable, and that she changed our lives hugely for the better. But if I sugarcoat things, then I'm not being honest.

URSULA: When I hear friends of mine who are unhappily married, or they're annoyed with their husband, even if they have loads of money, it makes me cringe inside. To think that someone is stuck living with someone else he or she can't stand, or is annoyed with: That's so much worse than changing wet sheets in the morning with Magdalena, which is something I hate. But I would choose those wet sheets every time over living with someone that I couldn't stand or having to spend every day trying to pep myself up for not getting into a fight with my husband. My marriage is easy, in the sense that I don't have to try that hard to love. And I'm happy.

I feel content, I feel at peace, I feel entertained. I feel loved. I feel all of those things. And despite the fact that this other part of my life can be difficult, I'd choose this basket of goods any time, over anything and anybody else.

~ ~ ~

Kate and J.D. Flynn, Colorado

When you think about sainthood, or holiness, how would you define those words?

J.D.: In our marriage and in our family, something we've learned is that holiness is a lot more visceral, a lot more physically and emotionally demanding, than the ephemeral, "interior castle" idea of holiness that I once imagined. I would've thought that, at some point, I'd be having an extremely rich interior life of affective intimacy with God. Well, maybe someday.

KATE: When we were first engaged, we talked about holiness and sainthood like, "We want to be stained glass windows together." We thought we'd have these deep daily prayers together. And yes, we pray together. And yes, we pray with our family. And yes, we pray on our own. But real holiness turns out to be the sacrifices and suffering in each day that God calls us to.

J.D.: Right. So the issue becomes: How do we live those sacrifices with love? How do we live not just for ourselves, but for our family and other people?

KATE: When you're younger, you have romantic ideas about what the "Christian life" will be like, or what discipleship with the disabled will involve. And probably that's good, because you're looking for some path to follow. Once you set out on the path, the challenge becomes, how do we keep our hand on the plough and not abandon it.

How long have you been married?

KATE: Sixteen years.

J.D.: We met at Franciscan University of Steubenville, liked each other, and started hanging out. And faith was important for us, even though we're very different people from very different backgrounds. I was baptized Catholic but grew up as an evangelical Protestant, and our family was very serious about that evangelical identity. In high school I started having problems with our faith, discovered the Catholic intellectual tradition, and started going to Mass. But I didn't have any formation. I entered Steubenville effectively as a Protestant.

KATE: I think we were drawn to each other because we wanted the same goal for life and marriage. In my case, my parents were Catholic, and they sent me to Catholic school, but they didn't practice the faith very deeply until I started getting serious about it. Then they got interested as well. They practice the faith now.

Have either of you had any serious doubts about the faith?

KATE: Sure, they pop up every once in a while. But then I get drawn back by the small things, the little wonders with God's fingerprints.

J.D.: If we don't have our devotional life in order, if we're not praying, that's when the problems start. But you know, the times of suffering for our family have been the times of least doubt. Our daughter Pia spent about a year in the hospital. And when she was sick, that was one of the richest periods of prayer and genuine Christian hope for both of us. So, I don't think our doubts, when they happen, correspond to the crosses as much as to the flat and easier times.

Why was Pia in a hospital? Cancer?

J.D.: She's had cancer twice. But the second time, she and Kate spent about a year living in Children's Hospital in Omaha.

Just for the record, what are the ages and circumstances of your kids?

J.D.: Max is 10 and adopted. Max has Down syndrome, fetal alcohol syndrome, and fetal meth syndrome. His sister Pia is nine. She's also adopted. She also has Down syndrome. And Davey is four, healthy, and a natural birth. The fetal meth and fetal alcohol syndromes have a much bigger impact on Max's day-to-day life than his Down syndrome. The last two years have been really hard for Max, and correspondingly for our family, because around age 10 is when a lot of the behavioral problems with fetal alcohol and fetal meth syndromes start to manifest.

OK, so you adopted children with special needs. That's a beautiful thing. But in the process, did you ever hear a little voice in your head saying, "What

terrific people we are; what a wonderful thing we're doing for these poor kids?"
Did you really understand the implications of what you were doing?

J.D.: We didn't adopt kids with special needs on purpose. We just
couldn't get pregnant, or had a bunch of miscarriages. So, we went
down the path of adoption. The agency asked us, "What kind of
children would you be open to adopting?" We were open to any
kind of child we could imagine. We didn't want to be consumers
shopping in a child supermarket. So, it wasn't like we were trying to
adopt a kid with special needs. We didn't know much about Down
syndrome, and even less about the other syndromes Max has. Then
with Pia, we weren't looking to adopt again, but we got a call just a
couple of days before she was born. Our agency asked, do we know
anybody? Well, sure ... us. So that's how we got Pia. And it has
been providential, because she and Max are best friends. They're
very connected.

What's the most rewarding thing, and likewise the most difficult, about your
situation?

KATE: Oh, the most rewarding thing is spending every day with
them. Our children have been a great blessing. All three children are
such a blessing. We have hard moments with Max, or with Pia's cancer and chemo, and Pia wandered away once for about three hours,
and that was terrifying. But I don't know if there are words to explain
how beautiful it is to spend time with them. And to see all three of
our kids accomplish great things.

How has your experience with Pia and Max affected your marriage and the
course of your family's development?

KATE: Well, we're often tired.

Oddly enough.

J.D.: With our marriage, I think we've handled all this pretty well
together. Things are good. It's been very good for our family. It helps
us to know what our mission is about and makes us more welcoming
to other people in their various struggles. The day-to-day [reality] is

just hard at times. Sometimes I feel like I don't get enough attention, and that irritates Kate, who's working just as hard as, or harder than, I am.

KATE: But I think those kinds of frictions probably exist in any marriage, right?

(Laughs) Yes. Trust me. Suann and I have 50-plus years of experience.

KATE: I think God knew what we needed in our family. He knew that J.D. and I needed each other to help each other get to heaven. And that entails some struggles and hardships. I think God also saw that we needed these children, and they needed us. We've talked about Max and Pia, and Davey was an extraordinary gift, straight from God, and completely unexpected. The kids have helped us grow to love each other more deeply and truly. And I don't think we could love the way we love, if it weren't for them.

There seems to be a hunger for perfectibility in American culture that's just not realistic; it's a national character flaw. And children with Down syndrome will never be "perfectible" in a utilitarian sense.

KATE: There's certainly an appetite for comfort and a fear of anything that looks like a burden. I think even many Christians expect a Christian life without the cross.

Do you think that Catholics in general, and Catholic leaders in particular, understand the nature and the scope of the problems facing the Church in this country?

J.D.: No. I want to be polite, but no. A lot of bishops are hobbled by their administrative role; they're good men dealing with problems that really do need attention, while trying to survive themselves. But that means they're not able to put the time into preaching the Gospel and being available to people in the pews.

The real question that I'm asking is this: Do they—and do we, the rest of us—really understand how dangerous this country could become for faithful religious believers and practice?

J.D.: No. And I don't think most Catholics, including a lot of bishops, fully understand what institutional disaffiliation is, why it's happening, and how we can respond to it. I don't think it's really on the radar at all.

Last question: Have your attitudes toward mainstream American culture and patriotism changed over your adulthood?

J.D.: It was eye-opening for me to realize I'd been wrong about Iraq. A lot of things like that. That was probably around 2010. And I remember going to a symposium that the bishops' conference was doing with some bishops and other people who worked in the Church. I was sitting at a roundtable with a Dominican priest. And the priest said to one of the bishops, "You still think that Camelot is coming" about the magical character and the glowing future of our country. He added that young people today don't expect that, or even want that. The bishop slapped his hand on the table and said, "No, I'm an American, and I'm a Catholic. And I'm tired of being told that those two things can't be the same."

It was revealing for me to see the difference between what the priest was saying, which corresponds to my experience, and what the bishop was saying. I don't think the Camelot idea exists for people who are 40 and younger. It might still exist for people Kate's age and mine, and others who are older, but it certainly doesn't exist for people who are younger. So, given the environment today, I don't really know what it means to be patriotic. I don't even know if I know what America is.

ॐ ॐ ॐ

Julie and Bill McGurn, New Jersey

Did your faith play any role in drawing you two together?

JULIE: It played a pivotal role. I had dated a lot of people. When I met Bill, I wasn't thinking about marriage at all. But he was a solid, serious, dependable person that I could rely on in a storm. I just intuited it. I could trust his judgment. In hindsight, I think I had to date those other people to understand how important that was.

You were 22.

JULIE: Yes. And Bill was 33. We've been married 29 years.

What about you, Bill?

BILL: When I was at Notre Dame, there were a few girls I was interested in, but it didn't work out. And then, after college, I lived all over the world. When I met Julie, I was looking for someone Catholic, but that wasn't enough as a label. For me, the pro-life issue was more important. And Julie was very pro-life; so was her family. We shared the same values, and our families were similar. So again, for me, the attraction was pretty instantaneous. I met Julie in February. And I decided by May that we'd get married, though I didn't tell her right away.

Very big of you to let her know.

BILL: Well, she said yes. And then I disappeared to Hong Kong in September until the wedding the following April. That's where I was based; I was on staff at the time for the *Far Eastern Economic Review*. I never had any doubts that the marriage would work, though. How could it fail? I'd offered her the deal of the century: 10,000 miles from her family, with a guy she barely knew.

JULIE: That's pretty accurate. It was a real leap of faith. But everything good in my life has been a leap of faith. We got engaged at the Republican Convention in 1992. In Houston. In a parking lot. It was a Ramada Inn.

And after the wedding, you moved immediately to Hong Kong.

BILL: We got married on a Saturday. We left for Asia the next day.

You're both intelligent adults at a time in the Church that's marked by a lot of division and confusion. Why do you stick around?

BILL: I've been angry at God at times, but I've never not believed, as we see so often in the Old Testament. I always remember Stephen

Dedalus in James Joyce's *Portrait of the Artist as a Young Man*, where Stephen is asked why he doesn't become a Protestant if he has so many problems with the Catholic Church. He answers something like, "Well, I've lost my faith but not my reason." In the end, for me, above the human chaos, the Catholic faith coheres.

Julie, what about you?

JULIE: I loved Popes John Paul and Benedict very much. But I'm uneasy about the hierarchy right now. I trust our Lord, and I trust our Lady. I know the Church will endure. But if the Church is a ship, it's laypeople now who need to pick up the oars and start rowing. Maybe we were too reliant on popes in the past to figure things out for us. As laypeople, we're as much the Church as any priest, bishop, or pope. It's dispiriting sometimes. I don't like not trusting our leaders in the Church. But I'd be a fool to trust some of these guys, based on what we've seen and know.

You have three children, all of them adopted very young from China. And you've raised them to be successful, highly intelligent young women. Why adoption? And why from China? Why did you do it?

JULIE: I suppose that was also a leap of faith. I remember, literally on our first date in Washington, D.C., Bill asked me how many children I wanted. I said, oh, about 12. And it was true; I always wanted to be a mother. I had no reason to believe I'd have any difficulty having children. So, when we were based in Hong Kong, and it just wasn't happening, that's when Bill saw a terrible documentary by a BBC crew who surreptitiously got into the state-run orphanages in China and saw how awful they were. The staffs would take the troublesome children, put them in a room, shut the door, and leave them there. So, we decided this is foolish; children right over the border are desperate for a home. It seemed clear to me what God wanted us to do. And I had confidence in him that it would it turn out well. And it has.

BILL: Julie said, "We can't fix China, but maybe we can help one child." The other two adoptions just naturally followed over time.

JULIE: One of the beautiful things about adoption is that it brought home to me in a very palpable way that children belong first to God. We're in their lives as stewards, and we love them. They're ours— but they're God's children first.

BILL: Our families were very supportive. Growing up, the girls' young cousins didn't know they were adopted. There was never anything awkward or strange about it. So, I've always been happy as a gender-and-ethnic minority in my own home. Our girls are, and always have been, a joy and a blessing. But I want to pick up on Julie's thoughts about the Church. Honestly, I have trouble trusting the clergy. It's hard enough to be a parent, without weaklings leading the Church. As I get older, I realize it's probably always been this way. The apostles fled from Christ when he was arrested, and one of his handpicked guys betrayed him. John Fisher was the only English bishop who resisted Henry VIII. But the current climate can still be pretty hard on a person's ability to hope.

What do you see as the major problems in the Church right now?

BILL: Well, one of them is the Vatican. We lived and worked in Hong Kong for a long time; [Hong Kong's retired] Cardinal Joseph Zen is a friend; I'm the godfather to [imprisoned dissident] Jimmy Lai. I think the Vatican's approach to China under Pope Francis has been very unwise. In the past, Chinese Catholics might be persecuted, but at least they could say "the Pope is on our side." I don't think they can say that now. If Francis were a layperson, his actions would be seen as venal, petty, and destructive. I don't think being a pope changes that reality. It's a near occasion of sin for me. So, I've resolved not to think of him. And that's the way I handle it. I don't want to feel more bad thoughts about the pope than I'm already dealing with. We have three girls we're trying to raise in a pagan world. I need help, and too often the Church gives us pablum.

JULIE: I want my priest and my bishop to tell the truth. I don't think that's asking too much. But so often now, Church leaders, at least some of them, seem to couch sexuality and other issues in nebulous terms. It makes me wonder if they believe what the Church teaches. And that's a problem.

To what degree does U.S. Church leadership understand the nature and scope of the challenges facing American Catholics?

BILL: I don't know. But Joe Biden is the most abortion-friendly president in our history. He boasts about his Catholicism, and our bishops are bumbling all over the place. That's the result of 60 or more years of muting the Gospel for the sake of "getting along" and not being clear. Biden's not the only culprit. There's Nancy Pelosi and others, all claiming they're Catholics in good standing. It's embarrassing.

You both come from families who love this country. How have your feelings about America changed over the last 20 or 30 years, if they've changed at all?

BILL: My dad was an FBI agent and a Marine. One of his classmates at Xavier Prep in Manhattan, where his faith was really formed, was Antonin Scalia. Before Scalia died he once told an audience, "Be fools for Christ. And have the courage to suffer the contempt of the sophisticated world." No matter what's happening in America, that's the obligation.

Julie, what are your impressions?

JULIE: About patriotism? Well, I vividly remember being a little girl in 1976, in our small Rhode Island town, and having a parade for the bicentennial. And I remember welling up with tears of pride. I still have that pride in our country, residually. But I know that kingdoms rise and kingdoms fall, and maybe we've had a good ride that's coming to an end. We need a spiritual revival, and it's not impossible. So, that's what I pray for. There's no other way we're going to do it.

What does it mean for you to be a lay Catholic? What's the lay vocation?

JULIE: Just be a faithful witness to Jesus Christ. In your day-to-day life, consecrate your thoughts and actions to *him*, to Jesus Christ, especially the hard and distasteful things.

BILL: Julie undersells herself, because, by any definition, she models the lay vocation. She's a great wife and mother. She organizes a bus to the annual pro-life march in Washington. She's served on the parish council. She ran a choir. She runs the Rosary Society. Most of the 20th century was a huge time for lay associations, the Knights of Columbus, the Rosary Societies, etc. They were humble. They just did the work. They rarely talked about a "lay vocation". I think if you talk a lot about something, you tend not to do it. And too often people want a paycheck, or an office and title; some recognition for obvious things that we should all be doing as Catholics anyway.

Last question: Is there anything I haven't asked you, that you feel is important?

JULIE: Well, I'd never leave the Church. As hard as these past years in the Church have sometimes been, I definitely believe there's a purification going on. And we just need to trust.

BILL: I'd never leave the Church, and I hope and pray our daughters marry good, faithful Catholic men. But to be honest, in the end, I'd rather see them marry good, *non*-Catholic Christian men devout in their faith, rather than some lukewarm Catholic guy. That would never be my ideal. But I could understand it.

JULIE: I remember one of St. John Bosco's dreams. In it he sees a ship—the Church—with the Holy Father at its bow. And it's on stormy seas filled with enemies. But he also sees two pillars: the Eucharist on one pillar and the Blessed Mother on the other, and that's where the Church finds safe anchor. So I keep coming back to those two pillars. Those are my lodestars.

CHAPTER SEVEN

Others, an Interlude

Views from the Outside

Work began on the [Cologne] cathedral in 1248 and wasn't completed until 1880, more than 600 years later. The man who laid the cathedral's first foundation stone knew that he'd never live to walk through its doors and worship there. But he believed it was still worth doing because he wasn't doing it for himself. He was doing it for the glory of God and for future generations. We need to have that same mindset today. We're no longer working for our own generation. We're working for several generations down the line.

—Carl Trueman

In the space of 80 years, the United States has gone from a continental republic with isolationist instincts to a commercial empire with global influence … and serious domestic tensions. What American Catholics think about their Church, their country, and the times is woven throughout the pages of this book. But many other believers, keenly observant but with very different roots, inhabit the same cultural space in today's world, and seeing things through their eyes can be instructive.

Born and educated in Britain, Carl R. Trueman is a Reformation scholar and a Church historian, a former fellow of Princeton University's James Madison Program, and a widely published author of articles and books, including the national best seller *The Rise and Triumph of the Modern Self* (Crossway).

The bishop interviewed for this chapter leads a major urban diocese overseas.

Richard Rex is Professor of Reformation History on the Divinity Faculty of Cambridge University, the Polkinghorne Fellow in

Theology and Religious Studies at Queens' College, Cambridge, and the author of *The Making of Martin Luther* (Princeton).

ॐ ॐ ॐ

From a conversation with Carl Trueman

You're a committed Presbyterian Christian, an ordained minister in the Calvinist tradition, and a Reformation scholar; yet you have many Catholic admirers of your published work and some close Catholic friends. Given the facts of history, isn't that a bit unusual?

TRUEMAN: I suppose it's a little unusual. Academically, my work in Reformation and post-Reformation thought helped me understand how much my own Reformed orthodoxy shares with Catholicism on such matters as the doctrine of God, Trinitarianism, and Christology; and how far some streams of evangelical Protestantism have drifted from the Nicene faith. I have more in common with a Trinitarian Catholic than with an Evangelical who, often without realizing it, rejects classical theism. I've also come to know many thoughtful Catholics personally and to realize that many of the caricatures that Protestants have of them simply aren't true, at least of the serious Catholics I count as friends. I hope I've dispelled some Catholic caricatures about Protestants too.

I've learned that a simple love of Jesus and his people is not a Protestant or Catholic monopoly. This also touches on the next point: I've received such Christian kindness from Catholics that it's only appropriate to be grateful. Finally, I think thoughtful Catholics and Protestants face many of the same pressures from the culture, and from within our own churches, that push us to betray our faith and our Savior. We're stronger when we pool our resources and articulate a forthright, robust vision of what it means to be made in God's image and living in the light of Christ's redemption. I give thanks every day for my Catholic friends.

The Christian faith, not just in the United States but throughout the developed world, seems to face a growing amount of hostility.

TRUEMAN: I think we're reaching a stage now in Western society where the conditions of good citizenship and the conditions of being a good church member are increasingly opposed to each other. And that presents Christians, individually and the Church as a whole, with a significant challenge.

Do you see any possibility of that changing in the future?

TRUEMAN: I'd never deny the power of the supernatural. The Lord could simply work a miracle and intervene. The trajectory today, though, seems locked in a negative direction, and I don't expect any serious change for the better in the next few decades, and maybe longer. When I teach students in my humanities courses, I always put a picture of Cologne Cathedral up on the screen. Work began on the cathedral in 1248 and wasn't completed until 1880, more than 600 years later. The man who laid the cathedral's first foundation stone knew that he'd never live to walk through its doors and worship there. But he believed it was still worth doing because he wasn't doing it for himself. He was doing it for the glory of God and for future generations. We need to have that same mindset today. We're no longer working for our own generation. We're working for several generations down the line.

And does anyone think like that right now?

TRUEMAN: No, we're a culture of instant gratification. It's easy to see that in the outside, secular world. But it also affects the Church. We like to see things happening in our own lifetime. I was amazed at how quickly John Paul II was named a saint. I'd always thought it took a long, long time.

Yes, that may not have been wise.

TRUEMAN: I don't doubt that he was a worthy recipient. But the speed was interesting. And it's because he had so many admirers, so many people who loved him. And they wanted him honored in their lifetime. That's a very modern attitude. The Church needs to wean itself off that spirit. We need to think in terms of eternity. We need to play the long game here on earth, rather than looking for everything to be done by the middle of next week or next year.

I'm convinced that renewal will come at the level of the local churches, the thick, strong communities we belong to that really shape who we are. And what I'd want to see there, from a Protestant perspective, is powerful preaching at the center of our Christian piety and common worship. Many Protestant denominations don't have the rich, formal liturgy that Catholics can draw upon; but Catholics, too, need better preaching on the whole Word of God; preaching that lifts people's minds and hearts heavenward.

You're teaching at Grove City College, a broadly Christian institution. What are the strengths and weaknesses of your students in terms of their religious consciousness?

TRUEMAN: It's difficult to generalize. A real strength among my students is their zeal for their faith; their desire to communicate it. As for the weakness: Sometimes they think that attending chapel during the week substitutes for being in church on Sunday. They don't have the consistent, transgenerational community that a church and Sunday worship provide. We tend to draw students from fairly culturally conservative or Christian conservative backgrounds. So, I probably see a higher degree of Christian commitment here than might be typical elsewhere.

I assume that your experience at Grove City College differs from how most Christian universities, including Catholic ones, usually operate now.

TRUEMAN: My younger son went to Georgetown, a notionally "Catholic" university, but at Georgetown, the surrounding culture had overwhelmed the Gospel in a big way. I got the impression that the administration was rather embarrassed by the school's Catholic identity. The irony is, I'm a Protestant, and I have no problem with it. I want a Catholic school to be distinctively Catholic, with Catholic convictions shaping the culture. My other son went to the University of Pennsylvania, the only Ivy League school not founded with a Christian affiliation. And of the two schools, I'd say Georgetown was the more secular.

When you look for practical sources of hope right now, what are they?

TRUEMAN: I'm seeing a lot of thoughtful young people who are very intentional in their identity as Christians. They're aware that the world is shifting and they need to stand shoulder to shoulder with each other. So, ironically, our very marginalization has a bright side. Marginal communities often become very strong and influential communities, though not overnight. It won't happen in my lifetime. It could take a long time. The Christian future may echo the past in what happened to the Quakers in England between the 17th and the 19th centuries. For many years they were derided as a strange group of religious eccentrics. But they ended up as captains of industry with outsized economic influence. So, it would be tragic if we simply took our current troubles as an opportunity for lamentation. Lamentation is perfectly legitimate up to a point. But it can't be the substance of our faith. We need to think and do the right thing. We need to be as kind and gracious as we can; but our theology needs to drive our practice, no matter the cost.

There's a tendency among some Christians, including Catholics, to see the current moment as apocalyptic.

TRUEMAN: It may or may not be apocalyptic in the sense of things falling apart. But it's obviously apocalyptic in the original Greek meaning of the word *apokalypsis*. It means "revealing" or "uncovering things concealed". Our current times are "apocalyptic" in that they lay bare the real beliefs and hidden character of people, and the true priorities and values of the Church.

To what degree, if any, does our current cultural and social confusion parallel events of the 16th century? The printing press helped to drive a theological and cultural revolution. Today, theology isn't a power player. But new technologies seem to be driving a quite radical social revolution—not just in terms of politics or the economy, but in how humans think about the nature of their own humanity.

TRUEMAN: The key analogy is the technological dimension, because the printing press really did reconfigure our notions of authority. The printing press changed everything. And we're seeing the same today with the advent of new information technologies. The worrying difference, of course, is that the printing press was merely one technological development, and it took Europe about 150 years of bloody internal conflict to reach some sort of stability and assimilate its impact. Today, we face technological innovations in a whole range of areas, and at a pace that society can't come to terms with before the next wave of innovation hits. Medical ethics is an obvious example. How can you have coherent medical ethics when medical technology is constantly changing? We don't have time to answer the ethical questions the last tech development created before the new questions arrive.

Doesn't the description that you just gave suggest the need for a centralization of power to manage all the confusion . . . and in a way that cuts exactly against Anglo-American political principles of decentralized power?

TRUEMAN: Yes, I think you're right. And it explains today's resurgence of authoritarian regimes, and the development of pervasive and invasive "social credit" systems. The same centralizing trends are gradually happening here in America—the vaccine mandates were an example—and the ability to administer and enforce them in a nation like the United States is unprecedented because of the technological ability of the authorities. It's interesting that an appeal to "experts" is now a standard way to shut down an argument. It's a power grab.

A final question: You were born, grew up, and were educated in Britain, but you've lived in the United States for more than 20 years. Based on what you've seen and experienced, to what degree are our political institutions healthy? It's fashionable these days to compare our current situation with that of the Weimar Republic in the last century.

TRUEMAN: The parallel with Weimar Germany isn't a good one. Germany hasn't existed as a country for very long and has no deep democratic instincts or institutions. Weimar was always a precarious regime. It came to power after Germany's defeat in a humiliating war, after which even more humiliating sanctions were imposed. So no, I don't think American democracy is about to disappear down the plug hole. I think the country's democratic institutions will survive. What *significance* they'll have, that's another matter. Big corporations now have huge political power. Unelected government administrative bodies carry a lot more weight than they ever did. I'm not willing to say our democratic institutions are vestigial. But I think they're going to play a far less significant role in all of our lives in the next 50 years.

ع‌ ع‌ ع‌

From a bishop of an urban, foreign diocese

My country is more secular than the States. Confessions are very low, and church marriages are in freefall; that's actually the most disturbing sacramental statistic for us here. So, being an active Catholic is quite countercultural. Except for some of the cities, Mass attendance is less than 10 percent. In my diocese it's higher, but overall, the process of secularization is moving at a pretty fast pace, not just here but throughout Western culture. And half of the bishops here don't even know there's a fight on. If they sense something's gone wrong, they can't make heads or tails of it. They're a bit like deer in the head-lights. They're in maintenance mode until they can get to retirement.

How Pope Francis affects this dynamic, or fits into it, isn't entirely clear. Among my young priests, I can think of one or two who'd be Francis admirers. But most are Benedict XVI men, and not be-cause he's the pope they grew up with. They're serious young men; they've often gone through a reversion or conversion. They went into the seminary very much against the cultural tide, and they want to give their lives to the priesthood. You're only going to do that if you take the teachings and tradition of the Church very seriously.

Francis speaks as often and as firmly as his predecessors on the life issues like abortion. He's very good on gender theory and bioethics, but you'd never know that from the media. So, some of the criticism he gets is very unfair. There's no doubt, though, that he's on a differ-ent page from Benedict and John Paul II. And that gives permission to people who want to push the Church in a more "woke" direction on issues like LGBTQ rights, the priority of environmentalism, those sorts of things. There's enough in what Francis says for them to claim, "Look, *we're* the faithful Catholics now. We're the ones in the main-stream Church. And the cranks who are still talking about abortion or evangelization are just backward."

There's a sort of classical-tragedy quality to Francis. His strength is also his weakness. He's made the Church accessible and even lovable to a whole group of people who were anti-Church or cynical or just indifferent to religion. They're attracted by his personality and symbolic actions, and also, whether consciously or not, by his fuzziness, his studied ambiguity. But this is also his downside, because it confuses and alienates a lot of faithful Catholics who already feel under pressure from an unfriendly culture. And he obviously dislikes America, so there's that. In the long run, though, some of this might be healthy because we had a string of great popes, and maybe we developed an exaggerated confidence in the role of the papacy.

I'm just really focused now on how the Church can recapture the imagination of people. And also how to build more of a community sense among our diocesan priests. That's a big challenge for a lot of diocesan clergy.

₂ᴡ ₂ᴡ ₂ᴡ

From an exchange with Richard Rex

When you look at the United States today, what kind of country do you see; what's the substance of its character, and has your view of it changed over your adulthood?

Rex: I see a deeply divided nation, pulled in different directions by contradictory impulses, some of them good. The inherent Christianity of the old U.S.A. has in some obvious respects weakened, but the "Protestantism" (distilled out of the liquor of Protestant Christianity) of U.S. culture remains strong, indeed rampant. This culture is so strong that, in the U.S.A., even the Catholics are Protestants (as, likewise, we tend to be in Britain). The spasms of ideological and moralizing angst which are currently convulsing the nation are, one might almost say, classic Puritanism with the explicit Christianity left out. To take just one strand of the problem, the "trans" phenomenon seems reminiscent of the subjectivism that lurks within the DNA of Protestantism. But if so, it's a subjectivism that breaks loose not only from the anchorage of sacred texts but also from the empiricism that tended to dominate 20th-century discourse.

In terms of cultural symbols, I look on with horror. The cult of abortion on the left is mirrored by the cult of guns on the right. In each debate, reason seems long ago to have been sacrificed to sloganizing and incantation. The dominance of electoral decision-making by those two issues and by money is the most obviously unhealthy aspect of American politics.

When I was young, and the Berlin Wall still stood, the United States seemed genuinely united. U.S. politicians respected and indeed backed their president even when he was of the other party. That respect seemed to survive even Vietnam and even Nixon. It's not evident today. But probably the roots of present discontents were even then being laid down. In sum, the contemporary U.S.A. is to my mind the closest to civil war of any of the world's free and developed states. All those guns ...

As a Catholic yourself, how would you assess the health of the Catholic Church in the "developed" nations?

Rex: Sickly. The mystical reason is probably that it's the poor, not the rich, who are blessed. And yes, we who enjoy comfort and riches tend to put our trust in them.

The differences between the turmoil of the Reformation era and the cultural turmoil/ambiguities of today are obvious. But are there similarities? And if so, what are they and why? In reading Hubert Jedin's great history of the Council of Trent, for example, there seem to be some broad parallels.

Rex: In each case we're seeing the explosive impact of a new idea or theology made credible by history and circumstance. "Woke" and kindred doctrines flourish in the soil of human rights, individualism, and consumer capitalism. They are not logical corollaries of those ideas and phenomena, but they're rendered plausible in terms of the words and concepts arising from them. In the same way, Luther's appeal to Scripture alone was made credible by the medieval concept of the Bible, itself subtly amplified by the invention of print.

The key question of our time is "What is Man?" And might it be that the "death of God" *necessitates* the "death of Man", at least in formerly Christian cultures?

CHAPTER EIGHT

The Investors

Making Things Run

As a general rule, how do you decide on whom or what to support? How do the mechanics work?

CAROL: *A lot comes from the heart; it's a heart thing.*

That's clearly true. But we've known each other a long time, and I've noticed that, yes, you give from your heart, but your head's very much engaged in it too.

CAROL: *We get involved.*

—Carol Saeman, Saeman Family Foundation

In the year 1212, two preachers appeared simultaneously—Stephen of Cloyes in France and Nicholas of Cologne in Germany—calling Christians to liberate Jerusalem. The city had fallen to Muslim control just 25 years earlier. Stephen and Nicholas were young and charismatic. Both burned with Christian zeal. Both claimed to have direct messages from God. Stephen had letters of commissioning straight from Jesus. In the case of Nicholas, God promised to part the Mediterranean Sea, just as he had helped the ancient Hebrews, so that pilgrims could walk to Jerusalem more quickly and miraculously convert the city's Islamic rulers.

On the matter of practical details, God was more ambiguous.

As many as 20,000 peasants and young people heeded the call and spontaneously started off on the trek. The resulting "Children's Crusade" is thick with legends, but a few of the facts are straightforward. After failing to gain the French king's support, Stephen's efforts crumbled. Nicholas, however, led his followers on foot over the Alps into Italy. They marched first to Piacenza and then on to Genoa. Many died of hunger, exposure, and fatigue. The waters at Genoa didn't part. Transport by ship cost actual money; money they didn't have. And the crusade collapsed from exhaustion, leaving the survivors homeless and desperate.

The story of the Children's Crusade has elements worth noting even today. It had a compelling mission; messianic leaders; an inspiring message; supreme confidence ... and a bottomless well of imprudence. Leading thousands of people hundreds of miles across arduous terrain, without proper food, water, tools, protection, and medical support, produced a predictable result: catastrophe. The lesson should be obvious. God inspires great things, but he expects a sensible degree of realism and planning from the people who listen to him.

The Children's Crusade lives on in dim echoes, because most U.S. faith-based work is organized on a nonprofit basis. Nonprofits, like every other enterprise, need money. Getting money and spending it wisely require certain abilities. Missions run on resources; major donors play a key role in making things happen and keeping them running; and no donor in his or her right mind will provide needed resources without confidence in the way things operate. As a result, for anyone starting or growing an apostolate the questions become: How do donors think? Why do they give? What do they expect, if anything, in return for their gifting? What do they see as their gifting mistakes and successes, and why? How should they be approached? What deters them from giving? And these practical questions presume that the person seeking donor support has already answered other questions: Is God *really* leading me to do this, or am I feeding my vanity? Do I have the skills and endurance, the humility and patience, to see the work through? Have I consulted and learned from more experienced others?

All of these questions need to be asked within a changing Catholic reality. In the space of a lifetime, American Catholics have gone from a distrusted but religiously vigorous minority to exceptional levels of political and economic influence ... with much diluted identity and decreasing Church affiliation. Resources will shrink as Catholic numbers decline. For people in apostolic work, it underlines the need to operate leanly, think creatively, and avoid duplicating efforts.

The donors interviewed in this chapter have long experience in supporting Catholic apostolic works. Some of their comments are unique; others are common to the gifting experience. But it's worth highlighting a few key points in the conversations. An apostolate's search for donor help will tend to succeed if it: (1) answers a legitimate need; (2) has a strong business plan; (3) has a clear leader with the intelligence, personality, practical skills, and commitment to carry it through; and (4) has a good support team, or at least the ability and willingness to build one.

Donors don't like to fund duplicative efforts. They don't like to be rushed or pressured or swarmed in potential donor-recipient relationships. They don't want to be the only source of a ministry's support, and they *do* admire an entrepreneurial spirit in apostolate leaders. Donors give to things they have a heart for. In effect, they "invest" in advancing the work of the Gospel. They want to see clean organization, regular accountability for the resources they provide, and in many cases, some form of personal engagement with the effort. And a little gratitude never hurts.

But at this point, we should let them speak for themselves.

ᘒᘒ ᘒᘒ ᘒᘒ

Timothy Busch, founder, The Busch Firm; founder,
The Napa Institute

In your view, what are the key things needed for renewal of the Church in the United States?

BUSCH: Actually, I think we're already in a renewal process. But because we're in the middle of it, we don't understand the progress we're making. It took a generation, 20 years or more, for the Church to tackle a sex-abuse problem that's prevalent throughout society, both secular and religious. But since the Catholic Church was the whipping boy for it, we've now gotten ahead of it. And I'm very proud of that.

Our next challenge, and we don't yet recognize it as a scandal, will be financial. I'm frustrated with the corporate governance of the

Church, where the bishop is the chief man in the legislative, executive, and judicial branches. It's what the Founders of our country identified as the weakness of other governments at that time, and they created a system of checks and balances. In the secular world, unlike the Church, the equivalent of a bad priest, a dishonest, crooked actor, is promptly dismissed. He's just very quickly *gone*. Renewal starts once you can identify, through humility, your weaknesses. Then you can go forward with your strengths. And we should never lose confidence because the Catholic Church teaches the truth of salvation through Jesus Christ, and the failures of her people can't undermine that.

As for our young people: The COVID pandemic really knocked them down as far as church attendance. And church attendance is critical to the renewal of our faith. So somehow we have to address that. But I'm not pessimistic. I was at the [2021] March for Life; 150,000 people showed up, and I was probably one of the oldest guys there. A lot of them were high schoolers and college students and the like; and no one going to that march and listening to those testimonies could walk away thinking that abortion is OK. So, there are some incredible seeds of renewal there.

Finally, I think the bishops get things right the more strongly they promote the Real Presence. The Eucharist is the heart of our faith.

You've mentioned in the past your respect for [the late] Cardinal George Pell and his concern for the lack of financial accountability in the Church. If you could change the way the Church does business, what would you do?

BUSCH: Well, again as a business guy, I'm really frustrated with the corporate governance of the Church. But everybody reminds me that I'm not Jesus Christ, and I'm not the founder of Church. So, I'll just suggest that if there's any issue of bad corporate governance, be it financial or otherwise at a diocesan level, that it should be taken up and investigated by the local metropolitan. Any person with common sense would wonder why the metropolitan doesn't already have that practical authority. And if the metropolitan is the subject matter of the complaint, then it goes up to Rome. That way, you've respected the Catholic teaching on subsidiarity, and you've left local problems in the local area.

You've had some unhappy experiences in the Church finance world.

BUSCH: A bishop can abuse his power. A bishop can be mentally unstable. I've been fired from a diocesan foundation board for asking hard but reasonable questions; and not just me, but others got fired too. This is the sort of arbitrary behavior that blows up in the face of the Church. You can't just pray this kind of problem away. Transparency isn't a word that we like very much in the Church, and it's led to the Vatican's financial disarray. Somehow we've got to eliminate that culture of corruption.

People like yourself are in a position to donate to good causes, but it's impossible to support every good project. When you and your wife, Steph, consider investing your resources in apostolic work, how do you focus your gifting?

BUSCH: I love that word "investing" because that's what it is. And it's been the greatest joy of my life. I started giving to the Society for the Propagation of the Faith way back in sixth grade, and it was always something that pulled at my heart. For Steph and me, what we support has to be faith-based. We have a bit of a preference for education, because we've both been educated through the various organizations we belong to. We especially see lay apostolates as the source of our faith. And we get involved; we don't give money as a rule to organizations where we're not on the board. Everybody donates differently, but that's what we look for.

It seems logical that people who have resources and share them with other people would want at least some evidence of proper usage in return.

BUSCH: Yes, that's right. I think in terms of leverage, because I'm in real estate. If I give a million dollars, how can I get an impact on the world of $10 million? So, that's how I operate. And again, I like to be involved. I had a very difficult conversation this morning with a guy from an apostolate who said, "Your job is to give; my job is to do. You have no business telling me what to do. And I'm very much offended that you're even asking these questions." Well, that's usually the sign of a guy who's got some problems, right? I mean, when you invest in a company and you're a shareholder, but you don't have a place at the table, there's usually something going on that isn't good.

What are the markers you look for in a leader or a project that's likely to be successful? How do you reason through that selection process?

BUSCH: That's a tough one, because unlike secular businesses, the Holy Spirit's involved. I really commit a lot of this to prayer, and it becomes obvious what to do. And it can be a bit scary when a kind of clarity comes to you and says, you know, this is something I want you involved in or this is something that doesn't make any sense. So, I have a board, and I engage them. I'm a guy who thinks I've got it all figured out. But I need to listen to other people I trust. Because, you know, that's a weakness. When you think you've got it all figured out, you don't.

To what degree does personality or manner of presentation affect your decision on giving? A good idea can have a not-so-good leader.

BUSCH: Character and competence are more important than vision, but you really need all three. Great character, bad vision doesn't work. Neither does great vision, bad person. And you need to have basic leadership skills or nothing gets done.

When people come to a wealthy person for support, they can easily be intimidated, even if they have a good idea and the skills to make it happen. How do you factor that in?

BUSCH: Sometimes people aren't at the top of their game. I understand that, and I never try to intimidate people. I know the process of raising money can be scary. I've been intimidated by other people myself. What I look for in an organization asking for help are signs of good or bad management.

What kind of timeframe do you typically give before pulling the ripcord on a failure or, on the other hand, a decision to continue your support?

BUSCH: Well, those are heartfelt decisions, right? Because when you do pull the ripcord, the whole organization can come tumbling down. What I try to do is influence a change of management, as opposed to ending support. And it's been a struggle over the years, because nonprofits can eat cash for breakfast, lunch, and dinner. By nature, they don't work on a profit model. As a donor, you have a duty to hold people accountable and demand transparency. Now, at the end of the day, if you exercise that duty, and they waste the money, shame on them. God always knows who did what.

It seems crucial for a recipient never to presume a donor's support; never to think that he or she "owns" or is somehow "owed" the donated resources. The money is the organization's for the task at hand. To lack a constant sense of personal and organizational accountability strikes me as a fundamental mistake.

BUSCH: Yes. Agreed.

Do you know the story of the Children's Crusade? Thirteenth century. Thousands of French and German children followed a couple of visionaries to liberate Jerusalem miraculously. Plenty of piety and zeal, and a worthy goal, but no money, no planning, no tools or transport or weapons. A complete catastrophe.

BUSCH: Not a surprise. Lay apostolates do their work in the world. They need to use the world's rules of financing, planning, and personnel, HR, that kind of thing, in order to accomplish their mission. They need to have those instincts and skills.

What are the biggest mistakes organizations make in getting started and seeking donor support?

BUSCH: They go again and again to the same people that donate to other organizations, instead of creating their own unique group of donors who are local, and supporters that are affiliated with the organization. And that's how certain big donors get targeted for everything, because too many people looking for financial help tend to be lazy. They should first drill down and find benefactors that are local, who can help get them started; if not with money, then with time and talent. We don't teach people how to raise money. We don't teach them that you don't meet a potential donor on the first day and say, "I need $100,000, and if you don't give it to me, you're a jerk."

You don't marry somebody on the first date; you need to get to know each other. And then, if your ministry can merge with the interests of the benefactor, which ultimately have a lock on his or her heart, then it's a win-win game. And you also need to think about widening your net. Will your revenue model solely be donations? Are there other sources of income that can help pay the bills, like CDs, textbooks, and videos?

Good point. But can't that also lead to mission creep; to overextending your efforts and losing focus? Successful founders sometimes have eyes bigger than their stomachs.

BUSCH: Yes, there's a temptation in a successful organization to bite off more than you can chew. That's why you need a strong and involved board.

What was your biggest mistake as a donor?

BUSCH: A school that I helped. I had no idea that people could take away a ministry that I basically paid for and think it was theirs to take. Today, everybody pretends it's a Catholic school. But it's not truly a Catholic school. And I'm embarrassed by that. So, I made a mistake. I have all kinds of excuses for why I made it. But it taught me not to make that mistake again.

For persons—new donors—just getting into the work of supporting Church-related causes, what's your advice?

BUSCH: My counsel for new donors is simple: Don't just give money, because you're going to hurt people that way. You need to sit down with the people seeking your support. You need to understand them and what they're doing, at least through your proxies, but preferably in person. Giving away money involves a conversion of your heart and soul, and that of your family's. So, that's my advice to the donor, get involved. Because if you don't, you're really not doing the right thing.

Now, as for the people trying to start a new ministry or organization, I think prayer is critical. That might sound trite, but the only time prayer isn't powerful is when you're not listening. And most of us don't really listen. This is why I love Adoration. You need to be really engaged with prayer, anyone involved in a founding; and then you have to start going around and just meeting people before asking for any money. Learn what your strengths and weaknesses are. Listen to people tear apart your business plan. What did they say that makes sense? Then correct the problems. That way you're not testing things on the fly.

You've had an impact with the things you support, and you've also had a higher public profile than some other major donors. Which means you also have your critics, especially on the Church left. Does that bother you?

BUSCH: If you want to get in trouble with somebody, try to change things. It's a part of our society, a part of life, that we just need to get used to. I've never lost one second of sleep because of criticism. If the *National Catholic Reporter* is unhappy with me, it's a compliment. Consider the source.

ॐ ॐ ॐ

Michael Crofton, CEO, The Philadelphia Trust Company

You're a donor to various Catholic causes and have been for years. You've also served on a diocesan finance council for a long time. Based on your experience, what are the practical issues over the next 20 years that you see as decisive for the renewal of the Church in the United States?

CROFTON: The Church needs to get smaller before it can grow. It's too institutional in outlook. It's weighed down by things, possessions. The Church has a tremendous amount of possessions; big cathedrals, nice to look at, but probably not needed anymore. Ten small churches are better than one big one, because you can build fellowship. And that's what's missing in our churches: fellowship. People go to Mass, they go home, and then they come back the next week. Basically it's a personal experience, rather than a communal one.

How have you seen that manifested in the work you've done on Church finance councils?

CROFTON: We have assets with very limited use, and the Church basically collapses under its own weight. It's a hard problem to address, but my own archdiocese, the Philadelphia Archdiocese, had to address it out of necessity because of the clergy sex-abuse scandal. It had to liquidate a lot of assets to raise money for settlements and other things. And that's actually been a good thing. It's much leaner now, and it can respond in a more meaningful way to some of the needs of its people.

Has that brought about attitudinal changes in terms of Church leadership?

CROFTON: There's a gap. Bishops tend to be consensus guys. They don't want to fix what isn't broken. They don't realize that a lot *already is* broken, and it needs to be fixed.

If you could change one or two things in the life of the Church, what would they be?

CROFTON: We should consider the Orthodox and Greek Catholic approach. A married priesthood, celibate bishops. That might help in fixing at least one big problem: homosexuality in the Church. A married priesthood wouldn't solve the whole problem. But it would help. And it might also make fellowship easier; priests and their families socializing with and closer to the laity.

Do you find that you're listened to as a layperson, in your dealings with Church administrative issues?

CROFTON: Not really. It depends.

So, where does a person like you, with real financial and money-management skills, fit in the internal structure of the Church? How do you think laypeople can exercise a real kind of Church leadership, rather than just offering advice to the clergy?

CROFTON: Laypeople need to have real authority. If a diocese is dying but the bishop doesn't delegate, and keeps all the authority for every decision to himself, there's a big problem. The laity should handle the material affairs of the Church, the clergy the spiritual side.

Donors like yourself get asked to support a lot of positive ministries, but nobody can give to every good cause. So, how do you decide what to help?

CROFTON: We give scholarships for education. We support pro-life causes, homes for unwed mothers, things of that nature. We make a decision based on our sense of the individual or group being financed. So, one of our big recipients is a school serving poor kids. We also give to a local community of missionary Sisters. We try to give as directly as possible to a specific need. We don't want layers of bureaucracy between our contribution and its use.

How do you judge whether you're getting a good return on your investment?

CROFTON: We give directly to the individuals who are in charge of the activity.

You know and can trust them, based on a track record of observing them, presumably?

CROFTON: We go and visit them. Quality of leadership is important. How close is the leader to the actual activity? How much gets spent on administration? If there's too much administration, we don't give them any money at all. In the case of scholarships, we want to give to the person who's directly benefiting from the help.

And how do you hold recipients of your support responsible?

CROFTON: We want to see growth where it's possible. So, we visit the people we help. We make sure that they're on track, that the leadership is dedicated. And you can tell that by meeting directly with them and talking with them. Basically, we put boots on the ground. I can go over to a school we support and see that the classrooms are full and the kids are happy. That's good enough for me. I can visit a home for unwed mothers we support and see the babies. That's good enough for me.

One other thing, though: We don't want to be the only funding source for any organization.

In other words, you're looking for an entrepreneurial spirit in groups you support to go out and find additional funding for their operation, so they're not totally dependent on you.

CROFTON: Yes, that's a requirement. They need to keep their institutions alive and prospering beyond what we provide.

As a donor, what's the biggest mistake you see other Catholic donors make?

CROFTON: Narcissism. Anonymous gifts are really the best kind, because they're true gifts. So, we actually give a lot of money out anonymously. If you're not anonymous, you risk doing it for business purposes or self-glorification. Or to make yourself feel good; in a sense, giving should hurt.

In any apostolate, there can be a big difference between a founder and a sustainer; the skill sets aren't the same. What are you looking for in terms of elements that suggest the longevity or the lack of it in an operation?

CROFTON: We go over the list of donors to things we support to make sure that other donors are coming back year in and year out, making the institution successful. And we want to ensure that the management turns over in a healthy way, so that the right people eventually take over from the founder, and have the same dedication and involvement.

I presume you're looking at the prudence of the leader; his ability and willingness to recruit to his weaknesses so that others neutralize those weaknesses?

CROFTON: Yes, absolutely.

What do you regard as your own biggest mistake as a donor? And what's your biggest satisfaction?

CROFTON: I never really thought about that. My biggest satisfaction is seeing the babies we've helped save, and the kids we've helped to educate. And I like to see the progress of programs we support. Once our money goes out the door, I don't want to have any influence over it. I don't want any strings attached to it. If the people we support are successful—and very few fail, because we check them out thoroughly before helping them—we'll keep giving them money. I just expect them to do the good works that they committed to.

For persons who have wealth and want to support good Catholic causes, what's your advice in terms of how to proceed for best effect?

CROFTON: They should be guided by their heart. And they should give money as directly as possible; in other words, not through intermediaries, but directly to the charity or ministry. The personal contact is important.

Is there a particular personality quality in the people you decide to help? One of the complaints I hear from donors is that they're often approached by people who expect help or almost demand it because they're doing God's work. In other words, "I've got a great idea, so you have a duty to give me your money to execute my idea."

CROFTON: That's very common. I like to give to people who are humble. Anybody who gets support from my family or my firm has a palpable humility. They're not blowhards. They're not out for their own ego gratification. They believe in what they're doing. They've dedicated their lives to it. And they often make very little money beyond enough to live on.

In the end, I basically give to people I know who are humble, who have good ideas, and have a record of doing good work. And then I let them run with it.

ح ح ح

Francis Hager, managing partner, The OppCap Group

You're an active Catholic working in the business world. When you look at the Church, what do you see as the decisive issues for her survival and renewal over the next 20 years in this country?

HAGER: Well, one of the big ones is how do we solve the "Gone at confirmation till the baptism of their first child" vacuum, which is a black hole for many of our young people. An alarm bell should be going off in our heads over the fact that a lot of young folks are sacramentized through the eighth grade, and then disappear from the parish until they're 30, if they come back at all. The reconnect rate with the Church for persons born, say, in 2000, is much lower today than in the past because of the pace of the culture.

What would you change in order to begin addressing the problem?

HAGER: We can start by examining which parish and diocesan programs for young people work, which ones don't, and why. We might learn things from the success of groups like FOCUS that can be adapted to the parish level; and also frankly from the Mormon community and the obligation their young people have for a year or two of mission. And our seminaries need to form their guys in that expression *esto vir.* "Be a man." We need priests with good masculine virtues, guys who are manly in a healthy Christian way and can inspire the young people around them.

You're a donor to various Catholic causes. How do you and your wife decide what you're going to support, and why?

HAGER: It's very easy if you're a Catholic of means to get scattered and overwhelmed with requests for help from good people with very worthy projects. But we've tried to go in the opposite direction, to concentrate on giving more to less, more support to fewer things, based on some sensible bets and what we think the Lord wants us to do. It's a kind of investment model. We want to leverage the dollars we give for maximum good benefits.

So, for example, we support the Collegium Institute for Catholic Thought and Culture at the University of Pennsylvania. But through Collegium we're also involved with the Penn Initiative for the Study of Markets, which is led by a Collegium-affiliated faculty fellow, Professor Jesus Fernández-Villaverde. Collegium provides the intellectual space for Penn students to get a greater appreciation for beauty, virtue, and truth. But it also gives us a way to create an intellectual safe harbor for economists around the world who might otherwise work in an environment hostile to their ideas.

I watched you for—what, two or three years?—studying the Collegium board before agreeing to serve on it.

HAGER: I'm interested in organized academic efforts that touch students with a pursuit of truth. So, I liked Collegium's principles. But the board situation was important. A divided board, a dysfunctional board, usually leads to unhappy endings. To answer your basic question, though, I like to invest on a for-profit basis. I like being able to see a couple of different ways to get a good return. And then I need to have confidence in whatever the organization's oversight governance structure is, that there's unanimity in the understanding of mission, very clear and owned by everybody involved.

Do you get directly involved in everything you support?

HAGER: If we make a gift over time that's a lot of money for us, we're going to be actively involved. We make sure that we know very well where those dollars are going. There's another layer of our gifting where we're not as involved. A project sounds good, and looks good, so sometimes we'll give it a shot. But those gifts are fractional relative to our bigger commitments.

What do you think are the biggest deficiencies in the way Catholic laypeople live their lives now?

HAGER: The bar for Catholic witness is set way too low; *way* too low. The fact that laypeople have an equal but different and complementary dignity compared to priests, and that we're called to genuine holiness in our daily lives, is something we don't hear enough at the parish level. The laity isn't really challenged to respond to what Vatican II proposes.

What was your own biggest mistake as a donor? And how did it happen; what short-circuited your normal reasoning?

HAGER: It was an enormously time-consuming and expensive venture with very well-intentioned people who wanted to use modern communications in a way that would be apostolic for the Church.

Hence, a nationwide Catholic radio network. And we got blinded. In my world, the financial world, there's a kind of "deal fever", where everybody gets so invested in doing something that they do irrational things in order to get it done. I think we had mission fever on this one; like, "we have to get this done." We lost patience. We didn't have a unified board. We didn't test our financial assumptions with the rigor that we should have. Basically, we ignored some standard diligence practices in putting together a new venture.

What's your advice to financially successful persons just getting into the work of supporting Church-related causes? For example, someone comes to you with a great idea and asks for your financial help. What are you going to tell him or her?

HAGER: The same thing I tell private equity firms and alternative asset management platforms in my "day job". If you think you're going to take a great investment idea, and a great group of individuals positioned to execute on that investment idea, and build a Blackstone or similar massive enterprise in three to five years, you're nuts. If an idea needs a lot of initial capital to successfully execute, the chances of getting that capital in sufficient size to take one big bite of the apple early on are very, very low.

In the [gifting] world, it's common to use a timeline for a gift, say five years, like we do with our Collegium gift, with very specific conditions that need to be met by the recipient organization. Then we see how it goes. And then, maybe, with tangible benchmarks achieved, there's going to be more capital behind it.

Real performance over time is the mother's milk of raising additional capital, both in the for-profit and nonprofit worlds.

❧ ❧ ❧

Frank Hanna, CEO, Hanna Capital

What issues, particularly in the United States, need to be addressed for a renewal of the Church to take place?

HANNA: Pope Benedict talked about the importance of "essentialism"; in other words, putting first things first. The Church will always

have God's grace, but here on earth we have limited resources, limited energy, and limited human talent to deal with our problems.
So, "both/and" thinking often won't work. We can address *either*
this problem *or* that problem, but not both at the same time, and
we need to decide prudently which to focus on first. But none of us
likes to prioritize, because that means some things will be relegated
to secondary or tertiary status. And so, we have battles about these
priorities, without actually reaching agreement on the purpose of the
Church, and the role of our parishes.

What's the Church supposed to *do and be* in the modern world?
We need a real and thorough analysis of that question, and few bishops have the time to step back and ask it. They're already inun-
dated with other more immediate duties. I'd like to see laypeople
get involved with those kinds of questions, to take a deeper dive into
what we need to accomplish. We know we're supposed to evangelize
the nations; we have the basic scriptural plan. But at the end of the
day, what does that actually mean in the way we structure our activity, energy, and material resources?

Do you know any bishops who think clearly and radically about these things?

HANNA: Not many, but I don't fault them. To go to the root of things
is to be radical, and most of our bishops are not radical; and I'm pretty
sure we don't want most of them to be. Pope Benedict XVI was actually a radical thinker, but he spent much of his time as something of
a professor. A bishop in his 60s with a tenure horizon of eight or 10
years, only has so much time and energy. And finally, making decisions about priorities means de-prioritizing certain things, and that's
exhausting and sometimes depressing. Closing an office or ministry is
like cutting a government program; these things have built-in constit-
uencies. I respect bishops. I'm grateful for their integrity and faith. But
maybe there's something systemic in our structures that both demands
too much and simultaneously inhibits what needs to be done. It's the
same with our government. I know a fair number of senators and
members of Congress. People like to say that all politicians are crooks.
It's not true. A lot of them really do want to fix things. But structur-
ally, governing a country composed of more than 300 million people
may require some systemic structural re-thinking. Otherwise, we end
up with $30 trillion in national debt.

For an example of this issue in the Church, we can look at Catholic education. How do we run Catholic schools? We tend to criticize the public school system for its bureaucracy and lack of flexibility or responsiveness. But then we ought not to do the same thing. We ought not to set up a diocesan superintendent and department of education and try to cookie-cutter a system across different communities of people. We tell the government to give parents a choice of the school where they send their kids. But if we really believed in choice within our own dioceses, we'd consider a scholarship system that parents could use for their children to attend any of our Catholic schools. We don't want to do that because they may all flock to our good schools, and we'll have a problem with closing the bad ones, which is one reason the public schools resist school choice, right? They don't want to close all the bad schools and have the spotlight on them. In the Church, just like in the government, we have massive infrastructure issues that we've got to rethink.

When we talk about structural issues, I wonder if we're overlooking an 800-pound gorilla in the room, which is that a lot of people really don't know their faith and don't really believe. They live their faith as a kind of positive ethical code, but it's not penetrating to their core.

HANNA: What's the most significant encounter the average Catholic has with the teachings of his or her faith during the entire week? It's the weekly homily. I'd love it if every homily could be great, but for starters, we really need to keep them from being boring. And if they're still boring, they should at least be short. Pope Francis has spoken to this topic frequently. How could we make that achievable? I might suggest one simple requirement: Somebody in every parish should video the Sunday homilies, and each priest should have the duty to watch his own homilies and learn from them. Every eighth-grade football team watches its game films. But most of our priests don't watch their own homilies, and for most parishioners, the homily is the main pipeline of their catechesis. Unfortunately, bad homilies chase people out of the Church. The homily should not feel like the penance one does to get the Eucharist. And speaking of penance, from a structural standpoint, making confession more available at better times than 4 P.M. on Saturdays

could make a big difference. We ought not to make going to confession so difficult.

*You're a donor to good causes. So, how do you personally focus your gifting,
and why do you focus on those things?*

HANNA: We've traditionally donated to spiritual works of mercy, as
I feel called to that, and I think it has a multiplier effect. When Jesus
trained 12 men intensely in the first "seminary", he multiplied his
effect. So, for most of my adult life I've been interested in Catholic
education. There are four chronological periods in life where significant biological change is taking place in the human brain. If you focus
on those stages of life, you have a chance of getting a disproportion-
ate return on your charitable dollars and efforts.

As an example, one of those stages is the period from age 18 to 21.
That's why I was involved with getting FOCUS chapters started at
schools here in Georgia. I've also been involved with K-12 education
for about 40 years now; what happens during that period is dispro-
portionately important to the rest of life.

As a side note, not everything we donate to has measurable efficacy.
At this point in my life I need a little more beauty and contemplation.
So, the other day, when a young couple approached me for help with
a sacred music project, which fits with my interest in beauty but also in
sacred liturgy, we gave them some help with what they do.

Generally, I'm looking for what might move the needle in a good
direction. And specifically, with any project, I'm looking for three
factors. One, is there a legitimate evangelical or corporal need that's
underserved? Two, do you have a credible plan for addressing that
need? And three, do you have a franchise quarterback who can lead
the team? You don't usually go to a Super Bowl without a franchise
quarterback. But you don't just go out and easily find and hire one;
they're rare. Starting something new is really tough, so don't think
you can just hire somebody as an afterthought to do the leadership
work because it doesn't work like that.

*But doesn't he or she also need a good team? A founder and a sustainer can
be two very different organizational creatures. To what degree do you look at
the bones of the organization?*

HANNA: Honestly, not that much, and that's partly because I tend to fund new initiatives. So, I'm particularly keen on assessing the leader. The rest of the team is certainly important, and becomes even more important for succession 10 or 20 years down the road. But if a founder's not willing to commit 10 to 20 years of his or her life to the project, it probably won't happen. You need that level of commitment from the founder. That's the problem. People sometimes have a great idea and think they can get somebody else to run it. No, that doesn't work.

Apple went bankrupt when Steve Jobs left. You can't just go hire another Steve Jobs; Apple only rebounded when they hired *the real* Steve Jobs back a few years later. So, my feeling is, if a project has a committed, creative founder, he'll probably build a good team. A great board is also nice, but it's not decisive. In the nonprofit world, board members aren't paid. Unless they're fully aligned with the mission, they're probably not treating it as one of the top two or three priorities in their lives. People think magic happens with boards, but I don't know of any institution in history that became great because of its board. I just don't know of any. So, the team is important, but the founder/leader is critical.

What's the biggest donor mistake you've made? And to what degree do you follow up and make sure that your money is actually being used in the proper way?

HANNA: On the issue of follow-up, I do, I ask for metrics. I come from the business world. That world has a lot of mechanisms for accountability. But measuring success is usually a lot easier in business than in charity. In apostolates, we can't actually measure the number of souls that get to heaven, so we have to use some sort of proxy measurement, and that's important, but really tough to do.

On the issue of mistakes, most of the mistakes I see come from a divergence of priorities. It's important for donors to know that when we give away money, it's no longer our money. It's not your money. You gave it away. So, unless arrangements have been made in advance for some kind of oversight or involvement, complaining doesn't make a lot of sense. You need to do your due diligence up front. Just like any marriage that lasts, expectations on both sides ought to be made very clear and agreed upon in advance.

Two final questions. First, imagine that I've suddenly got a lot of money, and now I want to be kind to the Church or religious apostolates. What's your advice to new donors? And second, I have a terrific idea for a new ministry. How do I go about getting the money to make it work?

HANNA: There's a saying among people who give money, a kind of platitude: "I didn't realize it would be tougher to give it away than it was to make it." That's not really true though. The reality is that people work for 40 years, 60 hours a week, to make their fortune, and then they hope to be just as effective at giving it away by spending four or five hours a week on it. That doesn't work. It's not harder to give it away than it was to make it, but neither is it easy to give money away effectively. So, sometimes it can become a chore or a guilt-offering. When this happens, we need to reorient. We always need to see our gifting as a blessing. I'd also suggest that it be done deliberately and thoughtfully, and that it's helpful to connect with and learn from the fraternity of donors already engaged in gifting within the Catholic Church. There's a lot of experience and knowledge that these folks are happy to share.

Now on the other hand, if you come to me for funding help with an idea, the first question I'll ask you is, are you willing to commit the next 10 to 20 years of your life to this apostolate? Because things tend to take longer and need a lot more dedication than you think. So, are you willing to make this project, after God and your family, the most important thing in your life? If you're not, donors will sense that you're hedging your bets.

Again, you need a franchise quarterback, a good business plan, and a legitimate market niche. If you start having success, you'll probably find that the funding available to you increases. Remember that many of today's leading companies didn't start out with somebody giving them a $10 million grant. Facebook started in a dorm room. Microsoft began in a garage. Start small and look first in your local community for a godfather. It's better if your support starts in your local community, because you can swing by and see those persons frequently, and the personal relationships really do matter.

❧ ❧ ❧

*Berni and Rob Neal, managing partner, Hager Pacific
Properties (Rob); multiple philanthropic boards (Berni)*

*If you were to name the key problem in American Church life today, what
would it be?*

BERNI: I think we're paying the price for allowing ourselves to assume
that we had community because we have this label called "Catholic".
But we never really built deep community. So when COVID hit,
and the church doors were shut, we didn't stay connected. In the
past, immigrant parishes in places like Philadelphia were very strong.
They were real Catholic communities. Today conditions are very
different, but we still need community.

ROB: I found it very telling that Facebook renamed itself Meta. It
speaks to how they envision humans will connect with each in the
years ahead. And not in a way that involves physical presence. I think
our Church is starting to learn how to deal with that. But we know
from the research—and Catholic Leadership Institute has done a lot of
great work in this area—that the outcomes we want to see in our local
parishes are all a function of "Father". If you have a great pastor, you
have a great parish, regardless of demographics, where the people live,
what they look like, and what their ethnic or racial profile is. If you
don't, you don't have success; again, regardless of any other advantage.
    It's personnel. It's all personnel. So, for Berni and me, one of the
big issues is how does a pastor get his skills and improve his skills?
There's a whole discussion to be had on seminaries and how we're
not only forming the men, but selecting the men as future pastors.
Because ultimately, we're talking about the concept of leverage. And
by far, the highest kind of leverage in the Church is the presbyterate.

*No donor can support everything, and a lot of good causes are out there. So,
what do the two of you focus your energy on?*

BERNI: I drive a lot of this. If I hear about something that intrigues
me, I want to get to know the founder and the mission really, really
well. Then I want to know their team. The team means everything.
So, usually I volunteer, or I get involved, for the first year or two

before we give any support. I want to understand their long-term game before I bring it to Rob, having done that kind of homework. Then Rob will do his own assessment.

ROB: We look for organizations in their earlier, formative years that are likely to become very effective as they grow. These early organizations are almost always dominated by a founder. And that can be a challenge, because it leads to a lot of redundancy within the nonprofit sector. Which just drives me crazy. You can have 50 people doing the same thing. Why? Because the founders involved are convinced that they were whispered to by the Angel Gabriel last night, and they've heard the word of God personally, straight from the top. The temperament of some founders is messianic. They can't scale or adjust their efforts no matter how wonderful their idea is. It's their way or no way.

The organizational life cycle is filled with examples of founders who could take a business from zero up to $50 million or $200 million or more—and then got lost thereafter. The same applies in the nonprofit sector. So, we want to know: Is this or that ministry founder someone who can scale? Or at least has the will and humility to let the organization scale?

When ministries come to you for support, what are the markers in your analysis that determine whether you're going to help them or not?

BERNI: Again, I need to know more than just the founder; I need to know the team. I need to know why team members have chosen to put their gifts into the organization. Because that says a lot not only about the founder's ability to choose good staff, but why the team feels that it's important to be engaged. Also, I want to stay really agile. I'm exposed to many different apostolates, even when I'm not serving on their boards; it gives me the ability to cross-pollinate on things like structuring compensation, for example.

ROB: I think of our gifting as asset allocation. Like I'm a hedge fund manager, and I'm managing our investments. And so the age-old question is, do you have a few stocks and hold them a long time? Or do you have a lot of stocks in your portfolio, and you trade in and out, and keep rebalancing? In my mind, we have a portfolio of nonprofit "stocks". We gave 40 grants [in 2021]. Our biggest grant was half a million dollars as part of a larger pledge. Our smallest was $1,300. And there were probably a dozen that were less than $10,000. Mrs. Neal likes to help a lot of little operations.

BERNI: There are two reasons for that. Some apostolates would be overwhelmed by larger grants. And some just need to know that you're supporting them, that you love them, that you're going to help them, but not solve all their problems. The Holy Spirit keeps us on our knees. The Holy Spirit does not give all of us lottery tickets and winnings for a reason. He wants us to be disciplined and work lean.

What's the biggest mistake you've made in terms of your gifting?

ROB: Sometimes you just fall in love with a powerful concept and for me, in this case, it was a group to help the homeless. I called this person, the foundress, a "homeless whisperer". She had a rate of success I'd never seen. Homelessness is such a challenging issue. It resists any kind of silver bullet. But she seemed to have it. She was taking maybe 50 percent of the people she met off the streets, gainfully employing them, and then tracking them. So, I started to invest. Pretty soon I was the chair of her new board, which I had formed. We gave them $45,000 in a couple of different installments. And then she promptly fired me. I was shocked, but this was good for us forensically. I didn't employ the rigorous techniques that Berni has developed in terms of watching an organization grow slowly and carefully before getting financially involved. I just jumped ahead. I ignored the warning signs.

What's your advice to people with new wealth who want to get into the process of providing support to religious ministries and good nonprofits?

BERNI: It takes nine months to make a baby; it takes about an hour to bake a cake. There's no fast way to have a lasting impact. You've got to do the homework. If you're somebody who has new money and wants to give to good charities, spend time with donors that you admire and respect, and ask a lot of questions. And don't give money until you've done the homework.

ROB: New donors need mentors; couples or individuals who've gone down the donor road before them. And by the way, sharing their experiences and providing their counsel is also good for the mentor couples. It's incredibly rich and rewarding.

BERNI: I'd just add a caution that when you're new, and you're giving away money, there's a tendency to think, "Wow, look at how important I am. Aren't you lucky you know me." That's a very treacherous place for the soul.

Last question. Joe Catholic just came up with this fantastic apostolic idea. And you happen to have the money he needs. What's the right way to approach you?

ROB: As Berni said, "You've got to build a team." We can get involved in that conversation. But usually what we tell people is, don't expect any financial contribution from us. We'll give you some ideas and share some of our hard-earned lessons. But we're not going to give you money. We're not going to point you to other donors, either. We'll tell you how to form a board. We'll tell you how to build a management team. And we'll talk to you about good governance and financial transparency, which a donor wants to see.

BERNI: We want to support the pillars of the Church: pro-life work, education, evangelization, priestly formation, things like that. We always ask ourselves how our giving impacts the horizontal and the vertical in Church life, and we look for efforts where they intersect. It's been quite the journey and very humbling for our spiritual life. We just happen to be on the giving side. That's a privilege and also a responsibility. But in the giving, we're also receiving.

≥∾ ≥∾ ≥∾

Director (anonymous), Catholic-focused family foundation

Over the next 20 years, what practical issue(s) do you see as decisive for the renewal of Church life in the United States? If you had one or two things you could change or enhance about the way the Church—first in the United States, but also the Church at large—does her mission, what would they be? And where do laypeople fit into that work?

DIRECTOR: We have no idea what the Church will look like in 20 years. We don't know if the Church will even survive as it's structured today. It's too unwieldly. We tend to share the view of then-Father Joseph Ratzinger when he described the future of the Church in his famous 1969–1970 German radio interviews. We'd like to see a Church that's smaller and purer.

We believe that catechesis—teaching the faith—will *always* be the most pressing issue within the Church. Laypeople can certainly fit into that work, and they should be involved. The key issue is determining whether the lay catechist really knows the material that he or she is presenting. Because the Church is so divided, it's important to be aware of the person's background in order to know which "brand" of the Catholic faith he or she is peddling. No more relativism.

No donor can give to every good cause. As a donor, where do you focus your gifting and why there?

DIRECTOR: Our foundation was established in the early 1980s, and we give almost exclusively to Catholic causes. If an organization that we support isn't Catholic, we expect them to follow the teachings of the Catholic Church. We give to parishes, schools, educational apostolates, and pro-life organizations, as well as one particular homeless shelter. We have trusted relationships with the organizations we fund. We prefer to give for general operations, so the money can be used where it's needed the most. We also like to fund things that really need the money, rather than big, well-established organizations. We prefer the underdog. We don't accept unsolicited requests. For this reason, we try to stay under the radar.

How do you decide on the worthiness of a request for support; what are the key markers of an apostolate's or organization's likely success, and how do you determine them?

DIRECTOR: Again, we have a relationship with all of our grantees. We know their organization, and we believe in them and their mission.

This isn't to say that we don't fund new organizations, because we do nearly every year. We also stop funding organizations for any number of reasons. The determining factor is the same, in other words, we know them, trust them, and we believe in the mission.

How do you monitor and hold recipients responsible for the support you provide? What kind of timeframe do you use for judging success or failure? What kind of feedback or reporting do you expect? How personally involved do you become in the efforts you support?

DIRECTOR: We don't have a formal reporting process. For example, we give a substantial amount of money to local parishes, and we don't expect them to give us a final report, even though some do. We do, however, make a point of having a once-a-year lunch, phone meeting, etc., with the point person from the various apostolates we support. Basically, we just want to know how they are doing, what worked for them and what didn't, new ideas, etc. We don't consider failures a bad thing as long as a lesson was learned. We really encourage people to be honest.

In your experience, what are the biggest mistakes that apostolates and organizations make in getting started and seeking donor support? And what's essential for an apostolate/organization in sustaining a success?

DIRECTOR: Before approaching a donor, it's very important to know personally the donor and his or her interests, even if it's just through your research. You don't want to approach a donor who has no interest in your particular cause. The biggest mistake of someone looking for money is overpromising. No matter the apostolate, it's always better to be conservative when speaking to a donor. The person seeking a grant has to be able to articulate his or her vision. A business plan is very helpful. It's wise to have at least a few donors secured before you approach someone unknown to you. A donor will frequently ask who else has agreed to fund the project. Success attracts donors. Sustaining success usually means that the organization is having an impact within its community. A new apostolate has to be constantly marketed, fundraising needs to be ongoing, and the product (whatever it is) has to constantly be improved and updated.

What was your own biggest mistake, and what has been your biggest satisfaction or success in your gifting?

DIRECTOR: We've made lots of mistakes. Granting money and asking for money are not perfect sciences. That being said, many years ago, we terminated two multi-year grants; one to a university and one to a high school. In both cases, we specifically stated that the school must maintain its Catholic identity, which it did not.

Our biggest "success" was giving a large grant, $1 million, to a very good and faithful new all-girls Catholic high school. It had a very hard struggle to survive, and we had to dip into the foundation's principal to provide the needed help. Each year, we only give away funds from the interest earned off the principal, usually around $500,000. It was an emotional time for everyone, but it did save the school. The school is flourishing today.

Last but not least: What's your advice/encouragement/caution to successful persons just getting into the work of financially supporting Church-related causes? And likewise, what's your advice to persons with a "great and urgent idea" for a new ministry that needs funding?

DIRECTOR: For successful persons just getting into financially supporting Church-related causes, the first thing is to come to terms with knowing that the money really belongs to God. This is very important. They also need to research the organizations they're interested in funding, and they need to talk with the person heading the organization. If all of that checks out, they need to give the money without any strings attached, even if it's a designated gift. This can be a real problem for many donors. Micromanaging the money can lead to disaster. I'm reminded of a donor, from my own nonprofit work, who gave money for Spanish-speaking students at a Catholic school to become proficient in English. He paid for a special program and a teacher to implement it. At the end of the school year, the children were tested and all but one passed the test. He wanted every single penny back, and as I remember, we gave it to him. Seriously, I have a million stories. I should write a book about that.

My advice to persons with a "great and urgent idea" is to pray, pray, pray, and then pray some more. You really need to know if this is God's will for you. Starting a new apostolate is very difficult, and I think it's nearly impossible without a strong prayer life. You'll need people of influence on your team. They can be of great help to someone starting an apostolate. The next thing is to research what else is out there. Is anyone else doing what you want to do? If so, you may want to join forces with them, or at least learn as much as you can from them. At some point, you just have to dive in. In the beginning, there's a significant amount of paperwork that needs to be completed just to get your nonprofit 501(c)(3) designation. So, be prepared to make mistakes and use them as learning experiences.

ح‍‍ ح‍‍ ح‍‍

Carol and John Saeman, The Saeman Family Foundation

Over the next 20 years, what do you see as decisive for the renewal of the Church in the United States? You've thought about these things for a long time, because you've been involved in supporting a lot of good efforts.

JOHN: God created a Church that teaches the truth, not a collection of opinions. We need to get back to the basics of our faith. And it's important that our seminaries produce men who are ready to defend and teach those basic truths that the Church has believed since the beginning.

CAROL: I'm amazed sometimes by how little Catholics actually know about their faith. If they were better formed or instructed, the Church would be much stronger, which is why we have such an interest in education.

Donors can't give to every good cause, so where do you focus your gifting?

CAROL: Most of our friends over the years have been into the arts, the symphony, things like that. But that was never our real interest. Our focus has always been the homeless or education to further our faith. Our main giving will always be to the Church and to Catholic education.

JOHN: Probably 95 percent of what we do on an annual basis goes to the Catholic Church. And of that 95 percent, about 70 percent goes to some form of education via the Saeman Family Foundation.

In Rome, you basically fund scholarships, correct?

JOHN: Yes, we have a program that we put together through Cardinal John O'Connor, back in the late '90s. He was then the chairman of the Papal Foundation. We wanted to make a major gift to the Church, and specifically to the needs of John Paul II. So, O'Connor went to the Holy Father, who said that as a young priest from Poland, without any knowledge of where his support came from, he was able to go to the Angelicum in Rome for his master's and doctoral degrees, and he was always very grateful for that. So, we created the St. John Paul II scholarship fund at the Papal Foundation. This year [2022], we have 95 scholars in Rome at various different pontifical institutes or universities, all from third-world countries. All are studying for advanced degrees. Whether you're a religious Sister or a priest, you're studying for either your master's degree or your doctorate. And these people will go back home to their countries and become leaders. They'll run the schools and seminaries. They'll become the bishops. We've been involved with about 1,600 students in the past 20 or so years. And it's a program that gives Carol and me and our family a great amount of satisfaction.

As a general rule, how do you decide on whom or what to support? How do the mechanics work?

CAROL: A lot comes from the heart; it's a heart thing.

That's clearly true. But we've known each other a long time, and I've noticed that, yes, you give from your heart, but your head's very much engaged in it, too.

CAROL: We get involved. I was working with a particular group some years ago, and we stopped giving for a couple of years because the leadership was in trouble and it needed to be fixed. I just wasn't willing to stay involved until they got their act together. And they did. And we've gone back to helping them again when we can.

So, how do you determine which specific apostolates or projects to help?

JOHN: Personal experience and personal referrals. If someone like a Cardinal Arinze or Archbishop Chaput, for example, comes to us and says, "I need help with such and such", we'll probably provide support. Unless there's some reason why we absolutely can't, we'll respond favorably. The cause needs to be good, but mainly we believe in the credibility of the person asking or doing the endorsement.

That raises the issue of leadership in the Church. Where does leadership fit into all of this?

JOHN: It's very important. Most of our support has gone to or through leaders in the Church we know and trust. Our giving is very much motivated by key persons we've come to admire and with whom we've developed relationships over time, and the needs they have in their missions. So, then we ask ourselves, how can we help them? And do their needs fit with what we're interested in? There's very seldom a time when you can't come up with a fit.

CAROL: We want to support people and things that are faithful to the teaching of the Church. Trust is a huge, huge factor, and not every bishop or Church leader inspires trust.

How do you hold people accountable? What are the markers you look for in the people and organizations that you support?

JOHN: Good question. We're probably not the best at that. We don't have a staff at the Saeman Family Foundation. Basically I field the solicitations, and Carol presents things to the board. So, we have to be very careful in our selection process, as opposed to coming in later on and trying to fix something that's broken. We're not structured to fix broken stuff. We're geared up to help drive the bus; to help new initiatives that have the backing of the leaders we respect.

A problem with some ministries trying to do good work is their assumption that, well, we're doing good, so you should give us money ... but don't pester us about what we've done with your investment. Have you had any bad experiences with your funding?

JOHN: The only time we've backed out on a commitment was to my alma mater, a Dominican high school in Wisconsin. I got a great education there. It formed me in my faith. It was a marvelous environment. So, we made a gift pledge of $1 million. We structured it to pay out in annual income at 8 percent interest. In other words, we gave them $80,000 a year for scholarships, and we specified in detail who would qualify for the scholarships and how: by academic performance, by income level, and by geographic location. So, after a couple of years, we hired a young seminarian to go in and field test what was going on. We arranged for him to visit the school and monitor classes. He came back and wrote a report. The school had totally ignored the conditions of our gift. So, we just shut the pledge down, and our money was no longer there.

CAROL: There was one other time. We were funding a halfway house for men. And we found out that the guys were bringing women in for overnights and doing other things that didn't fit with our convictions. Sometimes as a donor you get bitten, but overall we've been fortunate.

As donors, what do you see as essential for a ministry or project to achieve and sustain success?

JOHN: It needs to have a good business plan. And it needs to be unique and different in what it's doing. Oftentimes, Carol and I will look at a request for help and say, others are already doing that. Why would we want to help someone else do the same thing? An apostolate's mission needs to be clear and not duplicating other efforts. In fact, whenever we can, we try to bring people together who look like they have a common mission in mind. We don't need more of the same pasta.

Where's your satisfaction in all this?

JOHN: You don't always get to see the results of a gift. But, as I said earlier, our Saeman scholars in Rome are an enormous satisfaction. We've also helped FOCUS, and it's been hugely satisfying to see it so successful and doing so much good.

Let's say that I've just hit the jackpot in the stock market, and I want to give money to good causes. But I haven't done it before. As donors yourselves, what advice would you give to such persons?

JOHN: First of all, they need to identify an area of focus: Education? Halfway houses? Drug and alcohol rehabilitation centers? That sort of thing. You need to narrow the field down to three or four areas. The Daniels Fund, for example, has seven different mission areas. I'd guess our family foundation has four. Then you need to weigh how much money you have against what you can accomplish in a particular window of opportunity. When we die, everything Carol and I have goes to the Church. When the bell rings, whatever's in our estate is already committed. But if we had a windfall today, while we're still alive, we'd have a particular focus on institutions of higher learning like the University of Mary or Thomas Aquinas College or Christendom College; schools that are traditionally strong in their faith.

CAROL: In giving, you need to trust your radar. Sometimes, something about a project or the person pitching it just feels wrong; even if you like what you hear, the dots aren't connecting. Little details are the things that you look at. They're important. And if they're not quite right, you just need to say, whoa, let's think about this.

What about people who have a genuinely good idea and need donor support, what's your advice to them?

JOHN: An idea needs to have practical credibility, and it's got to have an economic test to it. For that reason, today, we don't do much in the way of start-ups. We were very involved with the Augustine Institute at the beginning, Denver's St. John Vianney Seminary at the beginning, and FOCUS at the beginning. But today, we're more in a mindset of giving to those ministries that have already been proven to be consistent with the teaching of the Church and with our own beliefs. So, we're not looking for new stuff, though we wouldn't completely shut out a good new idea, either.

Last question: To what degree do you tie your gifting to an organization's ability to raise other funds; in other words, to ensure that you and Carol aren't the sole donors?

JOHN: Early in the life cycle of FOCUS, Carol and I can remember sitting with Curtis [Martin] and asking him, "What would FOCUS do, if we gave you a million dollars?" Curtis didn't have a great answer, and, even though we loved FOCUS, we didn't give the million dollars. A year later, Curtis came back and said, "I have an answer for your question." He explained his vision for evangelization, for leadership development, and how FOCUS could double in size, and then double again. They had clearly defined goals and needs. He then said, "But this will require, not one, but two million dollars." So, Carol and I made the $2 million-dollar investment, but we also made it clear that if they doubled in size, we weren't ready to double our gift in the near future. Curtis told us, "That's OK, because we hope and plan to double the number of donors as well."

You had confidence they would raise the rest of the money.

JOHN: Obviously we did. They had a mission that we believed in, that Archbishop Chaput believed in, and that we'd already been supporting. So, it wasn't a difficult decision to make. It was the right thing to do. So, yeah. In the end, it really gets back to the quality, integrity, and mission of the institution and people that you're supporting.

CHAPTER NINE

Things That Work, and Why

Success in Seven Models

*[A] temptation for any apostolate is mission creep. Any expansion of scope
needs to be organic to the mission and very carefully thought through. It's best
to stay in your lane. Do what no one else is doing. And it's important to figure
out the one or two things you do really well, and then do them more, and better.*

— Mitch Boersma, Leonine Forum

If challenges facing the Church in the United States today are many,
so are the lay apostolates working to address them. In the previous
chapter, donors explained how and why they invest their resources to
support the mission of Catholic nonprofits. A list of worthy lay efforts
would be too long to include here. Catholic radio alone reaches millions of listeners through EWTN, Relevant Radio, and numerous
local efforts. But the seven different apostolates below all share some
common features: good leadership, careful stewardship, a clear, disciplined mission, and a record of effective results in an area of pressing
Church need. Each offers some useful lessons for anyone seeking to
serve the Church and her mission.

ॐ ॐ ॐ

FOCUS

FOCUS, the Fellowship of Catholic University Students, founded by
Curtis Martin, began with two missionaries at Benedictine College in

1998. Growth was rapid. As of 2023, it had missionaries on university campuses across the United States and in Mexico, Ireland, the United Kingdom, Austria, and Germany. FOCUS centers its mission efforts on college-age young adults. In its own words, it seeks to "form Catholic missionaries rooted in Church teaching, prayer, Scripture, and evangelization" who then "go out into the world, invite people into a joyful life with Christ, and walk with them as they grow in faith."

In practice, this means meeting college students on university campuses, building friendships, and "inviting them into a personal relationship with Jesus Christ ... walking with them as they pursue lives of virtue and excellence." FOCUS missionaries are extensively trained. Once in service, they pursue their campus/parish missions through Bible studies, outreach events, mission trips, and everyday accompaniment with the goal of serving and inspiring others—in this case, students who will one day graduate and work in the world—to share the Great Commission: "Go and make disciples of all nations" (Mt 28:19). The outcome has been obvious. FOCUS is now one of the most successful Catholic apostolates in the world.

In Curtis Martin's words

On what we need now as Catholics: We need to restore a Jesus-centered understanding of the Church. When we radiate the vibe that "the Church is an institution, and somewhere in there is Jesus", it's far less attractive. People want personal affinity. Peter didn't drop his nets in Luke 5 to join an institution. He was overwhelmed by a *person*. We also need a sharper sense of the evangelical imperative, a much greater sense of urgency. We're plagued by a misguided optimism that things in the Church are better than they really are. *We're* responsible for reaching the people around us. It won't happen without us. At no time in history have even half the people on earth known that Jesus Christ is the Savior of the world. We need to do better than that. And finally, in addition to being sacramental, we need to be more deeply biblical. The Word of God needs to become our words, so that the thoughts of God become our thoughts, and then our actions.

On the "why" of prioritizing university campuses: One reason is simple. My life changed as a college student. But the key reason is the nature of the college-age cohort. The years between 16 and 26 are a critical decade. It's where most life decisions are made. Prior to college, your parents tell you what to do. After college, for most people, your spouse and family demand your best efforts. But in those university years, you're both single and an adult. If God calls you, you can go anywhere, and you can follow him for the rest of your life.

You want to fix education? The next generation of teachers is students on college campuses today. You want to fix the marriage problem? The people likely to marry someday are right there in the same place. Ditto for fixing the priestly vocation crisis. Ditto for anything else that's broken. We need to be present on university campuses, because that's where young people in the right age group are gathered more effectively than anywhere else in our culture. And it's simultaneously the worst but also the best terrain for mission. Worst, because it's filled with hedonism and deconstructionism. But best, because the light shines in the darkness, and the human heart and mind have an instinct for the light. The Gospel will work anywhere and *does* work everywhere. Too often, it's just not proclaimed.

In Monsignor James Shea's words

I invited FOCUS to the campus of the University of Mary soon after I began my service as president in 2009. The most impressive aspect of FOCUS leaders and missionaries is their rootedness in the Gospel *kerygma*. They've shown (once again) that presenting a clear picture of the Gospel and call of Christ to young people continues to be attractive and powerful. They're serious and dedicated followers of Christ, and they pass on their dedication to their missionaries. Evidence of their success includes the sheer numbers of students they've touched, the impact of their SEEK conferences, the number of vocations to the priesthood and religious life and vocations to seriously Christian marriages and lay apostolates that they've produced, and the steady growth they've experienced. And, in my experience, it's an organization overflowing with the most impressive, highest-hearted people.

In a current board member's words

There are times when the FOCUS board of directors really annoys Curtis. I've seen it. But I think he also knows he needs that, and

I'm impressed by his realism. I tend to be on his side emotionally in issues; temperamentally, we're alike. But over time I've realized that the board isn't an accident that Curtis regrets. It's the structure he deliberately encouraged and accepted, like wearing a hair shirt. He felt it was something that would be good for him, and good for FOCUS. An organization like FOCUS works because of a charismatic leader, but that needs a responsible, experienced counterweight. Boards should never manage organizations; that's not their job. But there does need to be some degree of civil, respectful tension between a board and a charismatic leader to keep things on the rails. It helps the organization thrive. And with FOCUS, it has.

ૐ ૐ ૐ

The Leonine Forum

Named for Pope Leo XIII and his body of social teaching, the Leonine Forum (LF) is an outgrowth of Washington, D.C.'s, Catholic Information Center. Cofounded by the late Rev. Arne Panula and Mitch Boersma, the Forum seeks "to cultivate an emerging generation of virtuous leaders and empower them to live fully-integrated lives of faith in order to apply the social teachings of the Church within their professional and civic lives." Briefly put, LF is the premier lay Catholic leadership program in the United States. The application process is competitive. The program involves a year of study, lectures, group discussions, and fellowship. As of its tenth anniversary in 2023, LF has more than 800 alumni and alumnae nationwide, with Forum branches in New York, Chicago, and Los Angeles, as well as Washington.

Mitch Boersma, COO of the Catholic Information Center and Leonine Forum's executive director, previously held research positions at the American Enterprise Institute and worked as an independent writer and researcher. A graduate of the University of Dallas, Catholic University of America, and the annual Tertio Millennio Seminar in Poland, Boersma's published work has appeared in a wide variety of secular and religious outlets. Rev. Roger Landry, the Forum's New York City chaplain, previously served as attaché at the Permanent Observer Mission of the Holy See to the United

Nations. As of 2023, he serves as the Catholic chaplain for Columbia University.

In Mitch Boersma's words

On the reason for the Forum: The Church has a huge need for emerging Catholic leaders who are faithfully Catholic and known to their communities as Catholic. In other words, we need Catholic professionals able to witness their faith in whatever they do. The first step is knowledge. Young people with leadership potential need to have confidence in what the faith has to offer, not just for salvation but for creating a virtuous, happy life. They want more than just a normative set of dos and don'ts. So, we need to offer them a credible proposition for flourishing, and the courage to live and share it. In a cancel culture, that can be tough. It's not easy for a young finance guy who's trying to climb the ladder in a corporate environment to find other serious Catholics. The Leonine Forum is a proving ground for acquiring the knowledge, support, and relationships necessary for fellows to be strong witnesses to the faith in their communities and at their jobs.

On getting the idea: I'd had various fellowships myself. They were good, but also lacking in some ways. At the Catholic Information Center, we got a lot of traffic from very well-educated, professionally driven young people. Many of them were daily communicants. But they had no idea what the Church had to offer in terms of a deeper intellectual formation, or how to deal *as a Catholic* with social and cultural issues. A lot of smart people were passing through who didn't know each other, but should. I'm not a "front of the room" kind of guy, but I do know how to be the straw that stirs the drink. So, that's how it started.

On program nuts and bolts: We run on a very lean budget, but there's no charge to the fellows. We do insist on a serious commitment from everyone selected, though. The application process is pretty rigorous. And the program can be intense. In Washington our annual cohort ranges between 25 and 45 fellows, chosen from more than 120 applicants. Applicants need three years of grad school or professional experience before we'll even consider them. New York, Chicago, and Los Angeles each get 60 to 100 applicants a year for 30 to 35 spots. We looked at maybe granting a credential through a friendly higher-ed institution. But that's not what we're about. An academic stamp doesn't advance our mission. We're focused on equipping young leaders to engage their communities and evangelize their peers through the witness of their professional and personal lives.

On challenges: Finances, obviously. In any city we serve, the program needs to be sustainable. Otherwise it's a waste of time and energy. We've had offers in other cities beyond our current four. In each case, donors have been willing to contribute generous seed money. But we've turned them down because we don't yet have the ability to sustain the work. Another temptation for any apostolate is mission creep. Any expansion of scope needs to be organic to the mission and very carefully thought through. It's best to stay in your lane. Do what no one else is doing. And it's important to figure out the one or two things you do really well, and then do them more and better.

In Father Roger Landry's words

Most of the fellows we accept are in the 24- to 32-year age range. We do get a few outliers. We look for positive, well-integrated personalities. We want people who are intelligent and ambitious in a good way, obviously; but also affable, can cooperate well with others, and really want to form community. We work toward a balance of men and women from different professions and backgrounds. We also try for a mix of persons already knowledgeable about the faith and others who aren't, but eager to learn more. The feedback we get from the fellows is that the Forum is unlike any other young adult opportunity they've experienced. They get much more intellectual formation from this program, but it overflows naturally into the rest of their Catholic lives. It makes them better at worship and better at service. So, being involved with the Forum is frankly one of the most rewarding aspects of my priesthood. I see the hunger for substance these very gifted young people have, coming from so many different disciplines. They want to grow in a way that's exactly the opposite of arrogance. They come in hungry, and we feed them in the best way possible.

ॐ ॐ ॐ

Augustine Institute

In its own words, the Augustine Institute (AI) exists to serve "the formation of Catholics for the New Evangelization. Through our academic and parish programs, we equip Catholics intellectually, spiritually, and pastorally to renew the Church and transform the world for Christ." Its overall success has been striking. As of 2023, the AI offered three fully accredited master of arts degrees: in theology, with a concentration in Sacred Scripture; in pastoral theology, with a concentration in catechetics; and in biblical studies. Coursework options include both on-campus study and distance education. Auditors and non-degree seeking students are also welcome as class size permits. The institute also offers a wide array of sacramental preparation and adult formation materials, short courses, K–8 curricula, and high school apologetics resources. Its popular *Formed* streaming service delivers "award-winning studies and parish programs, audio content, movies, eBooks, and family-friendly kids' programming to help Catholics worldwide explore the faith anywhere, anytime."

The AI began as a discussion among friends, none of whom had business experience: Tim Gray, Curtis Martin, Jonathan Reyes, and Sean Innerst. The original plan imagined AI as a lay formation program attached to Denver's St. John Vianney Theological Seminary. The preference soon shifted to an independent, stand-alone institute to ensure lay control and flexibility. Early funding was raised with the support of Denver's then-Archbishop Charles Chaput. Today the AI is among the most influential Catholic apostolic enterprises in the United States. Tim Gray, Ph.D., serves as president. Christopher Blum, Ph.D., serves as provost.

In Tim Gray's words

On challenges in and to the Church: The average Catholic's experience of the liturgy needs to improve dramatically. That's the frontline problem. The music tends to be bad, most homilies are mediocre, and there's just not enough "there" to nourish the spirit. People need to be inspired, challenged, and motivated. Otherwise, they drift away. I'm not a fan of the old Latin Mass, but why do people seek it out? It's because they're getting an experience there of beauty, mystery, and the sacred that's absent from their local parishes. Why do Catholics end up in evangelical churches? It's because they're getting homilies in those churches that are deep and rich and immediate to their circumstances; the preaching feeds them personally. Meanwhile, many of today's seminarians just aren't being equipped to deal with the postmodern questions they'll face in a parish. It's a crude analogy, but there's an element of "customer service" that the Church can't ignore. A business that can't see or doesn't address the needs of its customers won't be around for very long. The Church isn't a business. She'll be around until Christ returns. But the lesson is still worth learning.

On the "why" of founding the AI: When we lost the religious orders, the teaching orders, after Vatican II, the Church lost her hold on the education of her own people. And because of that, she then lost her ability to have any real influence on and in the world. Education is the key to changing that by forming deep lay discipleship.

On lessons learned: I was trained as a biblical scholar. I had to learn to be entrepreneurial. That meant I had to find the people to teach me, and then I had to find the humility to learn from them. I've made a lot of mistakes. The key is to stop repeating them. Friends warned me against having a strong board of directors that might interfere with the mission. That's a mistake. AI has a strong, professionally diverse, mission-passionate, and very involved board of trustees. It has forced us, in a healthy way, to review constantly what we're doing, what's working, and why; to focus on the right priorities; to sunset things that don't work; and to be absolutely transparent in our planning and finances. Another important thing is building a strong team. We've got a great CFO. We have a faculty committed to the mission and to excellence in their teaching. And Chris Blum is our provost; he's smarter than I am; and he has no problem challenging and disagreeing with me when he finds it necessary. The team makes the difference. Good talent won't work for a leader who's insecure and focused on taking all the credit for himself. Quality people just won't put up with that kind of behavior.

In Chris Blum's words

A game-changer for the institute is that we don't have undergraduate students. Most of our students are online adults. Their average

age is 40. Our relations with them tend to be mission-oriented and professional. And we're not teaching math or English or accounting, things like that. So, we don't have an army of faculty members whose commitment is filtered through their particular disciplinary lens. Our people are all focused on the same mission. That makes a huge difference. The intensity and clarity of Tim's devotion to the institute's purpose is the other key factor. Does he bat a thousand on issues and projects? No. But he's got a better batting average than anybody else. And certainly better than I would have.

In the words of an institute board member

I have a high bar for agreeing to support any organization. It needs to pass a three-part test: The mission needs to be important; the organization must be committed to excellence and capable of *actually achieving* the mission; and I need to believe that I can personally make a difference. I expected the AI to have a commitment to excellence, but that's been exceeded. Tim Gray is highly entrepreneurial, but also a humble leader. He welcomes strong people around him, encourages them to engage in healthy conflict, invites their criticism, and delivers on the mission. To understate the obvious: Not all leaders do that.

❧ ❧ ❧

Catholic Leadership Institute

Catholic Leadership Institute (CLI) seeks to improve and support the quality of Church leadership. And it has been uniquely effective in pursuing that goal, especially given the social and cultural transitions now underway. The institute targets clergy as its main audience, since clergy have the task of pastoral authority. But it also supports lay and religious staff working in Church ministry at the parish and diocesan levels. CLI stresses that leadership is distinct from, and involves more than, developing better management skills, though such skills are valuable. Leadership is fundamentally a mindset and relational. It's not purely a matter of technique. It requires an honest self-assessment; building a team to enhance one's strengths and compensate for one's weaknesses; and an ability to inspire others to join in the mission of the Church in a mutually supportive way.

One of CLI's most useful aids, with more than 600,000 responses nationwide, is its Disciple Maker Index, "a survey tool that supports Church ministry with objective data, helping Church leaders recognize their potential and envision future possibilities through a deep analysis of attitude and belief, participation, relationship/satisfaction, and demographics." Today, much of CLI's work consists in mentoring, coaching, and consulting. Special programs exist for priests, bishops, seminary formation, and empowering lay leaders. Founded in 1991 by Catholic businessman Tim Flanagan, CLI is led (as of 2023) by Richard Clark as chair and Dan Cellucci as CEO.

In Dan Cellucci's words

On the current moment: One of the biggest crises we face now is the "aging out" of priests who get escalating responsibilities as their numbers diminish. And there aren't many resources to help them. No matter how good their intentions, it's very difficult for priests, let alone anyone else, to develop a whole new skill set and level of energy as they approach retirement. And the pool of laypeople who might be well-formed enough to take their place, assuming that were even possible, is also aging. So, we have a serious gap opening in the number of priests and laypeople ready to accept the demands of leadership. We're on the brink of a generational shift with a huge transfer of wealth and change in priorities. It will profoundly affect the Church. So, we need to look at better indicators than simply counting offertory [collections] and tracking Mass attendance to get a more accurate picture about where we are and what to do about it. Then we need to plan and form people to lead accordingly.

On CLI methodology: It's an overused word now, but CLI's approach has always been accompaniment. Adult education is moving away from conferences and seminars toward individual growth plans, coaching, and mentoring. It's a mistake to think that all the Church needs is some practical tools; just training guys on how to look at a balance sheet. The issues are deeper than that, way, *way* deeper. Today it's more about understanding the bigger picture, mission alignment, and building trust and team relationships. We've revised the curricula of our programs at least six times over the past 20 years. We actually do less "training" now than we did in 2000. We do much more personal and team coaching, facilitation, and consulting.

On the single biggest obstacle: Fear. I work with a lot of bishops and priests. They're all good men. None of them is unaware of where we are, what's at stake, and what's going on, in and outside the Church. But looking at what's ahead of us, I do think there's a great deal of fear and paralysis. There's also a hesitation to make the kind of changes we need because of the inevitable pushback and repercussions. But leadership means facing and handling those things. Change is going to happen, with or without a plan. And it'll happen in one of two ways: through crisis, which is always ugly, or through prayerful, carefully thought-through choice. The latter is the better route, though in no way easier.

In a pastor's words

I've been a pastor for more than two decades, and I have a parish that was already in good shape. But it just felt like we were ready to take the next step. So, I asked CLI to come in and do some priority planning and facilitating. If you look at the positive things that've happened here, and the even better place where we are now, I credit that to CLI. And frankly, I understand much better now how I typically work, and the kind of people I need to have around me to help me function. CLI had a big effect on our hiring process and how we share parish administrative tasks.

In a bishop's words; diocese in the central United States

There's always some resistance to new things, but in my experience CLI thinks with the mind of the Church. They love the Church, and they love the Lord. They want to support priests and bishops in the best way they can. And that's been the feedback from my priests who've gone through CLI's "Good Leaders, Good Shepherds" program. Their parishes are thriving and growing. They're better organized and focused in their ministry. And they're better able to engage and motivate their people.

In the words of a board member

I was always intrigued by the concept of leadership in the Church. I was very involved in my diocese at the parish level. Then I get on the diocesan finance council, ended up chairing it ... and watched, in frustration, a complete unwillingness to make and monitor important decisions. I think the things we failed to do were really grievous. CLI recognized early on that developing leadership is not a short-term proposition. It's not something you learn at a weekend seminar. Changing behaviors and teaching leadership are a long-term process. And to its credit, CLI has always committed itself to the kind of accompaniment program where you walk with someone through this journey for two or three years.

꒰ ꒰ ꒰

Real Life Catholic

Chris Stefanick, founder and CEO of Real Life Catholic (RLC), is widely regarded as one of the leading Catholic lay evangelists, perhaps the best, of his generation. Intelligent, articulate, energetic, and personable, he has a natural preaching and teaching skill with few peers, which accounts for his popular appeal and his effectiveness in reaching, and moving, everyday Catholics in the pew. He began his career in youth and young adult ministry; an irony, since he had "zero interest in working with teens". Yet he "fell in love with the work" and did it for the next 15 years. Over time, he extended his reach to larger and broader audiences across all age groups.

In the 12 months before COVID, Stefanick reached nearly 200,000 people in his public evangelizing events. The pandemic, in its duration, killed a key source of financial support and threatened RLC's survival. But it also forced the ministry into new and creative forms of outreach. Today, Stefanick's books, videos, radio spots, reality TV show, and educational initiatives—courses like *Living Joy: 9 Rules that Will Change Your Life*, *The Search*, *Joseph*, and *The RISE Challenge*—reach millions of people. Among Stefanick's many strengths is a talent for helping men recover their roles as unselfish, faithful husbands, fathers, and leaders with the courage of their Catholic convictions—one of the most urgent needs in today's Church.

In Chris Stefanick's words

On Church renewal: Reform lies in becoming a kerygmatic Church again. Our main problem is a crisis of faith. Plenty of Catholics "get" the compassionate messaging of the Church. Their compassion, though, flows from a kind of modern Arianism, a lack of real faith that Jesus Christ is the Son of God who saves and transforms us. Too many people see the Church as a bundle of rules and rituals, doctrines and regulations. Those things clearly have their place, but they only make sense in the context of a relationship. What I admire most about Pope Francis' teaching is his stress on the kerygma, the proclamation of the Gospel as a *source of joy*. Our other great need as a Church is better small-group ministry. Intentional groups based in Christian friendship have power. They're a kind of front porch for the Church. They're the best forum for evangelization.

On the focus of RLC: Most Catholics aren't overly theological. They're not interested in academia. But a lot of people in ministry geek-out on that stuff. People come to RLC events and materials because they want something practical to help them live their lives better; that gives them joy; that shows them the connection of faith to life. If they can't get that in their parish, they'll go to another church where they can. I have a friend on staff at Pastor Rick Warren's [evangelical] Saddleback Church. His coworkers acknowledge internally that they're "the largest Catholic church in Southern California". And Rick Warren is not "anti-Catholic". His staff is simply stating a fact.

On RLC methodology: In our "Reboot" parish events we work with the parish staff for six months before I get there. We push them to invite their whole town to church, and not only through social media or Catholic radio. That doesn't really work; too few people pay attention. The best contact is person to person. The invitation needs to be personal. It's the same blueprint Billy Graham used. So we typically draw 750 to 2,000 people even in small towns. In my first Reboot talk I invite people to make a decision for the Lord. In the second, I talk about how to follow Jesus in your everyday life in a way that makes you a more joyful person. And we don't charge the parish a fee. We sell tickets. That sounds counterintuitive, but it works. The point is, we don't have a top-down approach. To start a brushfire in the Church at large, we need a hundred thousand "micro-fires" where everyone is invited to become a missionary. If we want to start a grassroots movement, we need to lower the barrier for entry into leadership. So RLC provides the small-group resources to help people simply pray together, get to know each other, share a life, and form communities that they can then invite a friend to, someone who might otherwise be lost on the outside.

On dangers in the work: Taking yourself too seriously; burnout; stealing time from your family and ignoring their needs; starting programs simply because you think a donor might like them; getting lazy with donors who already support you and becoming complacent; failing to constantly critique yourself and learn.

In the words of a former RLC board member

The key to RLC's effectiveness boils down to five things: live events; easily shareable content; a focus on igniting small groups; and providing the resources to do so. The fifth ingredient is Chris himself. He's relaxed and easy-going with a very pure effect on people. But his brain just never stops. He's always working, always refining, always wanting to do better. He collaborates well with other ministries. He's a magnet for seekers, whether they're Catholic or not. In fact, RLC gets a lot of feedback from people who aren't Catholic. RLC is designed for people *outside* the Catholic hot tub, while giving people *inside* that tub the tools to reach disengaged family and friends.

❧ ❧ ❧

Collegium Institute

Modeled broadly on the Lumen Christi Institute at the University of Chicago, the Collegium Institute serves Philadelphia's University of Pennsylvania community. Penn, founded by Benjamin Franklin, is the only Ivy League school with no original religious identity. This poses both challenges and advantages for Collegium's mission. Simply put, Collegium seeks to draw "mainstream learning into conversation with the Catholic intellectual tradition and cultivates reflection on the *catholic*, or universal, questions that animate every human life."

Like Lumen Christi, Collegium is committed to advancing faithfully the Catholic intellectual tradition. Unlike Lumen Christi, Collegium is entirely independent of Church structure as a lay initiative. Collegium began and survived in its early years with the support of two senior faculty members and Philadelphia's then-Archbishop

Charles Chaput. But it has thrived because of its leadership and content. By its 10th anniversary in 2023, Collegium was offering a wide range of programming: Medical Humanities, Legal Humanities, Young Catholic Leaders, Global Catholic Literature, Catholic Humanism Fellowship, Grad Fellows Colloquia, Post-Classical Language Workshops, the Anscombe Papers Project, Philosophy of Finance, Genealogies of Modernity, and ongoing lectures and symposia. While remaining an independent 501(c)(3), it's also established a programmatic partnership with the University of Pennsylvania's Program for Research on Religion and Urban Civil Society (PRRUCS) through its Perry-Collegium Initiative (PCI). Dan Cheely, Ph.D., a Penn graduate and Collegium cofounder, has served as Collegium's executive director since its inception and as executive director of PCI since 2017.

In Dan Cheely's words

On the "why" of his involvement: Early on as an undergraduate I came to develop a vocational sense that the Catholic intellectual tradition would not be engaged seriously in a secular university unless there were some Christian scholars there committed to making it happen. A few years into my grad studies, my father told me he had just finished a transformative novena to Our Lady Undoer of Knots. He encouraged me to pray one as well for career guidance. That felt premature to me, having only begun my dissertation, but I figured, why not. On the novena's ninth day, I got a voicemail from my best friend in college with an idea he wanted to propose. And that was the seed of Collegium.

On the Penn environment: Unlike other early American institutions of higher learning, Penn was founded with a mandate to pursue useful knowledge for the common good. Distinctively, it hosted no divinity school. But has that been an impediment for Collegium? I'd say that, in many ways, it has been the opposite. Its history creates the conditions for open-field running. We don't have the problem of an institution's hostility to its own religious past. On the other hand, at the start we didn't have an audience poised to contribute to theological discussions. People tend to encounter us as something new and interesting. Many of the undergraduates and faculty drawn to our programs are not Catholic or even broadly Christian. Often they're not even religious. But they're attracted by the openness and freshness of the conversations.

On Collegium's purpose: American universities tend to have a utilitarian ethos. Penn itself features world-class professional schools in medicine, law, education, nursing, business, design, and communications. But the university also appreciates that the practical skills of a profession don't necessarily lead to a good life. We help draw our academic community into conversation with the capital-C Catholic tradition, but also with the lowercase meaning of the *c*, in other words, *catholic* as "universal". That's not the same thing as "lowest common denominator" Catholicism. It's the common pursuit of moral wisdom through our attention to the questions that make all of us human. So, in our programs we try to bring people together across disciplines to reflect on the unity of truth. That's one of our central goals.

In a senior Penn faculty member's words

Benjamin Franklin never meant Penn to be "secular" in the modern sense. He wanted an environment that would be nonsectarian; that wouldn't privilege any particular faith. He never intended faculty and students to set aside their religious identities. He never intended the disdain for religion that now marks so many universities. Too many students arrive at university today and find that it's the worst place on earth to ask fundamental questions and pursue them in an open-minded, thoughtful, serious way. When you go to a Collegium event, there's no doubt that it's Catholic. It's never wishy-washy. But it attracts a broad diversity of Catholics and non-Catholics alike: students, faculty, and other interested parties. That's remarkable. And Dan Cheely is an exceptional leader: intellectually alive and engaged, and not afraid of multiple and competing perspectives.

From a Collegium graduate, now teaching in the Ivy League

Collegium was very important to my formation, both human and academic. It has a keen sense of how to bring people together with a variety of ideas and views at the table. It has a good strategic grasp of areas to focus on in culture and the intellectual life. It's simultaneously faithful and open-minded but always with a strong Catholic voice and presence. So, it's the model for the kind of institute we're trying to start where I teach now.

ॐ ॐ ॐ

Napa Legal Institute

The Napa Legal Institute (NL) is a religious freedom organization focused on nonprofit law, public policy, and legal talent development. It provides "corporate, tax, philanthropic, and other strategic education" to Catholic and other faith-based nonprofits, and helps to equip them "with the tools and resources they need so they can protect their organizations and achieve their missions." Unlike allied organizations such as the Becket Fund for Religious Liberty and Alliance Defending Freedom, both of which contribute members to the NL board, NL engages in proactive education, not litigation.

As NL materials stress, "Securing religious liberty is a proactive activity, as most legal battles are already won or lost outside the courtroom. We educate leaders on the steps they must take now in order to ensure their nonprofits can avoid litigation, compliance-focused attacks, and unforced errors in the public square." Or as one board member suggested, NL is where a nonprofit goes for "a legal health checkup ... in order to avoid open-heart surgery down the road". John C. Peiffer II cofounded NL with entrepreneur Tim Busch, and serves as its president and general counsel. Josh Holdenried led NL as its vice president and executive director through its start-up and program development. He was later succeeded by Mary Margaret Beecher.

In Josh Holdenried's words

On NL's founding: The people leading religious nonprofits are typically very driven, very energetic, and very dedicated to the goals of their apostolates. They're animated by mission, not operational fine print. They don't always have the resources or knowledge to think about all the other elements needed to achieve what they want to do. One of those elements is the law. In fact, law is the area that's typically most opaque and challenging for faith-based organizations. You can fly by the seat of your pants with various aspects of management or human resources, because they don't always require specialized talent. With the law, there's no faking it. You need good legal counsel, and preferably before you get into a crisis. John and Tim looked around and saw that there was no organization within the current religious liberty ecosystem that focused in a full-time way on corporate governance, tax compliance, guaranteeing a nonprofit's religious identity, and similar issues. So, that was the motive for NL.

On the current cultural terrain: One of the problems plaguing our country now is a misunderstanding of religious freedom; what it is, and why exercising it publicly is one of our basic constitutional rights. Religious freedom is more than just "freedom of worship". The cultural left has a real genius for hijacking language. Words control thought, which then controls the conversation, which pretty soon leads to the nature of an idea like religious liberty being warped and stolen. Worshipping in a church, temple, or mosque is a good thing. But religious faith can't be squeezed inside the four walls of a church. If it's blocked from having public expression and effect, then it's just a personal idiosyncrasy. And that's what's happening. Christian content on things like sexuality, abortion, and the nature of marriage and the family, is being deplatformed by social media corporations. Christian ministries need to be very explicit about their religious identity and its employment obligations in their governance documents and hiring practices. Otherwise they're being sued to do things that violate their beliefs; and the reason is, they're not sufficiently "religious" under the law.

On advice for religious nonprofit leaders: I helped start NL with a very small team. And even with John Peiffer's good mentoring, I found that the amount of necessary detail involved was overwhelming. So, I have a lot of respect for what it takes to operationalize an idea. Faith-based leaders can be tempted to develop a certain hubris because they believe they're on a mission from God. And because of that, they might think they're buffered from some of the routine errors made by secular nonprofits. That's a mistake. Don't make it. It's a common misstep among Christian ministries and apostolates, and it can come with a very high cost.

In the words of an NL board member

People who are drawn to starting or running nonprofits have incredible drive and at least some form of unique, substantive talent. They're not generally "utility infielders", though, when it comes to running a business. Mission creep is a temptation for many, many non-profits. But the biggest problem I see in the nonprofit space is that people don't think of it as running a business. The fact that you have a 501(c)(3) after your name doesn't mean that you're not basically a business. You may be tax-exempt, but you're still an enterprise with all of the issues, challenges, and problems any business has. NL is a kind of vaccination against needing the services of the Becket Fund or Alliance Defending Freedom down the road. Think of it as preemptive care. NL doesn't engage in litigation activity. That's not its purpose. It has an educational role. It provides tools and resources to faith-based nonprofits on issues like tax, labor, employment contracts, agency issues, franchising, and health care. That's its special niche; that's the real value it offers.

CHAPTER TEN

The New Americans

Through Immigrant Eyes

In America everything is too easy. Where I grew up, life was very different and sometimes very difficult. In Colombia, yes there's some wealth, but there's also a lot of serious poverty; people with literally no food to eat and no money to buy even basic necessities. In America, nearly everyone has the chance to live decently. And that can make you lazy and even a little crazy. Because in most of the rest of the world, life is hard.

—Monica Marin Tafur

People come to live and work in the United States from all over the world. They arrive here from many different backgrounds, and for many different reasons. A 2023 CNN news story suggested that the decline of American Christianity is overstated because so many of those who emigrate here from other parts of the globe are Christians. That would seem to make sense, because Christianity is now the most persecuted religion in the world. But all such news is finally misleading. How immigrants integrate *once they get here* is what matters. And it's a statistical fact that immigrant religious practice tends to erode sharply after the first or second generation. The Catholic Church has bled out especially among Latinos. A Pew Research Center study found that the percentage of Catholic Latinos had fallen from 67 percent in 2010 to 43 percent in 2022, while those with no religious affiliation rose from 10 percent to 30 percent. And Latinos were the group that held the most promise for a Catholic future. This suggests that in some ways, daily American life has become a master class in consumerist appetites, unbelief, and addictions.

Of course, there are exceptions, as seen in the following interviews. And even small seeds can grow, with enough encouragement and support, into something extraordinary ... as Somebody famous has already mentioned (Mt 13:31–32).

३० ३० ३०

Cristofer Pereyra, founder and president, Tepeyac Leadership Initiative (TLI), immigrant from Peru

You're a husband, a father, and a ministry leader with a keen interest in the nation's moral and political health. So, when you step back, what do you see as the decisive challenges facing the Church and the Christian faith in general in the United States today?

PEREYRA: That's an interesting question. Because when I look at the terrain, for those who are alive in their faith—Catholics actually practicing their faith—the Church is as strong as ever. But of course, they're something of a remnant; a fraction of what the Church used to be. So, the biggest problem we have is the massive body of baptized Catholics who are completely disengaged, not well catechized, and just don't realize what a tremendous compass the faith can be in their lives. The Church has a lot of work to do in terms of evangelizing her own faithful. That's the low-hanging fruit. And that's where the Church should concentrate her focus and can be the most effective.

How did we actually get to this place? It was a very different environment just a few decades ago.

PEREYRA: It didn't happen overnight. Our grandparents or great-grandparents, at some point, just ceased to pass along the faith. I myself was raised "Catholic", but only culturally so. I was born in northern Peru, and Peru gave me a very strong Christian value system. But I didn't practice my religion. It was here in the United States as an immigrant that I came back to the faith through the marriage preparation program of the Diocese of Phoenix. And I've been wondering about that. Maybe I can answer your question best through the immigrant lens and experience.

What is it about this nation that makes third- or fourth-generation descendants of Irish, Italian, Polish, or German immigrants leave their faith behind? And why do the newest Hispanic Catholic immigrants lose their faith just as fast? I asked [Los Angeles] Archbishop José Gomez—himself an immigrant from Mexico—that question. He said it's the prosperity. This country enables people to believe that they no longer need faith. And I can see that clearly in the community I know well, the Latino community. They come here, first-generation Mexicans, Colombians, or whatever they might be, and God will be an important part of their lives. Then they'll nominally pass the faith on to their children, because many of them come here for the American Dream and end up working two jobs a week. They're so busy that they can't really pass on anything of substance to their children in terms of Christian values or faith formation. So the second generation is already cheated. But the children will go to college, and they'll do better than their parents, and *their* children will do better than *their* parents. Meanwhile their faith weakens or disappears. It doesn't have to be this way. But prosperity is not a friend of the faith in some ways.

When you met your future wife here in the States, was she more religious than you?

PEREYRA: Yes, but she wasn't really a religious person.

So, what made you catch the virus? What made you believe in a more vigorous way?

PEREYRA: For me, it was a very utilitarian, pragmatic way of looking at what the Church could do for me. I knew I wanted to marry my wife. I wanted to marry her because I loved her. And I thought Catholic weddings were beautiful. Catholic churches were beautiful. So, the beauty of my wife, the beauty of a Catholic wedding—those things attracted me. And then, as we had our children, I remembered the influence the Catholic Church had had on me; growing up it was definitely a positive. I thought I could find in the Church an ally in forming my children. So, I thought, raising my children Catholic will help me keep them and myself out of trouble. I still didn't believe strongly. And they didn't care much for the faith, individually. But I thought I could use the Church.

You're an honest man.

PEREYRA: I thought I could use the Church. That was the plan: I'll use the Church to raise my children. So, I ended up converting myself in the process. I forced myself to take my children to Mass every Sunday, and the homilies started making sense to me. I started reading. But the original seed was the marriage preparation process, which was very serious in the Diocese of Phoenix. Coming out of that, it made me take a second look.

So, what did your wife think about it? She marries this nice, good-looking guy. And suddenly he starts getting religion. How did that play in your marriage and in the formation of your family?

PEREYRA: We've had some difficult moments. She allows me to lead, but we've had times when she's said: "Hit the brakes. What's going on? You're not a priest, and I'm not a nun." We have different views. So, we've continued to work on our faith at different paces. She mostly supports my choices and the way we raise the children, even when she thinks I'm overdoing it. Now we're in a good place. I pray every day she'll fall in love again with the desire to be a saint.

Thanks for your candor; people need real stories of faith they can believe, not fairy tales. But let's scroll forward: Now you're a ministry leader. You're dealing with bishops and diocesan structures in the formal, institutional life of the Church. To what degree do Catholic leaders in this country understand the scope and the nature of the problems facing the Church?

PEREYRA: By the time you're a bishop, you have a pretty good view of the lay of the land. And lots of priests understand the problems we're facing. But I don't think most have any idea as to what to do about them.

That's less than encouraging.

PEREYRA: We can't put the whole burden of fixing things on the shoulders of the clergy. That's not their responsibility; it's ours, as laypeople. It's my duty to help transform the culture. And that's what we're trying to do through the work of TLI. The bishops are scrambling to find answers with programs and pastoral plans. And unfortunately, most of them seem to yield no effect. Changing the culture is the domain of the laity, and bishops and priests should form laypeople accordingly. The bishops' job is to provide a set of principles based on Scripture and Catholic tradition. Then it's up to us, the laity, to use those principles; to come up with the best policies and strategies according to our local circumstances, because dealing with an issue like immigration in the United States won't be the same as dealing with it in southern Europe, or any other part of the world.

So, if our goal is a renewal of the Church, how would we help that happen?

PEREYRA: I do the work that I do because I *know* Catholic renewal is possible. And it will happen organically. We're not going to rebuild Christendom overnight. It took three centuries just for the Church to exist legally. And then another 10 centuries before we could identify a Christian civilization. We can't get back to that overnight. So, I think it will happen organically. When you look at young Catholics, the ones actually practicing their faith, they're intensely committed. This is where the Holy Spirit is working very powerfully. They're the hope of the Church. And we need to invest in guiding them properly, so they understand that their mission is a life of Christian witness in the world, 24/7.

You're an American citizen now, but as someone immigrating here from the outside, what was it about the United States that surprised you the most, that really marked it in terms of its national personality?

PEREYRA: I came here when I was 15. And my first cultural shock—I had many—was that there are really two Americas, and sometimes they merge. What I admire is the entrepreneurial energy of the United States, its adventurous spirit, creating new things, exploring, and always moving forward. But at the same time, people can easily become too self-focused, too acquisitive, too individualistic, forgetting about God. Where I live in Arizona, my neighbors are just everyday Americans with a flag outside their homes. They're all about God, country, and family. And I'm grateful for that. They're about giving themselves for the greater good of their community and nation, and being mindful of their Creator. But then I see the other America, the one that's greedy for personal wealth and privilege and power; the one that looks down on the rest of the country and thinks it has no need for faith.

How would you rate the current health of our country's political institutions; its public environment?

PEREYRA: It's bad. It's very bad.

That is sobering. But also probably true.

PEREYRA: It's unimaginably bad. There's no truly "civil" discourse at all. In the past, a politician would at least *pretend* to be a gentleman or lady. That's gone.

It seems we've been building to our current political toxicity for a long time. Donald Trump, with all his flaws, simply forced it to the surface. Does that sound right to you?

PEREYRA: I agree. He's the one that revealed it. You know, I see a similar thing happening in completely different circumstances. My wife is from Mexico, and I know the Mexican reality very well. The cartels have been there for decades; a cancer in Mexican society that's been there for a long time. But nobody talked about it. They operated under the surface. When the government [under former President Felipe Calderon] declared war on the cartels back in 2006, that brought them up to the surface. Now they don't even pretend to respect the law. They do even worse things now. So, you can see some parallels between the two situations, the United States and Mexico, even though they're very different realities.

So, where's this leading? We can't sustain a poisonous political environment forever. Some sort of order will need to be restored, coming from below or coming from above. And coming from above, in a kind of "soft" or not-so-soft authoritarianism that seems to be growing, is the uglier of the two choices. Where does Tepeyac Leadership Institute fit into these issues?

PEREYRA: I find a lot of peace in refusing to cry about society falling apart. And I don't worry about the collapse of Christian civilization. We're already standing in its ruins. The first Christians were just 12 men who set the world on fire. So, I think we're back to that, and it gives me hope. Because there's never been a better time to be a faithful and committed Catholic.

That's a true observation. But how do you operationalize it?

PEREYRA: I was the director of the Hispanic ministry office for the Diocese of Phoenix. And as an employee of the diocese, I was sent to a secular civic leadership development program in Arizona. It opened my eyes to the reality of creating capable leaders. There's a national association of leadership programs. It has about 200 affiliates in cities around the country. They all focus on bringing professionals into their fold, running them through a formation experience, and then placing them into key leadership positions in their communities. This is where most of our political, business, and nonprofit officials get their feet wet with leadership and begin building networks. I felt very lonely at times because I was one of the few conservative voices during discussions in the sessions. But I realized that what these programs were doing was a good thing to do.

Right after completing the program, I went back to [then-] Bishop [Thomas] Olmsted and said we can do something better. We can make it Catholic. He liked the idea. He gave me his blessing. And he said, "Well, go do it. Do it for Latinos, but not just Latinos; do it for the whole diocese." So that's how we created TLI. We took the template, a good template, from the secular world, and reworked it for our purposes. And that's what we're doing. We're forming Catholics for leadership in civil society: board service, philanthropy, politics, business, education, etc.

And how does the TLI program work?

PEREYRA: We're mainly a one-time experience, a very intense, one-time experience; five months you're in, you're out, you're done, and we send you off. A lot of Catholic professional associations and guilds already exist. And I've seen from up close the struggle to sustain their chapters. We don't want to get into that game. We do have a type of "leadership society", which graduates can join to support TLI financially and help us continue our mission. They have some perks, and we arrange some events, both virtual and in person. We also have an annual alumni/alumnae retreat, which is probably the most important thing we do for them. Every one of our graduates has an opportunity to come back once a year to renew himself or herself in that retreat.

What's the age spread of people who enter the program?

PEREYRA: We don't have an age restriction. But candidates do need to be professionals in the workforce and out of college. We get a lot of persons aged 25 to 35, along with some people in their 40s and 50s. If they still have a few years left in their work life and want to grow as leaders, Christian leaders, we'll take them.

A final question: How do you form your graduates in thinking about where to use their skills? Everybody can't be a senator.

PEREYRA: Our job is to refine and nourish the talent God places in their hearts. We create a space in which they can hear that calling within the TLI program. And we press each of our program partic-ipants to be attentive to that calling. If God is calling you to engage the public square in politics, for example, that's good. We encourage you to say yes. But you can have an *enormous* impact at the local level. So, begin by thinking local. You don't need to be president of the United States. Think public school district. People of faith, people with Christian values, have completely ignored that space, and look at the wreckage of our schools, schools that shape the next gen-eration. Think public school district; think municipality; think city council. And then build from there. That's how you shape the future.

৵ ৵ ৵

Monica Marin Tafur, Catholic marketing director,
immigrant from Colombia

You're a wife, a mother, and active in Catholic ministry. You're also an immigrant and naturalized U.S. citizen. As a "new" American, how would you describe the main challenges and problems facing the Church in the United States today?

MARIN: I think we are very distracted, both as a culture and as a Church. Social media change the way we interact with each other on a daily basis; they're full of information, but in practice they're a kind of barrier to real connections. In Colombia, people are just naturally closer to each other. Without that closeness, without the ability to have longer and deeper conversations with each other, it's hard to share our faith and pass it along to anyone else. We end up isolated, and we don't take responsibility for shouldering our part of the Church's mission.

I also think we're afraid of sacrificing anything, of getting too personally engaged with anything that makes demands on how we live. There's a resistance to "getting involved". So, a lot of people go to Mass because it's an obligation, but they don't really understand the meaning of their worship; they don't really give themselves to Jesus. Meaningful things take time and personal effort, and that's the opposite of where the current culture is taking us.

How is Church life different in Colombia from that in the United States?

MARIN: The sacraments are more available, with Masses every day— morning, noon, and night. Confession is available whenever you need it. And the Church has always been the natural place for personal connections and friendships. The Church in Colombia is just more present and open to the people. I do think, though, that Church attendance is decreasing because of the country's political violence and other factors.

You've been working in a Catholic media ministry now for nearly a decade since immigrating. Do you get a sense that American Church leaders, and American Catholics at large, understand the nature and scope of the problems facing the Church in this country?

MARIN: I think the bishops are good men, and they do their best to defend the Church. But they're meant to be fathers of their communities first, and I wish sometimes they were closer to their people.

They can seem removed or distant because of their duties. They need to just "be there" for their people on a more regular basis. The power of a living, personal presence applies to everyone. It applies to marriages, families, parishes, and dioceses. It applies to spouses, and it applies to bishops.

How did you come to your faith? Was it an adult conversion or did you grow up in a devout family?

MARIN: My mother was Catholic, but she wasn't practicing. Growing up, I remember we would pray at night before going to bed. We'd go to church sometimes, and I remember feeling very loved, but my mom would never take Communion. I went to Catholic schools because we were a Catholic country. But when I was preparing to do my First Communion, the only gift I asked for was that my parents would go to confession and take Communion with me. It was the only gift I wanted. And after that, my mother converted and began practicing her faith again. My dad went to confession, and took Communion that day as well. I still pray for his conversion.

I had friends who were serious about their faith and very happy in how they lived it, and that had a big impact on me. And later I read Thérèse of Lisieux's autobiography, *The Story of a Soul*. That was the game-changer. I would walk to church and go to Mass by myself, just trying to figure things out. I knew God wanted something from me, something more. So, that's how it happened. And then I met The Work [Opus Dei].

When and how did you meet Opus Dei?

MARIN: Through my best friend in Colombia. I was maybe 17 or 18. She invited me to one of The Work's meditations. And it just clicked, because I knew I wasn't made for a normal religious vocation. I had a boyfriend. I was studying engineering in Manizales. I was partying and having fun with my friends. And I was still going to Mass, but I didn't have a sense of how I could live a real Catholic life until I joined The Work. That was maybe 25 years ago. The Work gave me Christian friendship and community. And that was very important in my early years, because it taught me that a person really can reach holiness, no matter what your age, just by living your life in a conscious, daily, dedicated Christian way.

In some ways the Church can seem like a pretty broken place right now. How do you maintain your faith?

MARIN: I've been blessed to truly know God in his Son Jesus Christ. We're all sinners. The Church is led by people who make mistakes and commit sins just like I do. I've made some huge mistakes in my life. But the flaws in priests and bishops never scandalize me, because my primary relationship is with Jesus. Neither the pope, nor the bishops, nor anyone else is responsible for my pursuing God's call to sainthood. It's *my* responsibility.

When you think about holiness, how do you describe it?

MARIN: It's learning how to love as Jesus did. That's holiness. We have the Mass and the sacraments to feed and guide us, but the main thing is having a relationship with God that leads us to love as Jesus did.

What do you see as the one or two things in the American personality that created the situation that we're in right now? Every nation has a particular strength and weakness. And when you grow up in it, sometimes you're not even aware of its character. But when you come into it from the outside, you might see things more clearly.

MARIN: In America everything is too easy. Where I grew up, life was very different and sometimes very difficult. In Colombia, yes there's some wealth, but there's also a lot of serious poverty; people with literally no food to eat and no money to buy even basic necessities. In America, nearly everyone has the chance to live decently. And that can make you lazy and even a little crazy. Because in most of the rest of the world, life is hard.

Just one more question. You were a successful woman in Colombia with two master's degrees. You had a professional life that was satisfying. And then you meet a man online, a man with a severely disabled daughter, and you take the risk of marrying him and moving to another country. Why? Why did you do that?

MARIN: Yes, that's an interesting question. I suppose most women wouldn't have taken the risk. When I first came to visit John [her husband], I asked him to bring along his daughter, Veronica. She has cerebral palsy, a serious seizure disorder, a feeding tube, and other problems. She needs total care. So, I had to know if I'd be willing to move to America, because I knew that Veronica would be part of our lives. I had a friend who cares for her disabled parents in Colombia, and she told me, you need to be *very, very* sure about this, because it's not easy. It won't be easy. And it won't get any easier.

But when I saw John doing everything he does each day to care for Veronica, I knew that he had a good heart. I mean, his heart is capable of loving so much. So, I'm just so grateful for John. And I'm so grateful for Veronica. I always tell our son, Thomas, that *he's* here because of Veronica. If Veronica hadn't been born, I wouldn't have met your father, because Veronica changed your dad's life. Veronica is the reason that we're the family we are now.

Veronica has taught us how to enjoy the little things. How little achievements are so important. When she learned how to brush her teeth by herself, that was huge for me. And she's taught us how to be patient. People sometimes say it's hard, you know, for John and me to have a daughter with so many challenges like Veronica. It isn't true. She's a blessing for our family. She has taught us how to be closer to God. And John is the man he is today because of her. Because of Veronica. She helped the seed of love grow in her father's heart.

CHAPTER ELEVEN

True Confessions

On the Problem and Its Solution

In ordinary life we hardly realize that we receive a great deal more than we give, and that it is only with gratitude that life becomes rich.

—Dietrich Bonhoeffer

My career began very far, both in distance and in content, from where it will end. I'll explain. I wanted to be a screenwriter. So, after grad school and a year working in New York, I moved Suann, myself, and our infant son to Los Angeles. I was lucky. I got a good agent, juggled three part-time jobs to pay the bills, and started to write. As it turned out, I was bad at writing for the screen, but very good at analyzing scripts. My agent also represented Burt Reynolds, Julie Christie, and other big stars of the day, and he would pass along to me the screenplays that were submitted for their consideration. There was no glamor in it. Basically, I served as their first line of garbage detection. In the evenings, working as a night guard, I'd read 20 scripts a week, paid at the lavish per-piece rate of $5 a screenplay. One or two would be worth moving up the food chain.

Over time, I began to read for producers as well. Every once in a while a gem would float by on the river of Hollywood effluence. And there came an evening when a then-unpublished book manuscript by a little-known novelist struck me as stunningly good. The producer I worked for laughed, said the text was "goofy", and declined to option it. The novel was titled *The Shine*. It's better known today as *The Shining* by Stephen King.

But why am I telling you this.

Here's why. Film done well has unique dramatic power. It's visual, absorbing, and immediate in its nature. Whatever truths it tells about the human condition linger a long time in the memory. Exactly such a film is *True Confessions*.

And yet ... "I *hated* that movie." So said a very fine priest friend some years ago when I mentioned the film. Looking back, I'm not surprised. Released in 1981 and based on the John Gregory Dunne crime novel of the same name, it's not a happy portrait of the Church, her people, or her clergy. But in the end, it always moves me. It's one of my favorite films, and I would argue that it's a profoundly Catholic one.

True Confessions begins and ends in the 1960s California desert. But the bulk of the story takes place in 1947 Los Angeles. It revolves around the Black Dahlia–like murder of a young woman, a failed actress turned prostitute. In real life, the Black Dahlia murder has never been solved. In *True Confessions*, the killer is finally identified, but he's irrelevant to the story's unintended consequences. The heart of both the novel and the film is the fractious relationship between two Catholic brothers: Des and Tom Spellacy.

Des, played in the film by Robert De Niro, is a rising young monsignor, chancellor of the archdiocese, right hand to the cardinal, and on the fast track to be a bishop. Tom (Robert Duvall, in one of his finest roles) is an LAPD detective; the "black sheep" son of their Irish Catholic family. Cynical toward life in general and the Church in particular, Tom Spellacy is the lens through which the story unfolds.

Tom is a complicated soul: resentful of his brother's perceived goodness, calloused by the meanness of the streets, but also protective of his brother's reputation. Des Spellacy is no less complex: smart, shrewd, ambitious, and (when necessary) ruthless—and also keenly aware of his own sin of pride, masked by a veneer of priestly piety. Onto Tom's police plate drops the case of the murdered young woman. Where it leads provides the rest of the drama.

John Gregory Dunne, the author, came from a Catholic family of six children. He knew the Church, and especially the Irish American version of her, from experience. His writing vividly captures the time and place, the language and culture, of the Church and a certain kind of Catholic life at the zenith of their social influence and political connections.

True Confessions takes place in the pious afterglow of the Second World War, 15 years before Vatican II and nearly four decades before the first hints of a clergy sex-abuse crisis. The story is a long way from sacred in its tone. But those who spent their childhood in the 1950s will remember the high esteem routinely accorded to the religion of the times; times quite different from our own. In effect, *True Confessions* is an exercise, unintended, in true instruction. Dunne's story is excessively harsh in its portrait of ecclesial life and its warts, but it's not entirely wrong. Over my 27 years in diocesan service, I met Des Spellacy, or versions thereof, more than once. I also met laymen like Tom Spellacy—and a lot more frequently than Des.

What *True Confessions* captures well is the human temptation to use the Church as fire insurance for the afterlife; or more tangibly, for personal advancement or profit. She can be a helpful tool and a very cleansing alibi for crooked actions wrapped in the vocabulary of virtue. And the temptation can easily grow as the social influence and political standing of the Church increase. Today this may sound absurd. The Church is steadily losing ground and numbers in the United States. As many as a third of priests approached to serve as bishop decline the office because of its demands. But we have the Church of 2023, at least in part, because we once had the Church of 1947.

Early Christian writers like Origen, Hippolytus, Tertullian, and Tatian all spoke forcefully against the corrupting effects of entanglements with worldly authority. Church attitudes obviously changed after Constantine's conversion. The vocation of laypeople, in particular, is to be leaven in secular culture, to sanctify the public sphere. But history teaches that alongside the great good that can be achieved through Christian engagement in public leadership, great harm can be done to the Church and her mission when her people and her clergy confuse material success with service to the Gospel. A comfortable Church, a colluding Church, a publicly esteemed Church can very easily become a dead Church. And when faith is merely skin deep, it's worth remembering that societies sooner or later shed their dead skin.

Simply put: Ambition, power, success, and public respect, like wealth, are not necessarily bad things. It's how and why we use or abuse them that matters. Especially for Christians, this should be obvious. Yet it's quite clearly not. But more on that in a moment.

ว๛ ว๛ ว๛

We need to remember who we are.

Memory matters. History matters. The past is our human diary; a record of who we are, what we've experienced, what works and what doesn't. That's why the French mystic Simone Weil warned that "the destruction of the past is perhaps the greatest of all crimes." And it's why, in his novel *1984*, George Orwell wrote that "he who controls the past controls the future; [and] he who controls the present, controls the past."

What Orwell meant is this: In the hands of ambitious people, control of the present becomes a tool to erase and rewrite the past. And once the past is reinvented, it becomes a tool to command and reroute the future. This is the spirit that drives so much of our current toxic culture. And it's why giving power to people who describe themselves as agents of progress, but include in their idea of "progress" the right to kill an unborn child, turning abortion into a perverse kind of sacrament, is so dangerous.

For us lay Catholics, this nation is our home. It's the mission field of our discipleship. But as a people, Americans have always been ambivalent toward the past. On the one hand, the Founders were shaped by biblical morality and Enlightenment thought. They admired the Roman Republic and the Classical Age. These things shaped the checks and balances in the structure of our government. They explain the importance of precedent in our legal system. They explain the architecture of the early public buildings in Washington. The Founders consciously created an experiment in ordered liberty. And they rooted it in lessons from the past. In other words, they made a country where responsibilities and rights, communitarian concerns and individual freedom, democracy and republican safeguards, law and impulse, reason and emotion, would balance each other and produce a healthy and dynamic unity.

The problem lies in the words the Founders themselves used. We're a *novus ordo seclorum*; an entirely "new order of the ages". As a nation, we're manufactured. We're a product of the human mind.

We're not really "organic" in the sense of ethnicity or even a single language group. Our system works very well when people share a basic mutual respect and the same broad moral convictions. And it doesn't, when they don't. That's where we find ourselves right now.

Americans have always been a nation of pragmatists and innovators with a fierce individualist streak. Dragging around the past as a kind of mortgage on the future is a burden. It interferes with our freedom to reinvent ourselves and everything around us. In some ways this is a strength. But it also means we forget things we need to remember, like the cost of self-indulgence.

The Founders revered the early Roman virtue of *pietas*. It was a mix of piety, duty, and maybe most importantly, *gratitude*. Self-mastery and self-sacrifice, grounded in a spirit of gratitude, are the pillars of mature adulthood. They're also the marks of personal character that make a real community possible. What we have instead today as a nation is an empire of desire. And that empire and its appetites are restrained by no overarching truth that judges us all and binds us together. We have only your truth and my truth. And then "truth" becomes merely an alibi for the arbitrary will of whoever has power and the ruthlessness to keep it. We saw where that leads in the last century. It's not a life or a society worthy of human beings.

Roger Scruton, the late British philosopher, once wrote that "St. Paul was right to recommend faith, hope, and love as the virtues that order life to the greater good." But he added that *false* hope, "hope detached from faith and untempered by the evidence of history, is a dangerous asset, and one that threatens not only those who embrace it, but all those within the range of their illusions." I believe those words are wise and true. They're true in the sense of *triewe*, the Old English root of the word, which means "trustworthy, honest, and real". So, it's the task of the Church to offer people *triewe* hope rooted in Jesus Christ and alert to the lessons of history.

For the Church, history as our shared Catholic memory does two crucial things. It teaches us humility, and it teaches us the real nature of hope. *Humility*, because history is one long lesson in our sins, mistakes, and failures. But also *hope*, because despite our best efforts at destroying our own baptismal dignity and the mission of the Church down through the centuries, here we still are. God is true. God is trustworthy. And he keeps his covenants.

Memory is the cornerstone of a sane and fruitful life. And it plays the same role for every community of purpose. It's why we need to look back to think forward. The past can be an escape route to imagined happier times. But for Christians, it's a grounding and a compass. Some years ago, while I was researching material for a lecture, a rabbi friend introduced me to the Hebrew word *zakhor*. It means "remember". The command to remember is the key to Jewish identity, survival, and hope. And so it is for us. The work of remembering who we are, what we believe as Catholics, and why we're here on mission in the world is sacred. It runs directly counter to our current American culture, which reduces us to consumers and cocoons us in a permanent present of appetites, distractions, and anesthetics.

The reason we can hope in the future is our experience of the past and its record of the constant saints among us. We moderns tend to think that the era of the saints is over. But we're wrong. It's always the era of the saints.

≈ ≈ ≈

It's always the era of the saints.

Those words, and the confidence behind them, belonged to the writer Georges Bernanos ... the same Bernanos who described the Church as an unending train wreck, save for one redeeming fact: her saints; the same Bernanos who went on to lament that "a cardinal is recognizable from so far away by his beautiful scarlet cape, while a saint is not in his lifetime distinguishable by the slightest detail of his clothing." His point was simple. When Scripture speaks of "the cloud of witnesses" who surround us (Heb 12:1), we rightly think of the holy men and women who have gone on to God before us. But they're also among us, living here and now, too ordinary to be noticed.

Saints are numerous. Saints are varied. They always have been. That's the nature of Christian life. Today's world, for all its noise and indifference, is no exception. And our saints include more than just the towering figures that populate our religious imagination; whose great works can loom over us like the face of Everest. If a famously difficult man like St. Jerome can be a Father of the Church and a model of Christian faith, there's room on the train for you and me.

Sanctity seems hard to us, Bernanos said, because we don't understand it. Many of us never seriously wonder what it is. But "saints" are merely people who one day become aware that they, and those around them, are each an *imago Dei*; we're made in the image of God. They consider what that means. They think about what it requires. And then—this actually *is* the hard part—they act accordingly. They pay attention to the real meaning of Christ's words in the Acts of Apostles: "You shall be my witnesses in Jerusalem and in all Judea and Samaria and to the end of the earth" (1:8).

Pious intentions come and go. Actions remake the world. That's why the book is called *Acts*.

I've always loved words. They have beauty and power. I've made a living using them, and the story behind each is often instructive. The word "witness" comes from the Old English *witnes*. It means "one who bears testimony". It has the same meaning as *martyr* in Greek. It's also related to the Latin verb *confiteri*, "to affirm, acknowledge, admit". We confess our sins, but we also confess our faith at the Creed in every Sunday Mass. In the Christian tradition, "martyr" has come to mean someone who dies for his or her faith. A "confessor" is someone who bears testimony to the faith, someone who confesses Jesus Christ in the face of hostility or persecution, but without suffering death. Christians are confessors by nature.

In that sense, every person interviewed for this book was chosen precisely to "confess" what he or she thinks and believes at a difficult time in the life of the Church ... so that we might consider and learn.

The America of 2023 is ruled by two mutually reinforcing features, neither consonant with a Christian life: ingratitude and fear. Each is masked by a screen of distraction. But the *ingratitude* is obvious. It undergirds our world of self-absorption; the deep well of material appetite that drives our economy and demands a relentless creation of new dissatisfactions and desires. The *fear* is less obvious but even more pervasive. It's in the air we breathe: fear of failing; fear of being worthless and powerless and alone; fear of being cast outside the herd; fear of losing what we have; fear of dying; all of which feeds today's permanent sense of emergency and transfers control of our lives to others. And just as love casts out fear (1 Jn 4:18), fear extinguishes love. We've built a loveless world. Now we're forced to live in it.

So, what shall we do?

The task of any "new reformation", any purifying re-formation of Church and world, begins with each believer. We don't really want to hear that. The personal sounds too small, too slow, too pious. We Americans compulsively think big. It's in our DNA. We want plans, policies, programs, and committees; the machinery that gets things done. But all such things are external and secondary to the deeper problem: ourselves.

The reason "personal conversion" seems so pathetically irrelevant to the Really Big Issues of life is that nobody wants to do it. We don't do it—*I* don't do it—because it's hard. It takes time and effort. It's easy to sign a petition or put a self-exonerating social justice sign on your lawn. But it's brutally hard to examine and know and speak the truth to ourselves; to honestly acknowledge our own sins and hatreds; to be grateful for what we have; to repent and convert; to forgive those people whose views and behaviors most offend us; to make ourselves useful in the needs and sufferings of others. But it's only when we do these things that life becomes fertile and rich; a magnet for the broken and lost; the beginning of a new world.

There's a line toward the end of *True Confessions* (the novel) that has always moved but puzzled me until now. In the course of the story, all of the once-worldly Des Spellacy's Church ambitions and influence, along with his reputation and pride, are destroyed. And yet he calls this his "salvation". Now, near the end of his life, he's the pastor of a small, dirt-poor parish in the California desert. In a moment of reconciling with his brother, he says this: "I have no gift for loving God. I still don't. [But I discovered] that wasn't a drawback as long as I could be useful, and out here in this godforsaken place, I am useful ... I'm useful to these people ... There's a kind of peace in that ..."

... as well as a kind of love. It's not sainthood, but it's the seed of a start. We need a lot more of it.

AFTERWORD

Homage to Good Men

Friends and Their Witness

I think many Catholics, Catholics who are active in Church life, have the feeling that their Church—the visible Church—is losing ground inexorably. But this is a wrong impression. We can never see everything. The Church is bigger than my parish, the Church in Paris, the Church in France, or the Church in the United States. One thing [Cardinal Jean-Marie] Lustiger taught me, or rather what I learned from him because he never taught it explicitly, is that you've got to see things from the point of view of the history of creation and salvation. Everything else is just shortsighted.

—Jean Duchesne

In *The Four Loves*, C. S. Lewis described friendship as "unnecessary" but also as beyond price. Friendship is "like philosophy, like art, like the universe itself (for God did not need to create). It has no survival value; rather it is one of those things which give value to survival." In a good friendship, "each member often feels humility toward the rest. He sees that they are splendid, and counts himself lucky to be among them."

Mothers shape the early lives of their sons. Wives anchor their husbands in reality and purpose. But men are made better men by the friendship of other, better men. Over the years I've known too many good men, too many good *friends*, to list here. But I offer the men I interview below—Jean Duchesne, Enrique Elias Dupuy, Joseph Fessio, and Charles Chaput, all of whom I've admired and treasured as friends for decades—as four of the very best of men. And each one

243

of them is a reason why the Christian life, lived and shared well, is infinitely rich.

೩ౚ ౚ৵ ౚ৵

Jean Duchesne, Paris

Husband and father, author, educator, and friend of theologians Louis Bouyer, Henri de Lubac, Hans Urs von Balthasar, and others, Jean Duchesne is cofounder of the French edition of the international theological journal *Communio*. He served for decades as confidant, friend, editor, translator, and largely invisible but irreplaceable aide to one of the greatest Catholic figures of the last century: Aron Jean-Marie Lustiger, the Jewish-born cardinal archbishop of Paris.

Where were you born? And do you have siblings?

DUCHESNE: My grandparents came to Paris from western France. My parents were born in Paris. I was born in Paris. My children were born in Paris. So were my grandchildren and perhaps soon my great-grandchildren. So, I'm afraid Paris is becoming a habit. I have a sister a few years younger than I am. She lives in southern France.

What about your parents?

DUCHESNE: Well, I have a complicated background. Both of my parents, when they were children, lived in the same middle-class apartment building. The Duchesne side of my family were good Catholics. They'd been mostly poor peasants and moved to the city to find a job. They were helped by Catholic Charities to adjust to the new working-class milieu in the suburbs. My mother's side was different. They were active laypeople in the French *laïcité* sense. My maternal grandfather was scrupulously honest, but a very secularized person, a good republican; my mother was a bit like him. He never went to church, even on Christmas or Easter. The two families barely acknowledged each other. And my parents never met because they went to different schools. So, the families were two distinct cultural networks, except for one detail. And that was dancing lessons. At the time, the children of good families were expected to learn how to dance for social events.

So, they fell in love dancing.

DUCHESNE: They married in 1934. My father served in the French army during the war. He was taken prisoner and sent to Germany, but he faked his papers as an essential worker on the French railways and escaped. I was born in September 1944. Paris had been liberated just a few weeks before.

You were raised Catholic.

DUCHESNE: My mother did not object to my being baptized.

But how did you come to your adult faith?

DUCHESNE: I did the usual catechism and sacraments. But I wasn't convinced about religion. I remember, on a retreat, reading a terrible story about some martyrs, and I thought: I'm not a candidate; I don't see my vocation as being butchered. I was skeptical until I was 20. And then a friend asked me to join him on a cultural expedition to Israel to visit kibbutzim. At the time, the kibbutz experiment was very fashionable, because it was a kind of a noncommunist socialism. So I said yes. I didn't do any research. I just filled in the forms. It turned out to be a Catholic pilgrimage that my friend had carefully concealed from me.

So, I went to the Holy Land dragging my feet, and when we reached Jerusalem, of course I was shaken by everything. But there's a difference between an emotional experience, discerning the reality and coherence of the faith, and then giving yourself up to it. So, I decided to do something radical. I would spend the night alone in the Holy Sepulchre. I told others in the group, so that no one would look for me. Then I stayed behind in the church and waited until everything was closed. And I hid in a corner; there are a lot of corners in the Holy Sepulchre. Have you been there?

Yes. And there are a lot of corners.

246TRUE CONFESSIONS

DUCHESNE: I had only one thing with me; it was a book for pilgrims. So I read. And I listened. There was an incredible variety of unexpected, almost indecent noises. Yells, moans, doors creaking, sometimes the singing of liturgies. There was one sentence in my pilgrim's book from Pope Paul VI that struck me; he had visited Jerusalem in 1964. He said that what matters is not whether [the location of the Holy Sepulchre] is really here, but rather, Who it was that brought me here, to this church, today. So, I said OK, I got the message. I didn't really know what I was doing, but I obeyed what I felt without knowing. The following morning, I showed up with my group for breakfast, because I was hungry. And then I discreetly looked for a priest who didn't know me too well. I had confession, and from then on I became incapable of saying no when something was asked from me that I could see was not merely coming from the man who asked it.

How did you meet your wife, Marie-José?

DUCHESNE: I met her two years later, on a pilgrimage led by Father Maxime Charles. Father Charles had founded the Centre Richelieu in Paris, the chaplaincy for Catholic students at the Sorbonne, in 1944. And one of his first recruits had been a young Jewish convert named Jean-Marie Lustiger. Lustiger then became a priest and then became his number two. And when Charles was promoted to the Basilica of the Sacred Heart in Montmartre in 1959, Lustiger succeeded him at the helm of the Centre Richelieu.

The move to Montmartre wasn't really a promotion, though, because Charles had made a nuisance of himself within the French Church. He was too successful. At the time, the French Catholic motto was "immersion"—submerging the faith into human realities so as to evangelize people discreetly, one milieu at a time. At least that was the theory. Charles, on the contrary, organized large, very visible groups of young people for pilgrimages to Chartres Cathedral. He managed to lead 15,000 students on the roads from Paris to Chartres. He organized a pilgrimage of 1,000 students to the Holy Land every summer. He had public meetings, filling the Paris equivalent of Madison Square Garden—15,000 seats or more—for debates on the faith. Things like that. And this was unbearable to many of his fellow clergy. So, he was made a monsignor and kicked upstairs. But once at Montmartre, he started what he called "biblical Adoration". Instead of just saying the Rosary in front of the Sacrament, he led people to read and meditate on the Bible, and to realize that the exposed Host was something living, something that spoke, and its words could be found in Scripture.

Monsignor Charles made you a leader in his student group at Montmartre, correct?

DUCHESNE: Yes.

And that group included Marie-José, but also your friends Jean-Luc Marion and Rémi Brague, both of whom went on to become significant philosophers, as well as the then-seminarian and now historian and theologian, Father Jean-Robert Armogathe. And together you founded the French edition of Communio, *the international theological journal.*

DUCHESNE: Jean-Robert was not part of the *Communio* founding group because he still was in seminary and his superiors at the time would have frowned on it as not "ecclesiastically correct".

How did you come to know and work with Lustiger?

DUCHESNE: I met him just after the Holy Land pilgrimage organized by Monsignor Charles. He preached a retreat at Chartres, and at the time I couldn't stand him. He was so insolent, so sure of himself, and every time we came across each other we quarreled, but it was a family squabble. I didn't like his arguing that disbelief was just moronic. Maybe our friction was because we had the same spiritual "father" in Maxime Charles. Lustiger was 18 years older than I, and 18 years younger than Monsignor Charles, so I could never figure out whether Lustiger was a father to me or an older brother.

So, you start by disliking him and end up with a very long-term and close working friendship; how did that happen? Meanwhile you're building your own career as a professor and author, so you have two different professional streams flowing at the same time. How did you reconcile that?

DUCHESNE: I didn't reconcile the two streams; they reconciled me. It just worked out that way. There was never a break in my relationship with Lustiger. We simply disagreed on certain things. And perhaps he was not always wrong (*laughs*). Lustiger was above all a pastor, a shepherd. For him, anything intellectual was purely instrumental. Such matters interested him personally, but a good idea was never "good" in itself; it had value only if it could be of some pastoral use. In his spare time he was more open, but on duty he had a kind of "pastoral utilitarianism". He thought Marion, Brague, and I were too intellectual.

Of course, Monsignor Charles had enabled that. It was Monsignor Charles who had connected us with the theologians Louis Bouyer and Jean Daniélou, who then put us in touch with Henri de Lubac, who in turn connected us with Hans Urs von Balthasar. This was from about 1967 through the early 1970s. All of them tutored us privately, at one time or another, at Charles' expense, and he never interfered. Balthasar also introduced us to his German friend Joseph Ratzinger, and all of them wrote articles for *Resurrection*, the student theology review we had at Montmartre that preceded the founding of *Communio*.

So, you developed an increasingly close friendship with Lustiger through your mutual friendship with Monsignor Charles. How did Lustiger become a bishop? And how did you end up assisting him for nearly 30 years?

DUCHESNE: It's a long story. In 1974, Jean Daniélou asked us to launch *Communio*'s French edition. *Communio* had been started in 1971 at the first meeting of the International Theological Commission, by Balthasar, Ratzinger, Daniélou, Lubac, and a few others. Balthasar took responsibility for the German edition, and Daniélou for the French edition, but he was busy and not a very good administrator, so he asked us laymen, the "young guys", to run it. Our first editorial meeting took place at Daniélou's home in Paris in March 1974; he had been ostracized by his fellow Jesuits for allowing himself to be named a cardinal. Balthasar was there at the meeting, along with Daniélou's editor from Fayard publishing. But Daniélou died shortly thereafter, and Fayard withdrew its involvement. We had to travel to Basel in Switzerland to ask for Balthasar's support. He bought us lunch at the restaurant of the zoo, close to his home, and I'll never forget how he anointed us just above the zoo's bears' den: "Just succeed," he said, "and I'll help you."

So, Balthasar came to Paris two or three times a year to talk with us and see what we were doing with *Communio*. And once we married couples—the Duchesnes, the Marions, the Bragues—started having children, we needed to find a place for him to stay because we didn't have room, and hotels were too expensive. At the time, Lustiger was pastor at Ste. Jeanne de Chantal in Paris. He had refused our invitation to join the *Communio* board for two reasons: He said that he was no intellectual, and that he already had enough enemies in the Paris clergy. But he was happy to have Balthasar as a guest during his visits to Paris, because he could have breakfast privately with him every morning.

Marie-José and I would sometimes attend Mass at Lustiger's parish because his homilies were unusual and interesting. There was a woman in his parish who would hold up a tape recorder during his homilies—people called her the Statue of Liberty—and then transcribe them with the help of others. But that didn't make pleasant reading, and Lustiger asked me and also the Marions to edit and rewrite them, to see if they might be publishable. So, I started doing some editing and publishing for him.

What year was that?

DUCHESNE: I think the book of homilies took more than two years to finish between 1976 and 1978 because at the last minute Lustiger didn't want his name on it. It was a painful business. He wanted it entitled *The Homilies of a Paris Parish Pastor*, without mentioning his name. And of course the publisher, Fayard, had no interest in releasing an anonymous book. In the end, Lustiger wanted the royalties for his parish, so he finally agreed to have his name on the cover.

Then in 1979, having been a pastor for 10 years, he felt that he'd had enough. He decided to find some religious Sisters in the Holy Land and work for them as their gardener, like Charles de Foucauld had done. Plus, being Jewish, he wanted to do his *Aliyah*, his return to Israel. But before he could do it, he received a letter from the nuncio inviting him to come for a visit. And that's when he learned he had been offered the appointment as bishop of Orléans. He told me later that he was disturbed by the news and wrote the pope a personal letter; John Paul II at the time. He asked if the pope knew he was Jewish; that his mother had died at Auschwitz; that he had been baptized in Orléans; that Orléans had a history of anti-Semitic rumors; and that he himself was unpopular with the Paris clergy and had a history of friction and conflicts with his fellow priests.

The pope wrote back promptly with a very short note, which Lustiger summed up in five words: "Yes, I know. Then what?" He never actually showed me the letter, but he took the job. The nuncio wasn't an idiot. He had noticed Lustiger and felt his criticisms of the Church in Paris were simply common sense. Of course, as bishop of Orléans, he immediately became a nuisance to his brother bishops for criticizing a new French catechism for young people because of its poor foundation in Scripture. He was also opening a seminary when other bishops were closing theirs.

Lustiger is consecrated bishop of Orléans in December 1979, then he's named archbishop of Paris in January 1981, just 13 months later. That's when you resumed your collaboration?

DUCHESNE: He wanted a text that would explain his pastoral approach to the Church in Paris. So, he asked Jean-Luc Marion and me to help him. He wanted to emphasize that what makes the Church "the Church" is not good policy. It's the Eucharist, which is both the means and the end of the Church. So, we worked on that project. We selected a number of his unused homilies for Corpus Christi. Few people realized that these thoughts on the Eucharist were the basic guidelines for his ministry. And then I told Lustiger, well, I'm afraid you'll have to continue publishing. Because publishing books is now part of your job.

Today audio-visual communications are omnipresent. But the Christian life, the spiritual life, needs a slower rhythm; something that's more meditative and that only the printed word can feed. The spoken word is more easily circulated, but it's also quickly forgotten. It's the same for the popular print media. But when it's collected and rearranged in a published book, it's substantive, and it drives the nail home. So, I spent the next 24 years fighting him; convincing him to publish things, so as to make the most of what had inspired him in various past circumstances but remained relevant.

How much of his work did he actually write? How much did you write for him?

DUCHESNE: I didn't "create" anything. I mean, the whole point was to capture what he had said; things that had been recorded, then transcribed. Then I cleaned up, rewrote, edited, and then published his words. It was an amazing process. Of course, I added linking material here and there. But I can't say that anything published under his name is mine.

But it seems that your relationship with him was a kind of conversation that introduced your ideas to him, and vice versa. Would that be an accurate statement?

DUCHESNE: Well no, because he was always leading me, and I was the follower. I only tried to organize things he'd said into structured books, without adding any serious material of my own. I was just the guy who said, "Let's try to build up something with your recorded statements on this or that current issue. That would meet a need." And then he would say, "You attend to it, but I'm not sure everything you'll find is worth printing."

So, looking back, what was it like working for Lustiger? What were his personal strengths and his personal weaknesses?

DUCHESNE: I don't know. I've never tried to look at the experience from that angle. He was always the one who asked first. I mean, I did make suggestions, and he didn't reject them all. Most of the time, he found things he thought I could do, and I would say yes and do the job, and keep doing it until it was finished or he asked me to stop, which was rare. But I never had a defined job, and I never was on the payroll. My mission was to help him, and this meant two things: one, that he (not I) knew best what he needed; and two, that I shouldn't burden him with any personal requirements, or expect any reward. A lot of my work concerned publications and books, contracts and translations, or foreign rights. And that implied following everything he did, to see what was worth publishing and could be inserted into a consistent, coherent whole. And also, almost immediately when he became archbishop of Paris, a lot of American Jewish leaders sought him out. And he had no one on his staff or in the Paris clergy who could manage those relationships, or take a phone call, or write a decent letter in English. And so that became part of my job, which included preparing his visits to the United States and accompanying him there.

And there were other tasks too. I wrote summaries of meetings that he couldn't attend, for example the National Ethics Committee, to which he had been appointed a member, or during preparations for the bicentenary of the French Revolution. There also was research for lectures he was to give, or background on candidates to the Académie Française once he had been elected to it (against his will), and countless memos on various mostly cultural events.

Together, Jean-Luc Marion and I also created what we called "the archbishop's club". Three or four times a year we organized an evening with an intellectual, and not necessarily a Catholic one, but someone who might stimulate Lustiger's interest in a relaxed way. We tried to keep him informed about recent trends in philosophy, linguistics, ethics, quantum mechanics, digitalization; those sorts of things.

Did he ever use the word "conversion" in regard to himself? He never diminished or discarded his Judaism to my knowledge; he always considered himself Jewish.

DUCHESNE: He would speak of the day when he had discovered that Jesus of Nazareth was the Messiah of Israel. He never spoke of himself as a Jewish convert to Catholicism. He rather called himself a baptized Jew. His idea was that Jewishness is acquired by birth and is indelible, and that he was no less Jewish than the Virgin Mary; the apostles Peter, John, Paul; or the members of the very first Church, in Jerusalem, as described in the Acts of the Apostles.

He also claimed that there have always been two Churches: the elder one, that of Jews; and a younger one, thanks to Peter first, then more systematically through Paul's preaching: the Church of the Gentiles, or pagans. And he argued that it made no difference if the latter had invaded so much space and apparently swallowed up the former. One of his great joys at the end of his life was the recognition of the Catholic Hebrew-speaking community in Jerusalem, with a special episcopal vicar, gathering together Catholic Israeli citizens, which means baptized Jews. He saw this as the revitalization of the original Jewish circumcised Church, reconnecting the whole of Christianity to its historic source.

If someone were to ask you, what are the essential elements of a lay Catholic vocation, what would your answer be?

DUCHESNE: I'd be very embarrassed, because for me there's really only one category: those who have been baptized. Among the baptized, everyone has his or her own personal vocation. The decisive moment in your life is saying yes to God. All the rest is just a matter of circumstances and divine providence. You just have to say yes to what's offered to you, because it comes from God.

When I look back, I've benefited from so many undeserved blessings—my wife, my friends, coming across a guy like Lustiger. But being a layman? I'm not sure that matters. If it did in my case, it was because I had opportunities to say yes also outside the formal structures of the Church. I was a college professor of English, and I enjoyed teaching. I was asked to join the national association of my peers, and I said yes. I was then asked to become president, and I said yes again. This meant attending a lot of meetings at the Ministry of Education and crossing swords with top-level civil servants and politicians. I did this for 20 years. This is what earned me the Legion of Honor a few years before I retired, which I take as a proof that I'd been troublesome enough (but not too much) in that unpaid representative job. Fortunately, the Ministry of Education is only a couple of blocks away from the archbishop's residence and office, which allowed me to jump from one place to the other in the same afternoon.

If I could work in those two different fields at the same time, in addition to my teaching duties, of course it was because I was a layman; because I'd been baptized; because I'd said yes to God and to whatever God sent me. Then everything else was possible, or at least much more than I thought I would have been able to achieve on my own, with my personal resources and ambitions.

When you look at the Church in places like France or the United States, what are your impressions?

DUCHESNE: I think many Catholics, Catholics who are active in Church life, have the feeling that their Church—the visible Church—is losing ground inexorably. But this is a wrong impression. We can never see everything. The Church is bigger than my parish, the Church in Paris, the Church in France, or the Church in the United States. One thing Lustiger taught me, or rather what I learned from him because he never taught it explicitly, is that you've got to see things from the point of view of the history of creation and salvation. Everything else is just shortsighted.

Our duty, here and now, is to say yes to God. And if we do that, God will give us the strength to do what he asks us to do.

𝒑𝒘 𝒑𝒘 𝒑𝒘

Enrique Elias Dupuy, Rome

Enrique Elias Dupuy is a member of the Sodalitium Christianae Vitae (SCV), a society of apostolic life for consecrated laymen founded in Peru in the 1970s. Elias served as a leader in the SCV-related Christian Life Movement in Colombia and Italy; as a local superior in SCV communities in Medellín and Rome; as a member of the Pontifical Council for the Laity; as a university pastoral agent; and 13 years as the SCV's procurator general based in Rome. In that role, he was the Sodalitium's primary liaison with the Vatican and its dicasteries.

From its beginnings, the Sodalitium was marked by vigorous apostolic activity. It played a key role in combatting Marxist influences in Latin American liberation theology throughout the 1980s. But the SCV's founder, Luis Fernando Figari, and its deceased vicar general, Germán Doig, were later found to have abused various community members emotionally and sexually, leading to Vatican intervention, the removal of Figari, multiple lawsuits, and a period of Rome-directed oversight. In the ensuing crisis, many community members left. Others, including Elias, stayed on to continue the Sodalitium's work and to help rebuild.

Let's start with some personal details.

ELIAS: I was born in Lima, Peru. I have two sisters and two brothers. My parents passed away years ago.

Were your parents, your family, practicing Catholics?

ELIAS: My mother was, for most of her life, until she divorced my father. My father had left her. So, basically she was the victim in that experience. It created the conditions for a very difficult life. She married again, four or five years later. She went to Mass on Sundays, but it was at the end of her life, maybe 10 years before dying, when she returned to full communion with the Church. She was very traumatized in many ways by the divorce.

And your dad?

ELIAS: My father was a nominal Catholic. He was a womanizer all his life. He never changed. He was pro-family, against abortion, and loved John Paul II, but his personal life was complicated.

You come from a well-connected, influential background.

ELIAS: My dad cofounded one of Peru's most powerful law firms. He was also a professor of corporate law and the author of a three-volume study of law that is required reading for most law students in Peru.

Where did you pursue your education?

ELIAS: I was taught by American nuns and priests in Peru from kindergarten through high school. Then I did theology and philosophy at the pontifical faculty in Lima, and my license at the pontifical faculty in Medellín, Colombia, which is connected to the Gregorian University in Rome. I couldn't do my doctorate because I'd gotten into a crazy, active lifestyle.

When you say crazy lifestyle, do you mean self-indulgent, secular? Or had you already become religiously engaged?

ELIAS: I had joined, full-time, this young new apostolic community, which involved extremely intense working days, no vacations, no holidays. It was a very demanding kind of apostolic life.

This is when you met the Sodalitium.

ELIAS: I was at school one day, and a boy beside me had befriended an older guy, a member of the community. We were like 16, and this older guy was 25. He had formed a Catholic group nearby, in a local neighborhood. The guy invited me for a meeting. And when I heard him say the "Catholic" thing, I immediately said OK, fantastic. I was pro-Catholic all the way. I had a very deep religious sensibility. There was nothing negative for me in the faith. So, I went to the meeting, and I just fell in love with everything. Everything.

Was the Sodalitium organized as a formal community when you first got involved?

ELIAS: It was just starting to get organized. It was very much like a Christian community of the first centuries. We would meet in members' homes; the kids and parents all got to know each other. It was a very beautiful experience of friendship.

Did you know the founder at that point?

ELIAS: This was 1979 or 1980. Luis Fernando wasn't my point of reference. But I'd see him after Mass to say hello. He was very friendly. There was nothing strange about him at that time that I could tell. Everything in those years, for me, was a fantastic experience of Christian Catholic life.

You're a very balanced man. You have a healthy personality. You come from a wealthy family. So, why did you choose to be a consecrated, celibate layperson? Why not a priest or religious brother; why choose this particular form of life?

Elias: You know why? Because in those days, there was nothing in the Catholic market that offered me a personal, authentic outreach, inviting me to something about Christianity that was really good. Nothing I came in touch with. There was Mass at the parish and religion in Catholic schools. But when it came to a vigorous, living faith, nobody ever said, "If you want your life to make a difference, come with me."

You were raised in a culturally Catholic country. Peru is "Catholic" in a way the United States could never be. But is there a negative in that—i.e., faith was sedentary and assumed, rather than evangelically preached and actively witnessed?

Elias: One hundred percent accurate.

To what degree was the Sodalitium influenced by evangelical Protestantism, which at that time was starting to be active in Latin America in a pronounced way?

Elias: It's a good point, but I think any Protestant influence on the Sodalitium was zero. The founder, Luis Fernando, had a calling after his years at Catholic school and Catholic university. He was a well-formed, motivated, very well-educated Catholic. Most guys from our socio-economic class in Peru were not like that; most were deeply touched by the liberal Enlightenment. So, the best schools might be "Catholic", but the leading families never promoted vocations from their own ranks. Almost never. There was this strange mix of Catholic sentiments and traditions, but not ideas. Thinking and studying took place at universities and in spaces where the faith wasn't the protagonist. The Sodalitium offered us something different.

   Most of the Catholic thinking in Peru in those years had become deeply sociological and political with a Marxist influence, especially in small circles at the universities.

What were those first years in the community like?

Elias: Apostolic, intense, outspoken, happy, positive—with no fear at all. It was unique. I don't remember anything like it in Lima. Later, the Charismatic Renewal had something like that too, but it was more of a popular style. It didn't have the same drive for impacting the wider culture.

Founders are complicated people. It's not so implausible that the same founder who eventually became a disaster for the Sodalitium could also, at least at the start, have the gift of sincere outreach and committed faith.

ELIAS: The community was so attractive because the apostolate we shared was manly in the best sense. There was nothing soft or weird about it. The last thing I could imagine, until very late, was that the founder could have a double life; and even worse, a life with homosexual tendencies. It just didn't seem possible. We were very strong in our fidelity, objectivity, intellectual formation, our commitment to truth and Catholic renewal; these things were essential to our everyday routines. It felt like we were engaged in a new reformation of the Church.

Of course, looking back with age and experience, it's easy to see that many elements of respect for members' spiritual freedom and discernment were ignored and abused by the founder and some others.

For me as an outsider, Luis Fernando is a mystery; the evil of the founder's sexually abusive side bitterly damaged individual lives, betrayed you and your Sodalitium brothers, and undermined decades of the community's good work.

ELIAS: Keep in mind two things. First, the ideals of the Sodalitium never changed. The spirit was always intense, beautiful, out of the box, crazy for apostolic work in a good way. That spirit was always alive in our imaginations. But after the first 15 years or so, things did begin to change. They got more rigid. The founder, because of his own inconsistencies, became more of a control freak, more eccentric, more of a problem especially in Peru; less so in our work outside the country. His worst side was well hidden from most people for a very long time.

Second, I've never been shocked by the sinfulness in the Church. Peru has a long tradition of priests who lead double lives. I've seen plenty of it during my years in Rome too. It's very sad, but it's very human. Only the Lord is our rock.

You've invested your life in the Sodalitium. Given the founder's actions and all the trauma and suffering he created, why have you stayed?

ELIAS: I never made my own bed until I was 17. I never cooked for myself. We had hired help for those things. And then in my teens I met this young community, and it was a magnet for me emotionally, spiritually, and intellectually. The guys invited me to a very ugly place in a very poor area of Lima, to a prayer experience. I don't know why I went. There was a young man leading the prayers; not very smart, but good and normal. We went into a chapel. There was a lit candle, an open Jerusalem Bible, and we read a Scripture passage—and I don't remember anything else after that, or what anybody else did. I saw the candle and just disappeared from the planet. I don't know for how long. Maybe a few minutes. But in that moment, Jesus spoke to me.

Not in words. There was nothing "Hollywood" about it. It was just an overwhelming, clear-headed certainty with a very specific content; like oh, no, I have to be a priest or consecrated in some way. And I felt an intensity of happiness and joy that I'd never in my life experienced before. It was so strong that I said OK, I surrender. There's nothing to fear.

So, to answer your question, I've stayed because of the blunt evidence of that calling.

But you didn't choose the priesthood.

ELIAS: In the beginning, I wanted that. But then the apostolic work and the manner of living I saw in the Sodalitium's consecrated laymen seemed like the obvious path.

Why was it obvious?

ELIAS: I don't know. My apostolic life has always meant putting on a parachute and jumping into places where there are no Christians. When I was sent to Rome, I knew nobody. And I didn't speak Italian well. But I took a bus to the university pastoral center in the Rome vicariate. I found the guy in charge. I volunteered to help. They appointed me to the school with the most radical left-wing faculty in Italy, the epicenter of the country's 1968 student turmoil. But I thought: Sure, why not? So, I had conversations about God and life with architecture students under the university stairways. It was crazy. So, that's been my life. And being a layman from a well-off family, I could mix with people who were very far away from the faith. I didn't make them suspicious or uneasy. For me, it was normal.

They could relax with you in a way they would never respond to a religious or priest.

ELIAS: Yes. Every priest has a formal importance because of his ordination. So, there's always a certain distance between laity and priests. With me, it's different. I become people's friends, play soccer with them, go to their homes, listen to their problems, offer them advice. In a very normal, human way, I can overcome people's prejudices, and once we become friends, any kind of conversation is possible. I think this is the way the apostles worked in the very beginning.

How would you describe the essential elements of the lay vocation, as opposed to clergy or religious life?

ELIAS: Being "out of" the world today is almost impossible, even for monks, because of cell phones, computers, and other electronics. So, every vocation today struggles with being "in" the world but not "of" the world. But that's *always* been the main work of the lay apostolate: to be in the world, to create a light in everyday affairs, a form of light, a way of being, that produces illumination around you, whatever you do in life. We're back to the first centuries of Christianity. People who know you and see you should perceive your joy, despite the desperations and conflicts of the world. You only get that kind of credibility from a life of personal charity and prayer, but it's powerful.

We're both in a Church where pastoral authority is placed, ultimately, in the clergy. So what does "lay leadership" look like? What does that actually mean?

ELIAS: Titles don't matter. The most important form of lay leadership is the spiritual power of a strong, virtuous, godly person. People love that sort of witness. They want to learn how to be like that. That's pure authority, and it's completely nonstructural. Being a good father or mother shapes the future. And leading prayer or social action or Scripture study groups is usually done much better by laypeople than by priests or nuns. All those things have direct influence on the actions of others.

The new movements and charisms that have emerged in the Church since Vatican II: What do you see as their main strengths and weaknesses?

ELIAS: The strengths are obvious. The movements tend to be ortho-dox. They have a strong fidelity to what the Church teaches and believes. And they create spaces for Catholic friendship and commu-nity; a context for real personal conversion, which is the exact oppo-site of the cold, bureaucratic reality of too many dry and decadent Catholic diocesan structures. The Church has become bourgeois and comfortable. That kills the Gospel. Either you're radical about the faith or young people won't follow you. And the new movements make being a Christian adventurous. The Gospel is an adventure; challenging and tough, but also fulfilling. An apostolate is an adven-ture, not a burden.

As for their weaknesses, contrary to their own self-understanding, they can be oddly clericalist, as if they hadn't escaped the last stages of the Trent mentality and the late 1500s. There's too much turf com-petition, too much eagerness to be "connected" at the Vatican, too much appetite for ecclesial influence, and as a result, a loss of their radicality and prophetic credibility.

You know Rome, you know the Church, you've traveled extensively in Europe, the United States, and Latin America. What gives you hope or anxiety about the next 20 to 25 years?

ELIAS: You can tell a lot about people's faith by whether and how much they want children. Fear of having children, or "too many" children, tells you what the priority is: God or money. Fear of chil-dren is killing the Church in the developed world. Hope comes from charity; from giving ourselves away to others. The poor and the suf-fering should be the priority of the Church, along with the right to life. If we embrace those two tasks, we'll become holy again. So, that's my hope.

The hostility of mainstream culture in the States, Canada, Europe, and most of the Latin American countries is a big concern. We're going to be humbled and beaten badly for a long time. That's going to happen. And it's not a bad thing that it happens, because we need conversion. God will give us hard medicine because we need it, and he really loves us. I'm worried, though, that the worst enemies of any real conversion will be the clergy; the cancerous realities of entitlement, inertia, and liberal culture that are still alive in the Church. They're the problem.

If you could change the way the Vatican operates, how would you do it? Or is the Vatican finally irrelevant to the foundational issues of current Catholic life?

ELIAS: If the Vatican were sane, healthy, and holy, it would be a massive tool for good. But it's not, and the truth is that nothing will change until the character of the people running it changes. I've been saying this for more than 20 years. The cancer is mediocrity, or worse, from the top on down. So, nobody should be waiting for any help from Roman cavalry. There is no cavalry.

ᘔ ᘔ ᘔ

Joseph Fessio, San Francisco

Joseph Fessio, S.J., is a Jesuit priest, founder of the St. Ignatius Institute at the University of San Francisco and founder of Ignatius Press. A friend of Henri de Lubac and Hans Urs von Balthasar, he earned his doctorate in theology under the guidance of then-Father Joseph Ratzinger at the University of Regensburg, Germany.

So, let's start with where were you born. And do you have any siblings?

FESSIO: I was born on an island in San Francisco Bay that begins with an *A*; not Alcatraz, not Angel, but Alameda. And I had one younger brother, now deceased.

And your parents were practicing Catholics?

FESSIO: No, not when I was born. They were both Catholics, and I was baptized. But when I was five or six years old, they decided they'd better start practicing because they didn't want their kid to grow up without a religion. So, I suppose that's one way children evangelize their parents. They get them thinking about more important things. I went to public grammar schools, but they wanted me to go to Bellarmine Jesuit High School, about 20 miles south of Menlo Park, where I grew up. So, that's where I went.

What about yourself? Did you believe? How did you come to your adult faith?

FESSIO: I went to church with my parents when I was a kid. And when I got to Bellarmine, it was pretty religious at the time. All my high school teachers, with one or two exceptions, were Jesuits. I remember in my sophomore year thinking, I'm a Catholic, but that's because my parents are Catholic. And that's not a good enough reason, because other parents are Buddhist, or Protestant, or Muslim, or atheist. So, I decided I needed to figure out whether God really exists or not. And I began to think about that. For me, it was just harder to believe that there *wasn't* a God, than there was a God. And I came to the conclusion that the Catholic Church has the most complete philosophy of life. It answers all the questions that can be answered. And so, from that point on, I was intentionally a Catholic.

Did any particular person influence you?

FESSIO: I had a lot of good Jesuit teachers. One especially, Father Gerald Flynn. We all looked up to him. He was a tough disciplinarian. He taught us how to think, how to study, how to learn. So, he was a big influence on us. But there were many others.

What about after high school; what led you to where you ended up?

FESSIO: I was aware in high school how blessed I was to live in a free country, to have an education, a family, a home, and everything.

And I knew that a lot of the world wasn't like that, and I wanted to give back in some way. I also knew that I wanted to get married. In fact, I had the year and date all picked out. It would be June 3, 1962. I'd be 21 then, June is the month to marry, and three was my lucky number. I wanted to be an engineer, go to South America, work with the poor, build roads and dams and things like that, and be a lay catechist. That was my initial idea. I wanted to remain a layman. I wanted to have a family. But I also wanted to give back something from what I'd received. So, I went to Santa Clara University and studied engineering.

What led you to the Jesuits? Did Ignatius or Francis Xavier have anything to do with your vocation as role models?

FESSIO: No, not at all. I figured that in order to be happy, a guy needs three things: a good religion, a good job, and a good wife. And I thought OK, I've got the religion part down. I'm a pretty good student, so I'll probably get a good job. The wife is the next thing. I had my eye on this one girl named Nancy Hardy. I liked her very much; she was a very intelligent young woman and also very attractive. So, we dated, and eventually I told Nancy about this plan of mine, you know, get married, go to South America and blah, blah, blah. And she said, "Well, you know, Joe, before we met, I signed up for the convent."

It turns out there was this nun at her high school, Sister Mercedes, a real vocation machine. There were like 21 girls in Nancy's senior class who entered the convent. I mean, this nun was really something. So, anyway, I thought, "Well, I'm going to talk Nancy out of this." I was a debater and good at that sort of stuff. And I kept thinking about it, and prayed about it. Then one night I was sitting on the floor in the engineering building, leaning against the wall and feeling depressed. And the thought came to me, I'll be a priest. That's what I'll do. I got in my car, and I drove up and knocked on Nancy's window. "Nancy, I'm going to be a priest." So that's the edifying story of my vocation.

OK, so now you're becoming a Jesuit. You're ordained. Let's pick up the story a little before you and I met. How did you get the Ignatius Institute started? Forget Ignatius Press for a minute. How did you get the institute going? And why did they kill it?

FESSIO: I need to step back a bit. I was a Jesuit scholastic and not yet ordained. And I taught at the University of Santa Clara. I was the only scholastic there in 1967–1969, which was a pretty tumultuous time after Vatican II in San Francisco; Haight-Ashbury, that whole thing. Father Arrupe, the Jesuit superior general, had said that we should be "men for others" and think about the poor. So, I thought, "What can I do for the poor in Santa Clara?"

So, I went to the principal of the biggest grammar school in East San Jose, the poorest area in the South Bay Area, and said, "Look, I want your teachers to pick for me 50 eighth grade students. I don't care if they're black, white, Hispanic, or whatever. But here are the two criteria. Number One, their teachers think they have college ability. And Number Two, they're likely to drop out of high school. I called it Project 50. So, we had these kids on the Santa Clara campus, gave them six weeks of remedial stuff, and took them on field trips to let them know what it would be like with a college education behind them. And of course, I was trying to fit in with the kids. I was growing a little beard, playing guitar, that sort of thing. My Jesuit superior was a tough old army chaplain from World War II, Father Copeland. And here's this one young scholastic, playing a guitar and growing a beard. He was very upset about it.

Well, the guy who'd been president of the University of Santa Clara the year before, under whom we'd started Project 50, had become the Jesuit provincial. So, I went up to San Francisco, met with him, and said, "Look, I don't want to be a rebel. I want to be a good Jesuit. I'll shave my beard." He just laughed at me. He said, "Well, you know Joe, have you ever thought about going to Europe for theology?" I said, "No, do you want to me to think about it?" He said, "Yes, I want you to think about it." So, C. M. Buckley, a Jesuit friend, had driven up with me, and as we drove back between San Francisco and Santa Clara, I decided to go to France for my theology, because that's what C.M. had done.

In other words, because I grew a beard, I ended up in France for my theology. And I got to know Henri de Lubac, who at the time wasn't appreciated, because he was seen as too "conservative" by his

Jesuit brothers. I became his private secretary. I wrote letters for him.
And he was my mentor, one of the truly great men of the Church.

Great story.

FESSIO: Yeah, a great blessing. So, when the time came, I asked Lubac
what I should do for my doctorate. And he said do it on Hans Urs
von Balthasar; he's the greatest theologian of our time, and maybe of
all time. Now, Lubac was a very measured person. He never went
overboard in his praise. So, that made an impression on me. So, I
asked him where should I do this. He said, "There's a very fine young
theologian in Regensburg named Ratzinger. I'll write him on your
behalf." So, I went to Regensburg for two years, 1972–1974, and did
my doctoral work on Balthasar under Joseph Ratzinger. How do you
earn a gift like that? You don't.

Anyway, I came back to the United States and the University of
San Francisco in 1974, where Father Buckley was. He and some other
Jesuits had been wondering how to restore Jesuit education, because
it had really gone off the rails. By 1974, 10 years after the Council,
men were leaving the Society of Jesus in droves. Even the provincial left. So, we decided to start a program that would reconstitute
the traditional Jesuit *ratio studiorum* within the university. I was the
youngest and didn't have any responsibility. So, I did the research. I
went to the registrar's office, got a bunch of catalogues, and designed
the thing. Then we discussed and prayed about it. And that's how we
started the St. Ignatius Institute in the fall of 1976 with 61 students.
My codirector was a layman named John Galten—and by the way,
talk about lay apostles! Do you know John Galten?

I met him several times.

FESSIO: He's just gold, just tremendous. We used to do retreats
together, and we had a reading club to discuss various books. Every
so often I'd bring in a book by Lubac or Balthasar or von Speyr and
translate a chapter or a few paragraphs for them. John was the one
who said this is really great stuff; this should be available in English.
So, we decided to start Ignatius Press. That was in 1978. The goal was
to put Ratzinger, Lubac, Balthasar, and others in English.

How and why did the Ignatius Institute get taken away from you?

FESSIO: It was always controversial. In those days, all you had to do was repeat the articles of faith and you were a right-winger. And the institute became very successful, which led to a lot of hostility and jealousy.

I remember when you were fired, I don't think it was presented as you being "fired". It just suddenly was a different kind of organization. Does the institute still exist, by the way?

FESSIO: In name it does.

But what happened? The institute's design was an instinctively Jesuit kind of project. The way that the Society in general, and the California Province in particular, unraveled—it's still a mystery to me.

FESSIO: I'll give you a clue. When we began Ignatius Press in 1978, I'd gotten the rights to a John Paul II book, his doctoral dissertation—which, by the way, wasn't very good in my view, but who cares what I think? Anyway, I had wanted to make Ignatius Press a university press, both for the benefit of the university and for the benefit of the press. The university's president Father John Lo Schiavo heard about my plan. And he wrote me a personal note. It said, "I understand that you have the rights to a book by Pope John Paul II, and I want to make *very clear* that this should have nothing to do with the university." That was the mentality toward John Paul II.

Why were they so hostile to John Paul II?

FESSIO: I don't understand it. I just do my job.

(Laughs) OK, but why stay with a religious community that's so punitive and causing you that much pain?

FESSIO: I was asked that same question by a provincial. And it involves a little backstory. This was prior to my tertianship, which every Jesuit takes before final vows.

I was down in Santa Barbara for a meeting. Three Jesuits ran the thing, and they had Mass around a table with no vestments or maybe just a stole over lay clothes, winging the words of the Consecration, and so on. After Mass I approached one of the three guys, who later became a bishop. He asked, "Well Joe, are you comfortable with that?" I said, "It's not a question of comfort, but whether the bishop approves it." "Oh, yeah," he said, "the bishop is fine with it." So, I thought OK, I'll find out. I wrote a letter to the bishop; in this case, the cardinal archbishop of Los Angeles. And I simply said, "Here's what happened in this Mass. Can you, and if so, *do* you, give approval for this?"

So, I got this letter back [*reaches for bookshelf*]. It's dated April 2, 1979.

Dear Father Fessio,

I write in response to your letter of March 14. The situation you inquire about is distressing to me, but not unknown where members of the Society gather. The documentation on the Sacred Liturgy is abundant and clear. No one except the authority of the Church is allowed to proceed on his own initiative to regulate the Sacred Liturgy. Every liturgical act is a public act even though performed in private. It is distinctly forbidden to celebrate Mass while wearing only a stole over non-clerical clothes. Likewise, no private authority may alter the Eucharistic prayers. With as much insistence as I can communicate, I disapprove of the circumstances you inquire about. I think they are unworthy of the loyalty which the Society holds to the Holy See, and a source of scandal to those who are aware of this kind of conduct. God's blessing does not fall upon it. Nor mine.

With every best wish, I am very sincerely yours,
Timothy Cardinal Manning

That's the strongest letter (*laughing*) I've ever seen from an ecclesiastic. And he copied my provincial, because I had copied my provincial in my own letter to Manning. So, the provincial called me in. He asked me why I went over his head. But I said, "I didn't go over your head; you're not between me and the local ordinary when it comes to the Mass." Then he said, "What about charity toward your brother Jesuits?" And I said, "Well, if I were doing something wrong, I'd want someone to warn me; that's a charitable thing."

So, he said, "I can see you're not psychologically ready for tertian-ship." And that was the end of my tertianship at that time. I finally did, later, go to Siberia for my tertianship. But before that, I got called in another time by another provincial. He said to me, "There are rumors that you think the Society is corrupt." I said, "Yes, those rumors are true. I do think 'corrupt' is an accurate descriptor, in the sense of being incapable of internal reform." So he asked me, "Then why do you stay?" And I said, "Well, I made vows to God that I would live my life as a Jesuit. If you marry a woman, and she becomes a prostitute, she's still your wife."

Only you could enjoy that story, Fran. It fits your sense of humor.

It's a gem. But what about Siberia? That's a different Jesuit province, obviously. Why Siberia?

FESSIO: I later had a very friendly provincial. He suggested that I should go to El Salvador. And I could do my tertianship there. I thought that would be great. I could learn some Spanish. So, he wrote to the Central American provincial, and the answer he got back was this: "We will not permit Father Fessio to enter the province." So, my provincial said, "I'll give you the required retreat. But you need to find a place where you can do some ministry." I had friends with Aid to the Church in Need, and through them I eventually found a Jesuit bishop in Novosibirsk, Bishop Joseph Werth. Just a great man, a great Jesuit. And so I went to Novosibirsk, Siberia, to do my tertianship. And I loved it. I was there for three or four months.

You've worked closely with laypeople most of your life. In your experience, what are the most difficult issues to overcome in building an effective clergy and lay cooperative enterprise? You did it. What were the problems?

FESSIO: My greatest blessing as a priest has always been the laypeople I work with. I've never had any problems. And here's why. We've always started with a common faith, a serious Catholic faith. We believe the same things. We serve the same Lord. We read good books, pray together, and love the Church. I've always been a vanilla Catholic: Mass, Rosary, Divine Office, personal prayer, and fidelity to the Magisterium. Private devotions are fine, but we need to stay with the core. Problems come when solid, faithful Catholics can't get along because of some fixation on a particular devotion or claim.

What about our current culture? It seems to confuse the nature of the Church and the role of the laity in the minds of a lot of laypeople. Secular and Catholic ideas of "equality" are not really the same thing at all. The Church is a different kind of creature from a routine political entity; neither a democracy nor a clergy/papal autocracy; short on instrumental power, but long on legitimate moral authority. Such things easily get mixed up.

FESSIO: We're all called to love and follow Christ. That's our main vocation. For me, the lay vocation is primarily marriage and family, to have children and raise them in the faith to make the world a better place. Of course, it's compatible to have a family and also to have a career, both for men and for women. But the main role of the laity is to sanctify the temporal order. And family and work are the biggest parts of that. I don't think the lay vocation is liturgical. Things like serving as a lector are great, but you're not going to be a better layperson simply because you're a lector.

The role of the clergy is proclaiming the Word of God officially, celebrating the liturgy, and being pastors and leaders for the believing community. But supervising the finances, building the church, running the school, and so many other practical matters: You don't need to be a priest to do any of that. All of the vibrant parishes I know are ones where the initiative mostly comes from the laypeople.

You have a long record of engagement with the Church as an international body, and you've had some very significant foreign Catholic friends. So, how do you compare the average American lay Catholic experience and mentality with their foreign cousins?

FESSIO: Europe has been dying for some time, religiously. But vibrant lay movements and leaders do exist in places like Poland, Hungary, Slovenia, and Croatia; there are some incredibly good people there. Africa is where the growth and the future of the Church lie right now. But I think our situation here in the United States is actually very healthy. We've had two generations now of John Paul II and Benedict XVI priests. We have a network of 600 Catholic radio stations, all of them—every single one—faithful in their content. We've got some wonderful blogs, schools being started, things like the Augustine Institute, the Chesterton Academies, and lots of other positives, including very good seminaries. Thirty years ago, the seminaries were a mess. That's completely changed. And of course, the pro-life movement is very strong.

How would you rate the legacy of Pope Francis?

FESSIO: I wouldn't venture an opinion. Legacies are always retrospective. The legacy of any pope is judged, in part, by the number of faithful priestly, religious, and lay vocations his ministry inspires. John Paul and Benedict inspired thousands. Time will tell if Francis can demonstrate the same.

If you could do one thing in the life of the Church right now to begin the process of renewal, what would it be?

FESSIO: Honestly? I'd simply apply the canon law for excommunication. It would make the Church stand clearly for her beliefs despite whatever beating she might take. It's the one thing that would speak the truth most forcefully; it would say, this is what it means to be Catholic. You're free not to be Catholic, but you're *not* free to abuse the fidelity of other Catholics by claiming to be Catholic when your actions say the opposite.

Last question. This one's for laypersons seeking to serve the mission of the Church, especially people who want to start a new apostolate, or work inside diocesan structures. Do you have any advice for them about how to think clearly about their ideas before they jump into the work?

FESSIO: There's actually a recipe for this. An infallible plan. And it works every time. If you see a problem, get together with some friends who see the same problem. And say, well, we're going to pray; we're going pray *together* and ask God for guidance. The guidance will come. That's how we started the Ignatius Institute. We regularly prayed and had a private Mass together. We did that for a whole semester. No answer. So, we thought OK, let's make a pilgrimage. So, John Galten and I went on a pilgrimage to Guadalupe with this group of hippies. We went down there, prayed, and came back. And what we needed to do became clear. That was the start of the St. Ignatius Institute and Guadalupe Associates, the official entity that operates Ignatius Press. Together is the key; two or three or more in prayer, asking God: "Not what I want or we want, *but what do you want? What can we do? What will serve you best in this situation?"*

That's the answer, right there.

ॐ ॐ ॐ

Charles Chaput, Philadelphia

Charles Chaput, a Capuchin Franciscan, is the archbishop emeritus of Philadelphia. He previously served as archbishop of Denver, bishop of Rapid City, Capuchin provincial minister, parish pastor, and seminary instructor. A past White House appointee to the United States Commission on International Religious Freedom and a U.S. delegate to the Organization for Security and Cooperation in Europe, he's the author of four books, and numerous articles and lectures. He served as a delegate to international meetings of the Synod of Bishops in Rome in 1997, 2015, and 2018, and served a term on the synod's permanent council.

Looking back on the 2020–2021 COVID pandemic, a few things seem clear: among them, a lingering spirit of anxiety and restlessness in the culture. How would you describe COVID's impact on people's attitudes toward the Church, their mortality, the afterlife, and religious faith? Was COVID just an accelerant of trends already in process?

CHAPUT: I have all the obvious worries about future church attendance. I don't know if or to what extent fears about the virus had an impact on people's attitudes about their mortality, the afterlife, and religious faith. But yes, COVID clearly accelerated trends already in process. And our culture is very good at distracting people from the fact of their own mortality, and whatever might come next.

In the country's public square, who were the pandemic's winners and losers? The virus greatly increased people's dependence on government and expert counsel at a time when government is less and less favorable to religion.

CHAPUT: The winner in terms of consolidating power, at least in the short term, was the Democratic Party, which is really the party of our elites now. The country's mood can always change, but it does seem that the pandemic increased people's dependence on government and "expert counsel". I've been happy to see more people standing up for religious freedom in the wake of the virus and its severe public health restrictions. But I don't think that's really the attitude of most citizens.

In his book Rubicon, *the historian Tom Holland draws parallels between the last stage of the Roman Republic and our own political tensions today. The differences are striking, but so are some of the similarities. Does that sound plausible to you?*

CHAPUT: Yes, it does seem plausible, and I do worry about our country's commitment to its Constitution. By design and for good reasons, we're a democratic *republic*, not a pure democracy. I think many states will fight to keep a strong voice in the federal system. But the majority of our people tend to live in large cities on the coasts. So, in some sense, they have more voting power. Also, our country is a mix of both current immigrants and immigrants from long ago. Many new immigrants haven't gone through the traditional, formative, school civics classes. As those people of different cultures come to political power, they'll have a huge impact on the future shape of our nation and its institutions.

It's clear that people today have much less concern about religious freedom than they did when our nation was formed. Because they themselves are less religious, they don't value religious freedom nearly as much as earlier generations. And that, of course, may cause great harm to the Church down the road.

Are ideas like the supernatural, angels and devils, transubstantiation, and an afterlife—so often loaded with medieval imagery or complex-sounding doctrine—really credible to a 21st-century person?

CHAPUT: Interest in purely superstitious things actually increases when people lack or lose a genuine faith. I visited Japan just a few years ago with a friend. Tokyo was an extraordinarily modern, hi-tech city in every respect. But palm readers were everywhere. Our guide, a woman with a doctorate in Japanese history, stopped to have her palm read every day. She was convinced that it was vital to do so. And here in the United States astrology has never really gone away. Now it's big again. The human heart is, by nature, very interested in the spiritual and supernatural. So, I don't think people are finally atheistic. Everyone believes in something, some kind of a God or godling. But many aren't willing to accept the teachings of an orga-nized Church community.

In America, we've always had a pragmatic, materialist streak—that's why we're good at technology—but it's been in high gear since the end of World War II. In practice, we're the most materialist soci-ety in history, and we've channeled our hunger for "something more than this" into psychotherapy and boutique spiritualties.

One could argue that we're living through one of history's periodic inflection points, a new kind of Re-formation or Great Reset, this time stripped of the-ology. Does that kind of thinking sound like melodrama?

CHAPUT: It certainly feels like a Great Reset to me, in the Church especially because of Pope Francis and his ambiguous style. I've had to re-think the role of the papal primacy and infallibility because of things that have happened over the past eight or 10 years; things he has said and done. Whether it's truly a Great Reset for the Church will probably depend on the next conclave. As for our country, we've been heading toward a Great Reset for a long time. Both George W. Bush and Donald Trump were moments of pause, but there seems to be an inevitable shift toward a different understanding of our repub-lic. Things aren't clear yet. But it's definitely not "melodrama" to notice and engage these concerns.

What do you think the Church will look like globally in 20 years?

CHAPUT: I have no idea. But with the appointment of the kind of cardinals that Pope Francis has named, the governance of the Church at the highest levels is obviously going to be more international. John Paul II and Benedict XVI had a high regard for the Catholic Church in the United States. Pope Francis has a different view of our country and American Catholic life, and he's moved his focus in a different direction, but it's not clear where that direction will lead.

Based on your interactions with Rome as a bishop, can the papacy and the Vatican endure, and should they endure, as currently constituted; in other words, in their current form? If they need to change, what needs to change and how?

CHAPUT: No, I don't think the papacy, as it currently conducts business, can endure. It won't be financially possible. As the Church shrinks in the wealthy nations, the sources of income will diminish. The papacy's present form is a Renaissance court. A lot of it is symbolic. That can't continue, no matter how much financial support comes from the Vatican Museums. The *appearance* of strength, of course, resides in the international structures of the Church, especially in Rome. But it's a very expensive superstructure. It's hard to see how it can be sustained.

We need to return to a simpler view of the papacy. Not so much as an international political entity with its nunciatures everywhere, but more simply as a community of faith, with the pope being primarily the bishop of Rome, to whom cases are referred when disputes develop in the Church. He certainly is the universal shepherd in the sense that he has a special responsibility to care for the unity and fidelity of the churches. But the pope will no longer—nor should he any longer—be seen as a universal pastor in the sense of having his fingers in all the dioceses.

Will history judge the Francis pontificate as a success?

CHAPUT: I'm not in a position to know. History is an exercise in looking back on the past. It shows that popes are vulnerable to mistakes and sins and character flaws, sometimes very serious ones, just like the rest of us. I do think the current pontificate's understanding of "synodality" is flawed, and the process leading up to the 2023–2024 synod has been defective, with a tendency to predetermine the results. That will have an impact on its credibility, and therefore its value, long-term. And it depends on what one means by "success". Success in a Christian sense is fidelity to the consistent teachings of the Church, and conversion of the human heart to Jesus Christ. Christianity is more than a system of ethics that can be adjusted to fit the mood of the world on matters like politics and sex. Our mission is to "make disciples of all nations" with a Gospel that's beautiful and salvific, but not always welcome. That's what matters. And it determines the success or failure of any pontificate, including the current one.

In your experience, what are the main strengths and weaknesses of the selection process for bishops? What were the biggest surprises in your own early service as a bishop?

CHAPUT: The main strength of today's process is that it keeps secular powers out of the selection dynamic and reserves the decision simply to the Church. When the Holy See gave that prerogative away in China, it made a huge mistake. It was a mistake in Europe when it was done in centuries past. How would I improve the process? To start, I'd insist that every diocese have a mandatory, functioning diocesan pastoral council, as well as a priests' council. These would be consulted automatically in any selection of a new bishop, both for what's needed for a diocese and to surface good candidates for that service. As for the biggest shock to my early ministry as a bishop, it was the ambition of bishops to become archbishops and cardinals, and also the lack of a common commitment to the essentials of the faith among bishops.

Given today's challenges to the Church, how would you improve the formation of our priests? What are the main challenges bishops today face in preparing men for fruitful priestly life?

CHAPUT: Seminaries like the ones in Denver, Philadelphia, and elsewhere are mainly very good. I'd hate to see any of that given up, though no structure will ever be perfect. The primary deficit in today's priestly formation is that, in my experience, there's little clear support for young priests after they're inserted into parish life. If I had to do it over again, I'd insist that the diocesan clergy office spend at least a quarter of its time with newly ordained priests, helping them adjust to life in parishes for the first three years of their ministry. It can be a challenging road.

Can Catholic schools survive? Is there a better way to educate our young people more durably in the faith?

CHAPUT: I support Catholic schools, but I don't see how many of them can survive financially in their current form. That's already being demonstrated by the lack of commitment on the part of parents to enroll their children. It happens for a lot of reasons, but a big reason, even for very faithful Catholics, is that they simply can't afford the cost. And why would you pay for a "Catholic" education that's not very Catholic if you can find a good education elsewhere? Parochial and diocesan support for things like homeschooling and other options would be a much better way to use available funds. And it would make Catholic education much more affordable. But in many places, any innovation would be difficult because of resistance from traditional structures like the diocesan Catholic schools office.

Given the changing political weather in "developed" countries, can Catholic social and charitable ministries, especially those that partner with government agencies and take public money, survive?

CHAPUT: Local dioceses should do all they can to cooperate in their social and charitable ministries with government agencies. And they should take public money in doing so, as long as they don't compromise on any, and I mean *any*, moral issues. The Church provides a huge benefit to the general public in her charitable works. There's no reason to refuse government help in doing that. Public authorities might drive us out, but that burden ought to be on their heads, and not on ours.

What does a concept like the "collegiality" of bishops really mean? Is it more aspirational than fact? What does it look like in action?

CHAPUT: Collegiality is very hard in a conference as large as the U.S. bishops. Things would be much more effective here if we were divided into three or four regions. And each one of those regions would be separate for reflection on moral and doctrinal issues, which is the area in which collegiality would be most important. I don't mean we should have four USCCBs, but four reflection groups. And the chairmen of each of those groups would get together for national coordination and organization. Candidly, I don't think episcopal conferences like the USCCB, as they're presently configured, are worth the time, staffing needs, and expenses. They can sometimes create as many problems as they solve. The biggest problem is that bishops find it impossible to speak clearly with one voice on issues of disagreement within the conference.

It's very hard to come up with a common policy on serious issues when a small group of bishops opposes the principled position of the majority of the conference. And, of course, the conference has no authority other than moral authority. So, even when we do speak on an issue, there's no way to enforce it.

The quickest way to reform the USCCB is to limit the money it has. That means reducing offices and staff. I can't think of a single useful thing that the USCCB did for me in my more than 30 years as an ordinary. Not one thing. If national issues arise that need to be worked on, we should have the kind of national council that created the Baltimore Catechism, called together only for specific purposes. And it would need only a modest staff.

Can celibacy survive as part of priestly life? Should married deacons be allowed to remarry on the death of their wives? Given that sexual sin is part of every human vocation and profession due to human nature itself, what do you see as the real cause of the clergy sexual abuse crisis of the last 30 years?

CHAPUT: Celibacy is an essential element of priestly life. By "essential" I don't mean essential dogmatically, but essential for the good health of the Church. If you compare the Roman Church with the Orthodox Church, you'll see clearly what I mean. The Orthodox have all the issues we have, plus the problems of unfaithful marriages, financial corruption based on family need, and a lack of courage in order to protect family members from being harmed. Celibacy has lasted so long in the Roman Church precisely because it's been effective. And the missionary activity of the Church has been very much dependent on it.

Yes, married deacons should be allowed to remarry on the death of their wives. They're accustomed to married life, and it's very hard for them to give that up after their spouse has died.

As for the clergy sex-abuse problem, celibacy had very little to do with its causes. The sexual revolution in the 1960s saw a huge drop in safeguards around chastity, including clerical chastity, because of psychological theories at the time. You and I both lived through those years, so we know from personal experience how big the changes were. Twenty years from now, the prevention and awareness steps the Church has taken will have shown good results. Some of the unusual policies we have now might not be needed. But the passage of time is necessary for anything like that to happen.

What are the main burdens of priestly life that laypeople typically don't see or understand?

CHAPUT: Probably the loneliness of priests; men who are temperamentally prone in that direction. Also, there's an ambivalence in many laypeople. They want priests not to be on pedestals but then, in practice, they put them on pedestals. I'm always amazed at the number of lukewarm Catholics who are astonished at the clergy abuse problem and other priestly scandals. Why would they expect priests to be free from the very same temptations they themselves face and often give in to? The things laypeople sometimes expect of priests are unrealistic. On the other hand, I don't think laity are demanding enough on matters like preaching. Somehow priests ought to be evaluated by their parishioners. And a mechanism should exist by which that can be done; something that doesn't require a whole new cluster of bureaucratic diocesan procedures.

Everyone talks about the importance of the lay vocation, but pious words can easily become clichés with little substance. How many Catholic laypersons really know what those words— "lay vocation" and "lay leadership"—mean? What should a form of faithful lay leadership in the coming decades look like, especially since the role of the clergy is so fundamental to Catholic identity?

CHAPUT: Understanding the nature of lay leadership and the lay vocation requires a willingness from both laity and clergy. Priests have the duty and authority to lead by virtue of their ordination. But laypeople are not second-class Christians. As Benedict XVI stressed, they're fully equal cooperators in the mission of the Church. This needs to be taught more effectively in seminaries. Priests should have genuine lay friends. Of course, having *only* lay friends can be unhealthy for a priest if it leads to his being isolated from his brother priests, or to a weakening of his priestly identity. My point is, the main focus of lay leadership is out in the secular world. That's their mission field. But laypeople can also provide support and leadership inside many Church structures. And that shouldn't be discouraged.

At the local level, every parish should have a functioning pastoral council marked by candor. The relationship between a pastor and his people should be respectful, mutually supportive, but also frank; honesty animated by charity. This requires a high degree of maturity from both priest and people. The fact that canon law only requires parishes to have finance councils says something negative about the seriousness of the Church regarding lay leadership on the pastoral level. But institutionalizing all of this like the Episcopal Church did with its houses of laity, clergy, and bishops would not be a healthy thing. Having those separate houses really does confuse rather than embody the Church's understanding of the right relationship between clergy and laity. The apostles had a very lively interaction with the first Christians that didn't emphasize one aspect over another.

The 2020 election of Joe Biden as our second Catholic president aggravated divisions in the Church on issues ranging from abortion to same-sex marriage and transgender rights. Is the John Courtney Murray style of thinking—i.e., Catholic faith and life are basically compatible with, and favorable toward, liberal democracy and the American experiment—still realistic? Some impressive Catholic scholars would argue that today's growing hostility to religion in American politics is simply the logical end result of our political system.

CHAPUT: For me, Murray's thought is still generally valuable and realistic. I very much admire faithful Catholic thinkers, men like Patrick Deneen and Michael Hanby, who raise hard questions about our culture and our political system that otherwise we too easily gloss over. But even now, there's still a lot of good in our country. The founding didn't determine our current problems; we created them by our actions. Now we need to do what we can, to save what we can.

Finally, what are the greatest worries, and the greatest sources of hope and confidence, that you've dealt with in your daily ministry as a bishop?

CHAPUT: The greatest worries I have are the decline in Catholic numbers, the strange kind of leadership we currently get from Rome, and the men applying for seminary. They're good, talented men ... but also too few in number. My greatest sources of hope are today's lay movements and the intense commitment I find in a lot of young, energetic Catholic people. Sometimes there's an "otherworldliness"—and not the healthy kind—about these groups and young seminarians that bothers me. But overall, the good outweighs the bad. And that's a reason to remember that God never abandons his people.

ACKNOWLEDGMENTS

It's common for an author to thank his spouse at the end of a book's acknowledgments. That would be unjust here. She belongs first in line. My wife, Suann, worked with distinction in Catholic education for 40 years. Her professional experience, her love for Jesus Christ and the Catholic faith that shapes our family and our life together, and her practical help with advice, criticism, research, proofing, and mental-health counseling (when needed) were vital to this text. There's no way to thank her adequately. But she already knows that.

I owe a deep debt of gratitude to the Saeman Family Foundation, the Eleanore Mullen Weckbaugh Foundation, Steph and Tim Busch, Carol and John Saeman, Michael Crofton, George Marlin, Berni and Rob Neal, and Terry and Michael Polakovic for their friendship and support throughout the development of this project. Whatever good emerges from this book belongs to them. I'm grateful to Professor Vincent Phillip Muñoz and the Napa Institute for the privilege of serving as the inaugural senior research associate, 2020–2022, at the Center for Citizenship and Constitutional Studies, which Professor Muñoz leads at the University of Notre Dame. Sincere thanks go as well to Bill Barry, my agent, friend, and a man of outstanding skill and Catholic character; and to Father Joseph Fessio, S.J., and Mark Brumley at Ignatius Press, both of whom have been faithful friends for decades.

Certain elements of chapters 1 and 11 have been revised and amplified from material previously appearing in *The Catholic Thing* and *Catholic World Report*. My thanks go to the editors, Robert Royal and Carl Olson, for their permission to use. Thanks also to Ryan Anderson and Mitch Muncy at the Ethics and Public Policy Center (EPPC) for inviting me to present some of this book's early thinking to my EPPC colleagues; thoughts which were later solidified in these pages. And it's impossible to tally up the debt I owe to Archbishop Charles Chaput, O.F.M. Cap., for the conversations, projects, and ideas we've shared over 26 years. They inform and shape this entire book. My gratitude, along with my admiration, will always be there.

Thanks also go to the scores of good people interviewed as the substance of these pages, many of whom remain anonymous. It's easy to go down a rabbit hole of worry and frustration about problems in today's Church, and thereby to miss the larger picture. But there's really no excuse for that. The Church is bigger and purer, younger and more alive, than the flaws of her people and leaders, and the hostility of the world. She always has been, and she always will be. Now is no exception. The First Letter of John reminds us that love casts out fear. Our job is to live like we believe it.

Finally, any mistakes and inadequacies that might survive in this text are mine alone. I own them, nobody else. Just me.